W9-CFR-101

DRAWING AND PAINTING
Plants and Flowers

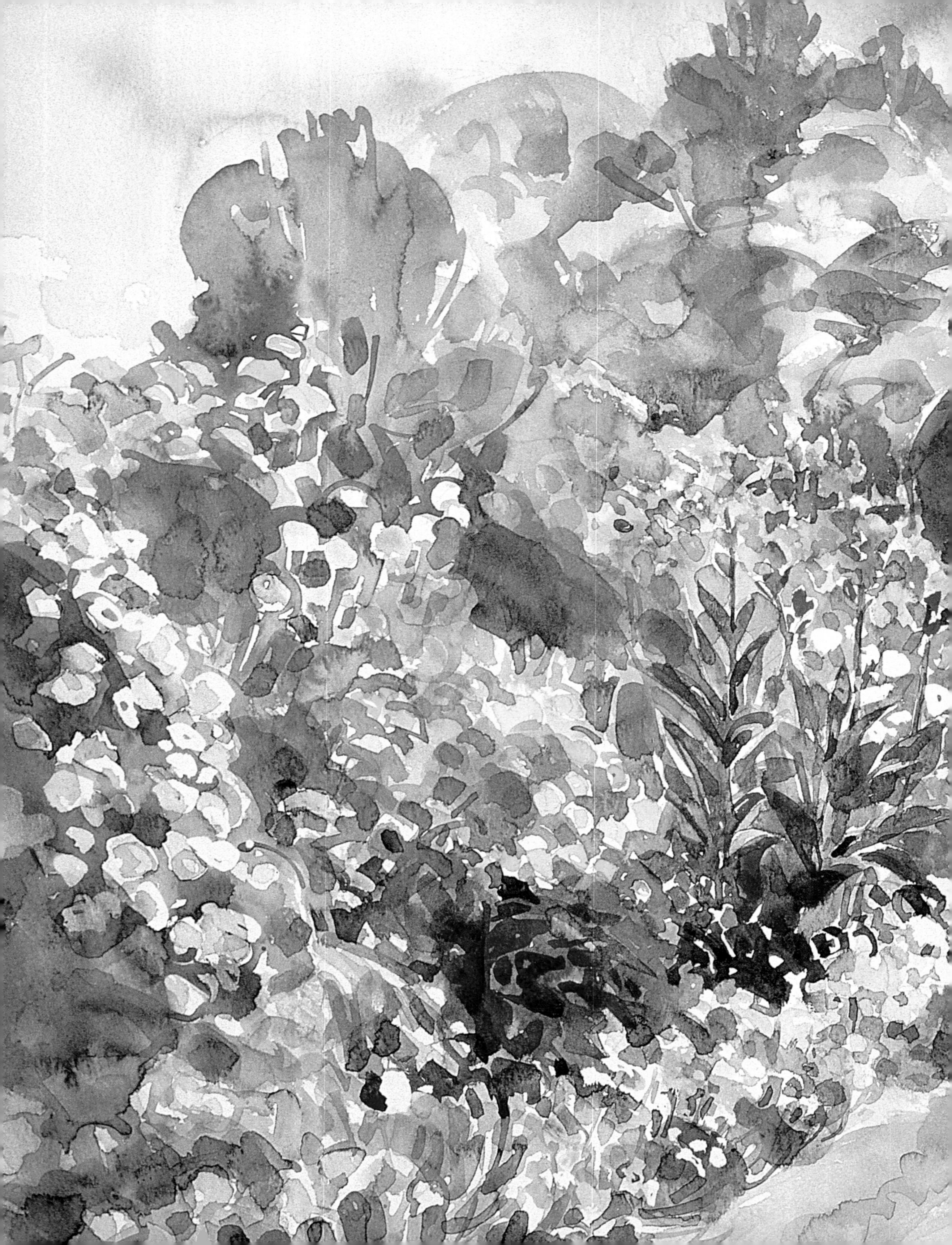

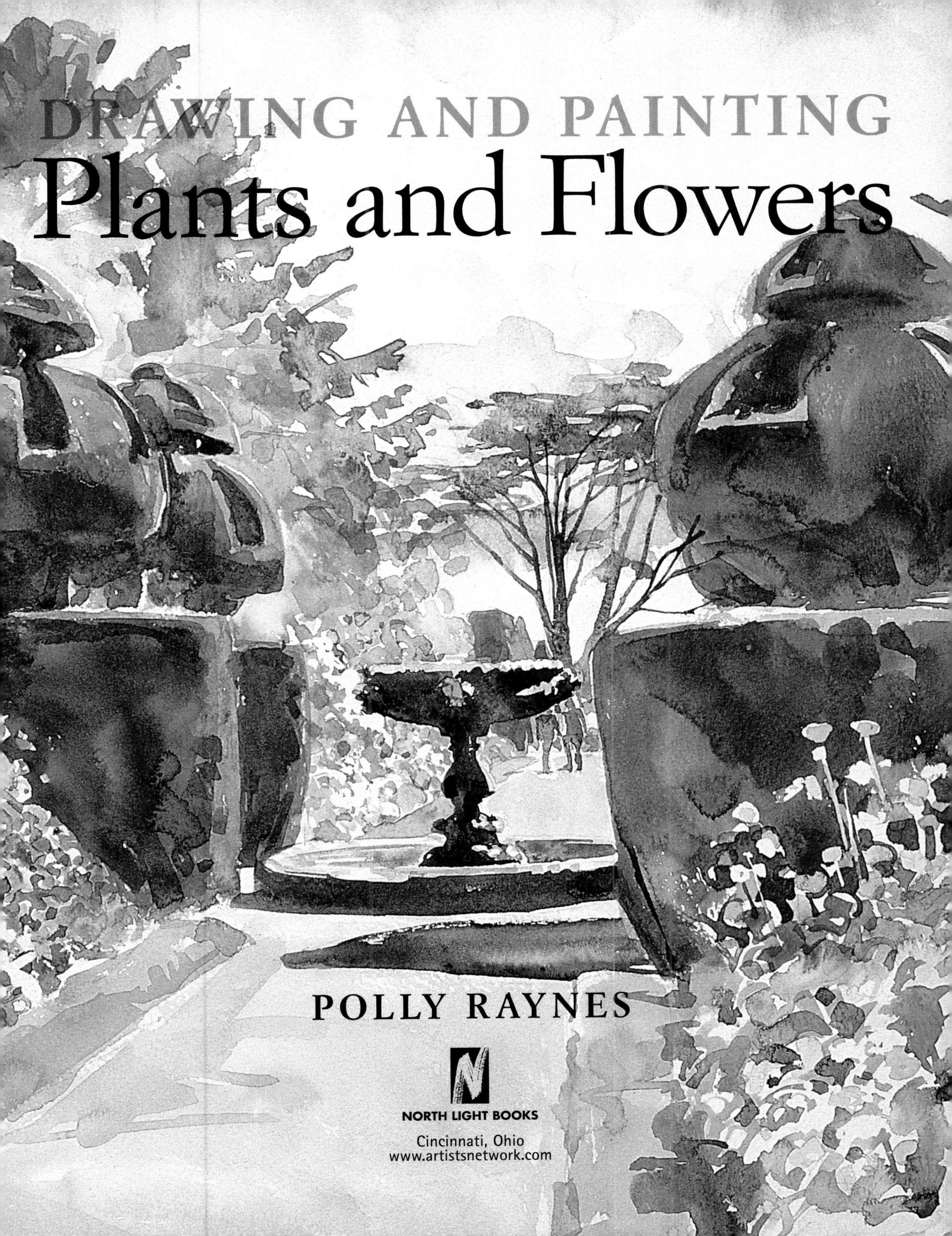

DRAWING AND PAINTING

Plants and Flowers

POLLY RAYNES

NORTH LIGHT BOOKS

Cincinnati, Ohio
www.artistsnetwork.com

First published in Great Britain in 2003 by
Collins & Brown Limited
64 Brewery Road
London N7 9NT

A member of **Chrysalis** Books plc

First published in North America
in 2003 by North Light Books
an imprint of F&W Publications
4700 East Galbraith Road
Cincinnati, Ohio 45236

9 8 7 6 5 4 3 2 1

Library of Congress Cataloging-in-Publication Data
is available.

ISBN: 1-58180-396-6

Editorial Director: Roger Bristow
Project manager: Emma Baxter
Editor: Ian Kearey
Design manager: Liz Wiffen
Designer: Liz Brown
Photography: Duncan McNeill

Color reproduction by Bright Art Graphics, Singapore
Printed by Times Publishing Group, Malaysia

Contents

Introduction 6

Part 1: Techniques **8**
Getting started 10
Anatomy 18
Developing your studies 24
Composition 36
Putting it all together 48

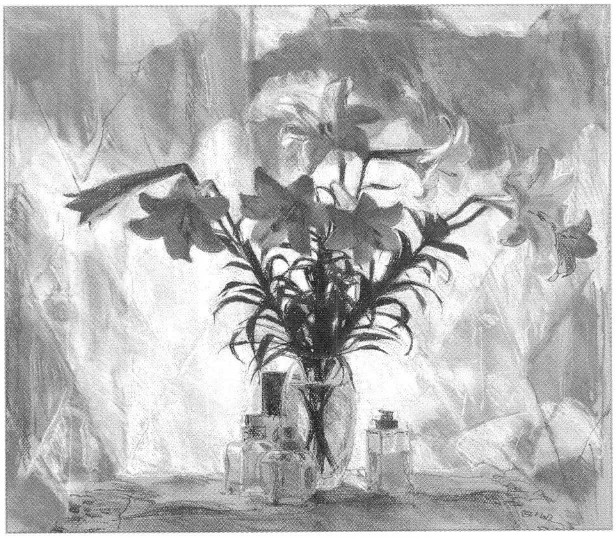

Part 2: In practice **50**
Public garden 52
Wild plants 56
Daisies 61
Ponds and water 64
Exterior architectural setting 69
Winter scene 74
Spring scene 79
Summer scene 84
Fall colors 88
Botanical gardens 93
Informal set-up 99
Formal interior with arum lilies 104
Interior with lilies 108
Dried flowers 113
Interior and exterior set-up 118
Presentation and framing 125

Index 126
Suppliers and acknowledgements 128

Introduction

The subject of flora has a rich history, and plants and flowers have been a favorite subject for artists for thousands of years. Nations and cultures around the world have incorporated flowers, trees, and even herbs into the symbolism surrounding their religions, nobility, and conquering armies. Even a simple green sprig carries the power of life and hope when we think of the white dove of peace bearing an olive branch.

"Arum"
This image, by artist Ann Hale, shows the subtle beauty of a detailed botanical painting.

The richness of painting that we see over the centuries illustrates the devotion and reverence that people have shown for particular species. Ancient Egyptian tomb paintings demonstrate that lilies and irises were revered by their kings, and Persian carpets are embellished with decorative interpretations of flowers, fruiting trees, or cypresses. Plants on wall paintings in Pompeii show how important flora was to the Romans, and medieval monks adorned their manuscripts with plants and flowers of all kinds for pure decoration, as well as for their symbolic messages.

Plants were revered for their medicinal properties—both to cure and to poison—their scent, visual beauty, and flavor, whether the plant was fruit, vegetable or herb. Collections of illustrated works helped physicians identify plants' medicinal uses, and an early work, *De Materia Medica* by Dioscorides, was used as a reference book for about 200 years.

Aristotle completed plant studies with meticulous detail, and these remarkable works, or *florilegium*, were highly popular in the sixteenth and seventeenth centuries. World exploration was at its height, and new discoveries inspired and fed the insatiable appetite of

Study of medieval border
Here, I have explored the decorative, rich color and patterning produced by medieval monks. The rhythmical swirl of the foliage, and gold embellishment create a wonderful, rich, and yet restful image.

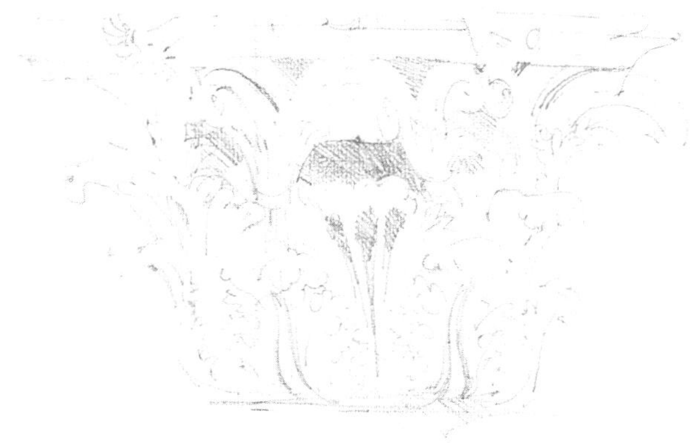

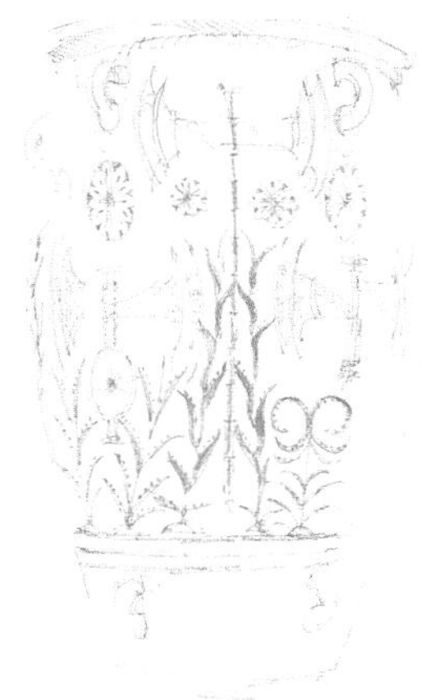

Ancient decoration
Near left: *On this Cretan vase, a stylized image of lilies grows among the religious emblem of the double axe. Lilies of this Minoan period are widely considered to be influenced by the Egyptians, as they also revered the lily.* **Far left and below:** *The Greeks and Romans showed their admiration and joy of flora with decorations ranging from capitals on columns to drains.*

wealthy collectors. Redouté is probably the best known botanical artist, with some of his best commissions, *Les Lilas* and *Les Roses*, recording some of the Empress Josephine's collections of plants. Although strict, botanical drawing of this kind is not the subject of this book, it is wonderful to look at and be inspired by these works, and to see the various, rich interpretations of flora that artists have painted throughout history.

The use of color in plants is often influenced by religious symbolism, white being a sign of purity, and red signifying martyrdom and Christ's blood. Names or nicknames show how emotionally, psychologically, and medicinally we respond to flora—for instance, forget-me-not, love-lies-bleeding, passion flower, lovage, lungwort, feverfew, and hemlock.

Flowers and plants are an intricate part of our lives, given as gifts to celebrate love, marriage, birthdays, anniversaries, and all kinds of personal achievements. They are also used to apologize and to commiserate with, and share grief over death.

Fashion, though, can change the way that we see them—the lilies that my grandmother associated with death, I see as a clean, pure, architectural plant that resides by the coolness of my pond. Poppies drawn by an Edwardian lady are going to be different from the same flower in a silkscreen print by pop artist Andy Warhol. And, of course, all of this makes flowers and plants a particularly personal subject to paint.

The following chapters will introduce you to the rudiments of plant study, giving you the confidence to explore different materials to achieve your interpretation of this colorful, textural, decorative, delicate, and yet powerful subject.

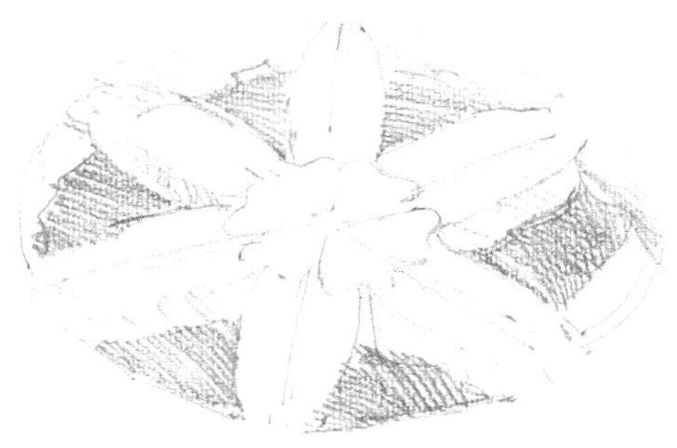

Pebble mosaic
This early Greek pebble mosaic shows the exquisite subtlety created by simply using carefully graded river pebbles for color and size.

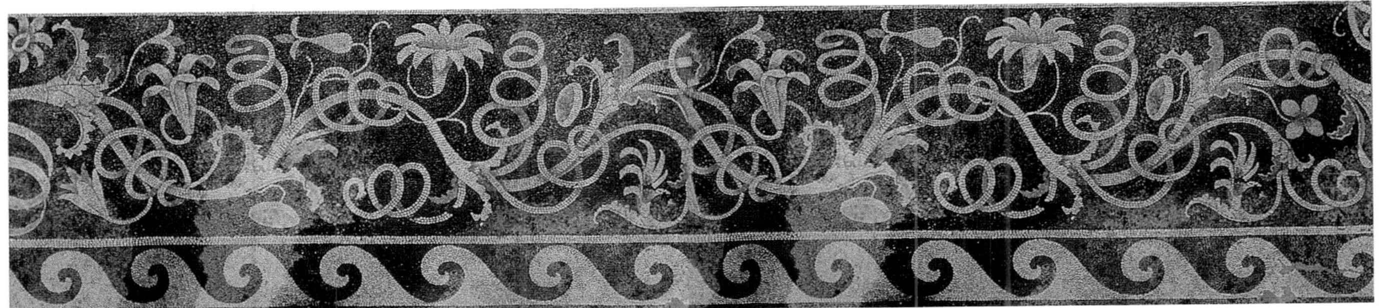

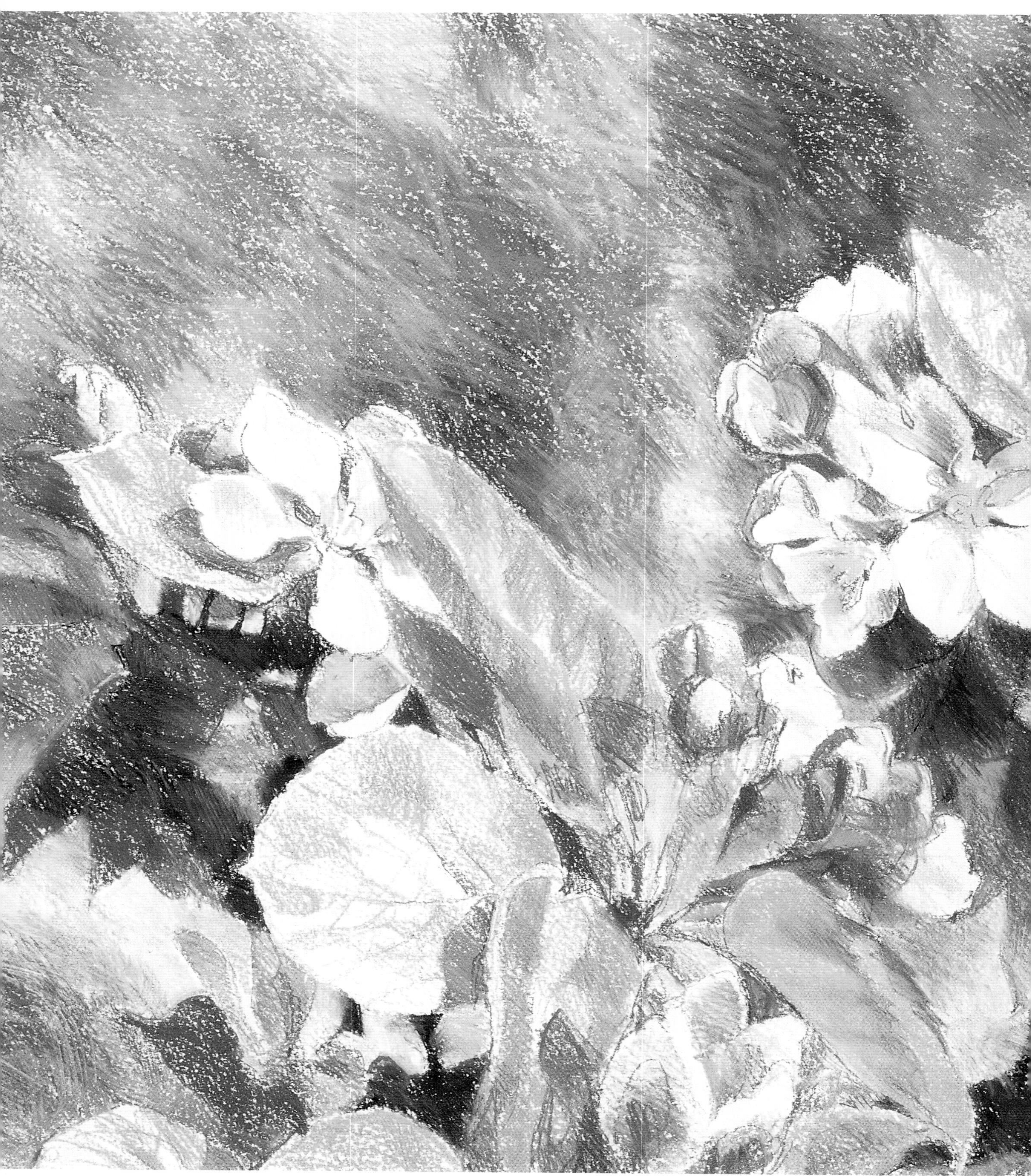

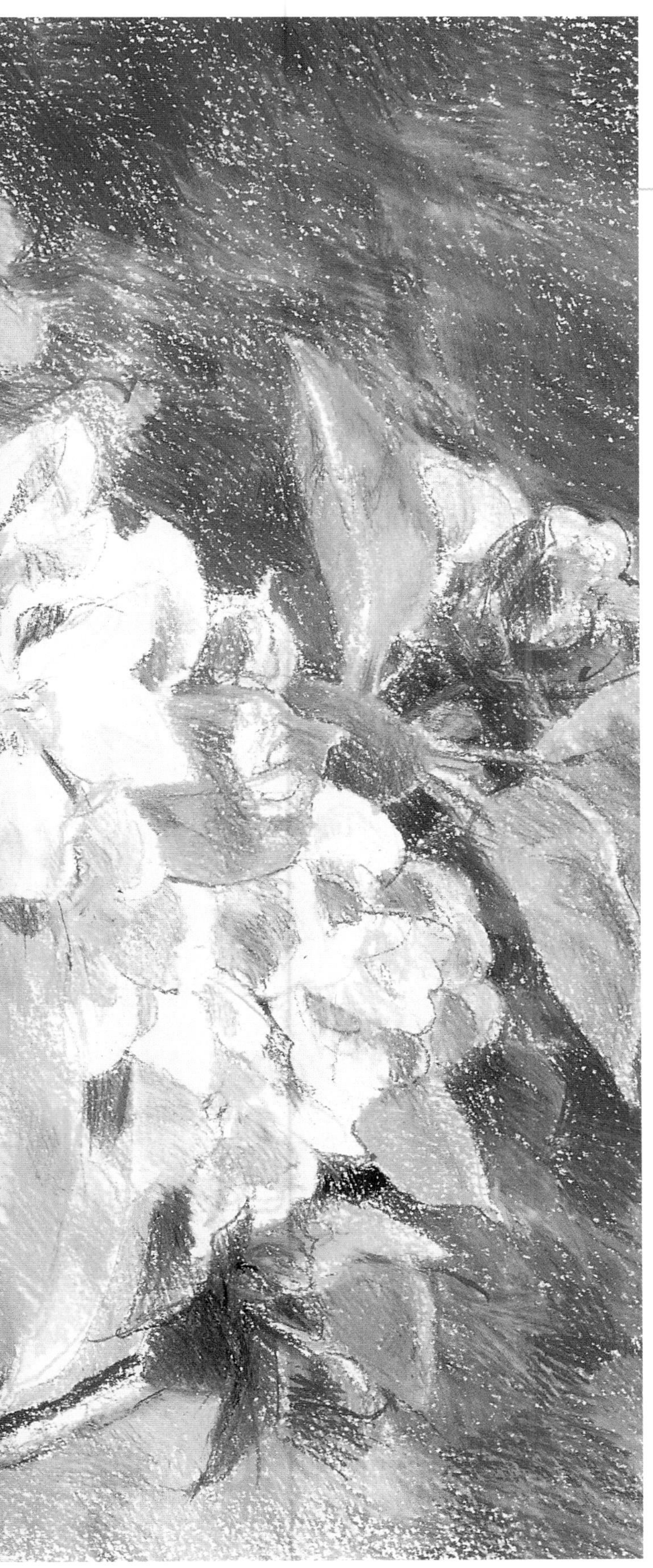

PART 1

Techniques

Technique really is just the way we choose to put pencil to paper, or for that matter, ink, pastel, chalk, charcoal, or paint to any surface, be it card, wood, canvas, stone, or plaster. It can be as simple as that—no special effects, just laying material or materials onto a surface.

Nevertheless, a certain amount of knowledge can be invaluable, and sometimes essential, for some materials react strangely—water cannot thin standard oil paint, and watercolor does not sit well when painted on wood. There are fun things to try out that can expand your range of possibilities with perhaps limited materials, giving you a new dimension of texture, or paint quality to explore.

Technique can sometimes get you out of trouble when things go wrong, or it can help you improve your expertise so that mistakes are minimized—and you can relax and enjoy the experience of creating artwork, rather than worrying at every stage.

A change of material, technique, and direction can be refreshing—try applying light tones in pastel work after working with watercolor, for example—but do not become so immersed in clever technique that you lose your direction in the picture as a whole. The choice of techniques is a careful balancing act that relates at the same time to the composition, subject matter, and your approach to it.

Getting started Pencils, Conté, and monochrome mediums

This can be as simple as you want to make it—a single flower or leaf can be all you need for a still life, and, together with a pencil and paper, it is all there.

It rarely stays that simple, though. Looking at the wealth of available choice of mediums can be confusing, even when just considering the simple method of "black" marks on paper. Black can be silver, sooty, all tones of gray, or a deep blue-black, with textures encompassing coarse, fine, dull, shiny, solid, and translucent. These marks can be water-resistant, or soluble in water to form washes, or can just be smudged.

CHOOSING YOUR MEDIUM

When considering your approach to your plant subject, look at how it holds itself. Is it strong, angular, woody or gnarled? Perhaps charcoal, Conté, or wax pencil would help express its character or movement. In contrast, the fine texture of the pasque-flower or the fragile hanging head of a snowdrop would probably ask for a more delicate approach— here, a graphite pencil

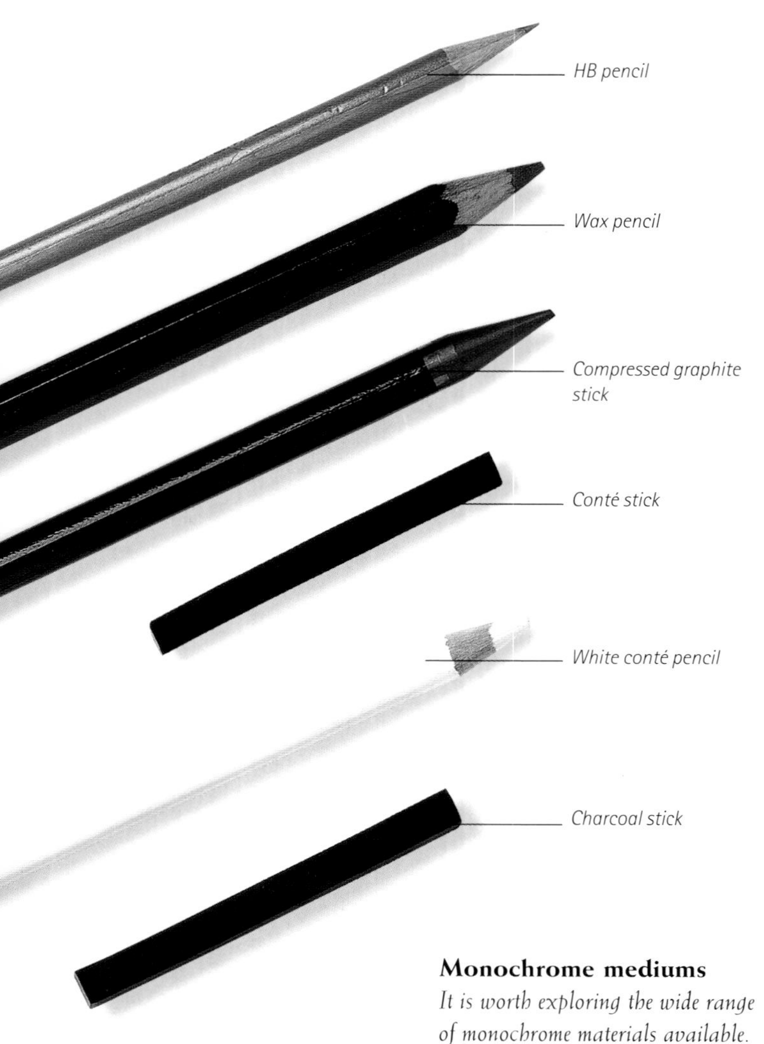

Monochrome mediums
It is worth exploring the wide range of monochrome materials available. Different applications often ask for a certain type of pencil or stick.

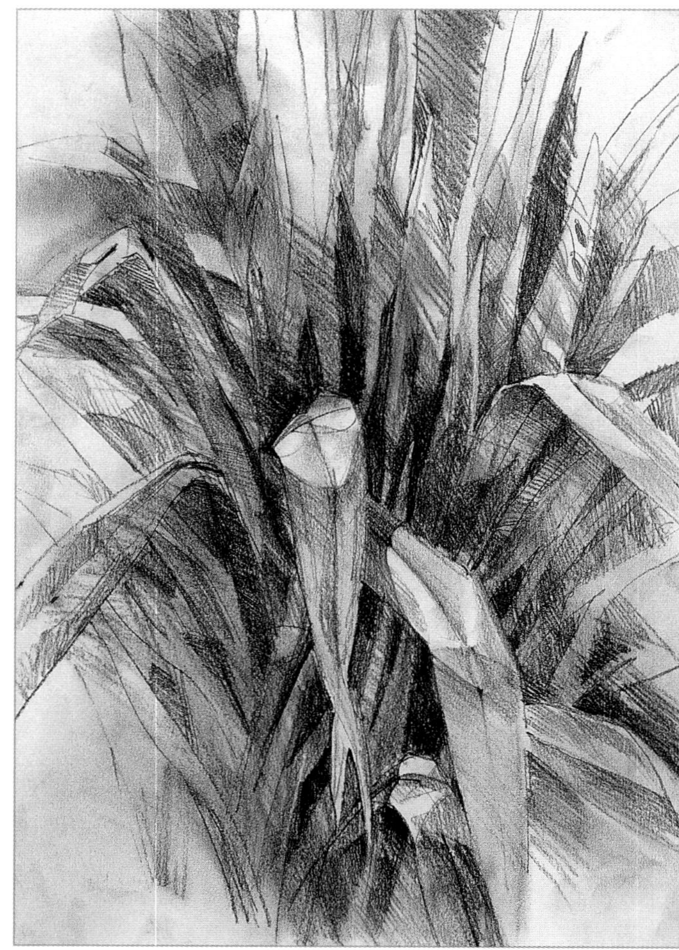

Study in tone
A soft, Conté pencil gave me a full range of tone for this study of light and shade. The softness of the Conté gave me a chance to smudge the tone a little, without losing the quality of line.

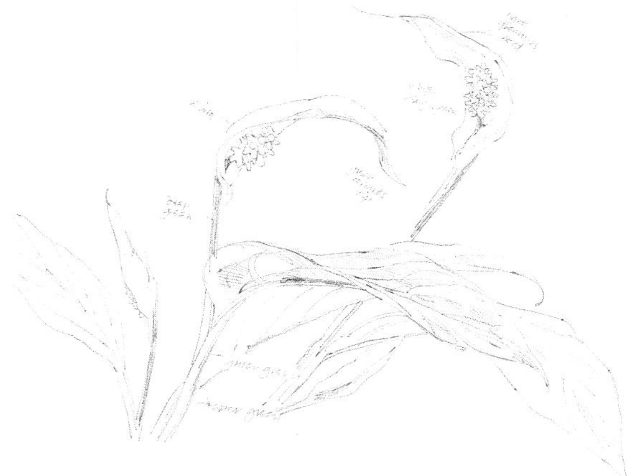

Aide-memoire (above)
When working in monochrome, written notes can be very helpful to jolt the memory of certain color details.

Tonal study in pencil (right)
This study, with a 5B pencil, helps describe the form and solidity of the subject. I was interested in the fleshy leaves and unusual plant structure.

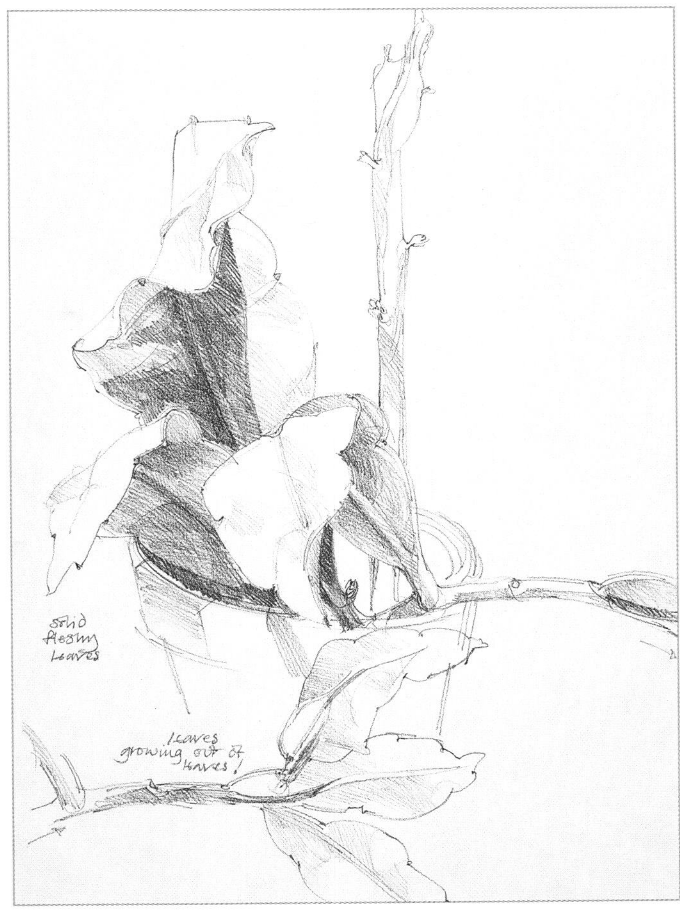

or compressed graphite stick might be appropriate. The scale of your drawing can also greatly affect what you use. A Conté stick that may look crude on a small scale can have power, as well as great sensitivity when swept in large movements on a full sheet of paper or board.

There are no rules. A primrose can be drawn two feet tall. It's all about looking, analyzing, and interpreting. You can reduce elements down to their basics, or develop the detail and texture, as you wish.

SURFACES

Different surfaces, or supports, add to the variety of marks that can be made. Smooth paper lends itself to a drawing with more and finer shading, whereas textured paper deepens the tone and exaggerates the texture with, for instance, wax or Conté sticks. Colored or midtone papers can work well when you introduce white or light-tone Conté or pencils to widen your tonal range.

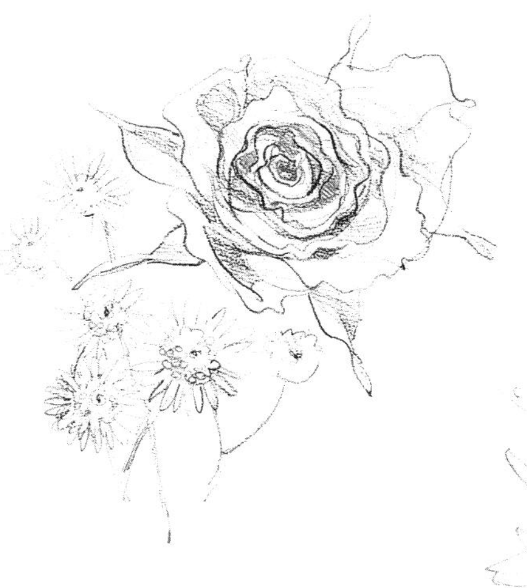

Pencil plus another medium
Pencil studies can be enhanced by introducing another medium—in this case far left, Conté: When quickly sketching a flower, look at its overall shape. Is it circular, triangular, or even rectangular? Keep this in mind, as the whole can get lost when you concentrate on the details.

Pen and wash

Images in black and white need not be just in a dry medium. Obviously you can paint in monochrome with oil or acrylic, but for study purposes, pen and wash is a wonderfully fluid way of drawing.

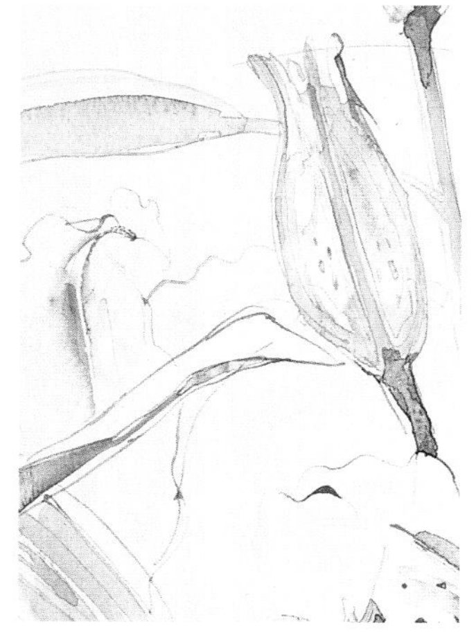

NIBS AND MARKS

You can achieve great detail with fine nibs, or softer, wider lines with bamboo or reed pens. Metal nibs can give you scratchy, energetic lines, while bamboo glides more easily across your surface in a smoother rhythm. Ink can be watered down to create a light, delicate line, or marks can be washed when still wet to give a blurred effect. Try dampening the paper first, and your subsequent marks can bleed, adding to your range of textures and effects.

Home-made drawing implement
I cut off a bit of dying leaf from the base of this plant and used it as my tool for drawing. The possibilities are endless!

Simple color marks
Color pen work, even in its simplest form, can still communicate a great deal about the likeness, form, and color of the subject.

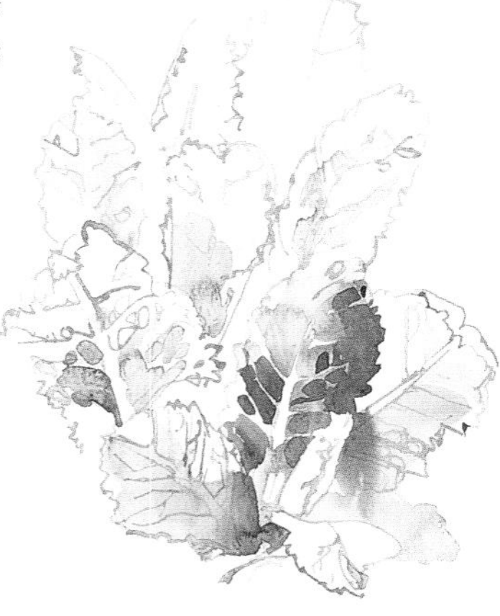

INKS

Ink that is waterproof can be useful if you want to keep your marks clean, but still be able to wash areas to create midtones. Check how waterproof it is, however, as some are not as good as they promise to be, and some bleeding can still occur.

The word "experimentation" comes up again here, as there are no real rules about making marks with inks. Anything can be dipped in ink, whether it be a trimmed feather quill, stick, or plant stem—after all, that is what a bamboo pen is. Brushes are lovely and expressive for drawing, especially when you consider what can be done with an oriental brush.

Bamboo pen (above)
Using a bamboo pen gives a broader, softer, wider line, and the nib flows easily over the paper.

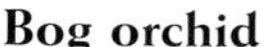

Bog orchid
When studying this plant, I used wash line and hatching to develop the structure, tone, and mottled patterning.

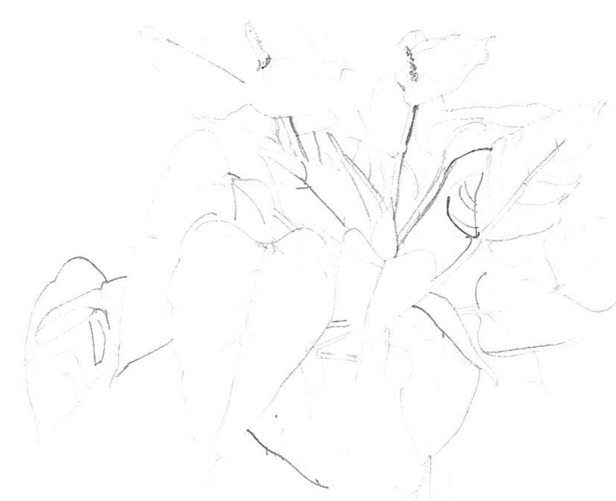

Contour drawing
You can convey a lot about a subject with pure, linear work.

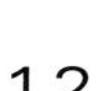

Colored pencils and watercolor pencils

Color is hard to ignore when studying flora. There are many different ways of approaching the recording of color in your subject, using dry mediums.

A popular method, used by many artists, is to study the subject in purely neutral line and tone before applying color in the latter stages. If you are up against time, you might find study sketches useful, where you draw tonally and then indicate color with notes and small swatches, either on the drawing or alongside.

COLORED PENCILS

I like to work in color right from the start if possible, whether in line, areas of wash, or both. Colored pencils and watercolor pencils are very useful and versatile for this quick process of recording. They are clean to use, easily transportable, and you can get a wonderful range of colors. They can be sharpened to give either a fine point or a broader edge, which is perfect for line work, as well as for shading and hatching. Use the pencils broadly and you keep the texture open, or shade with them delicately to produce smooth, detailed work.

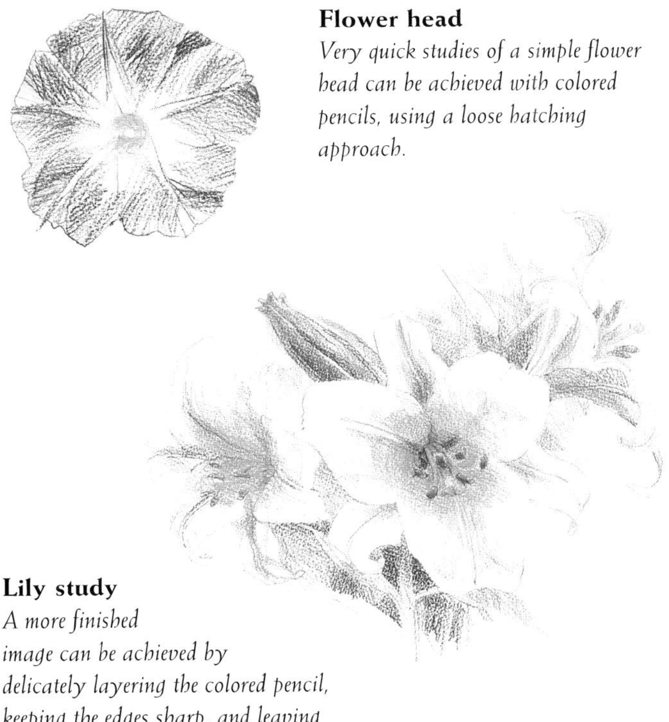

Flower head
Very quick studies of a simple flower head can be achieved with colored pencils, using a loose hatching approach.

Lily study
A more finished image can be achieved by delicately layering the colored pencil, keeping the edges sharp, and leaving the areas of white clean where needed.

WATERCOLOR PENCILS

Watercolor, or water-soluble, pencils have all the advantages of colored pencils, and more. By adding water, either to the tip of the pencil, or to the marks on the paper, you can blend the colors more easily and create washes. This saves time if your alternative is to constantly shade with pencil—more importantly to me, it adds a freshness, and creates more variety and texture in the artwork.

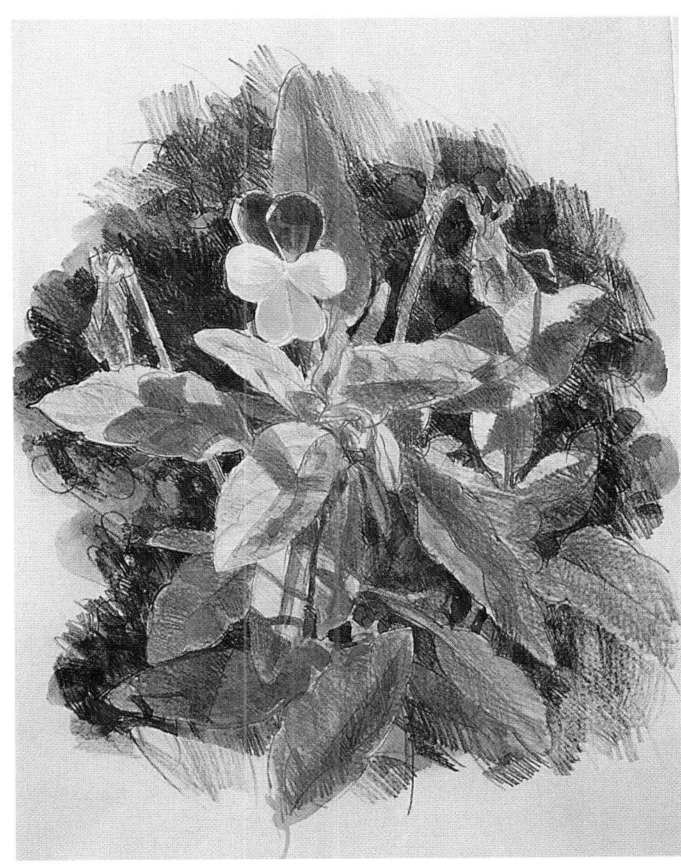

Watercolor pencil study
This viola was catching the light. I vignetted the tone around the plant, washing pencil to strengthen the colors by brushing clean water over the pencil marks.

WATERCOLOR PASTELS

Where colored pencils are wonderful for detail and more subtle shading, watercolor pastels have vibrantly rich colors with a chunky, textured line of oil pastel. The great surprise when adding water is the wonderful richness and power of the colors as they blend and wash, which is superb for large, quick sketches as well as finished artwork—I think of big, architectural plants or a tropical scene. For delicate areas I sometimes use a brush to wet the pastel—almost like a watercolor pan—and apply small touches of color with just the brush.

ROSE HIPS

The richness of the red in these rose hips against the color in the foliage is translated beautifully in these rich pastels.

Some light areas of wash were created using paint running from adjacent hatched areas, moved around the paper by a wet brush.

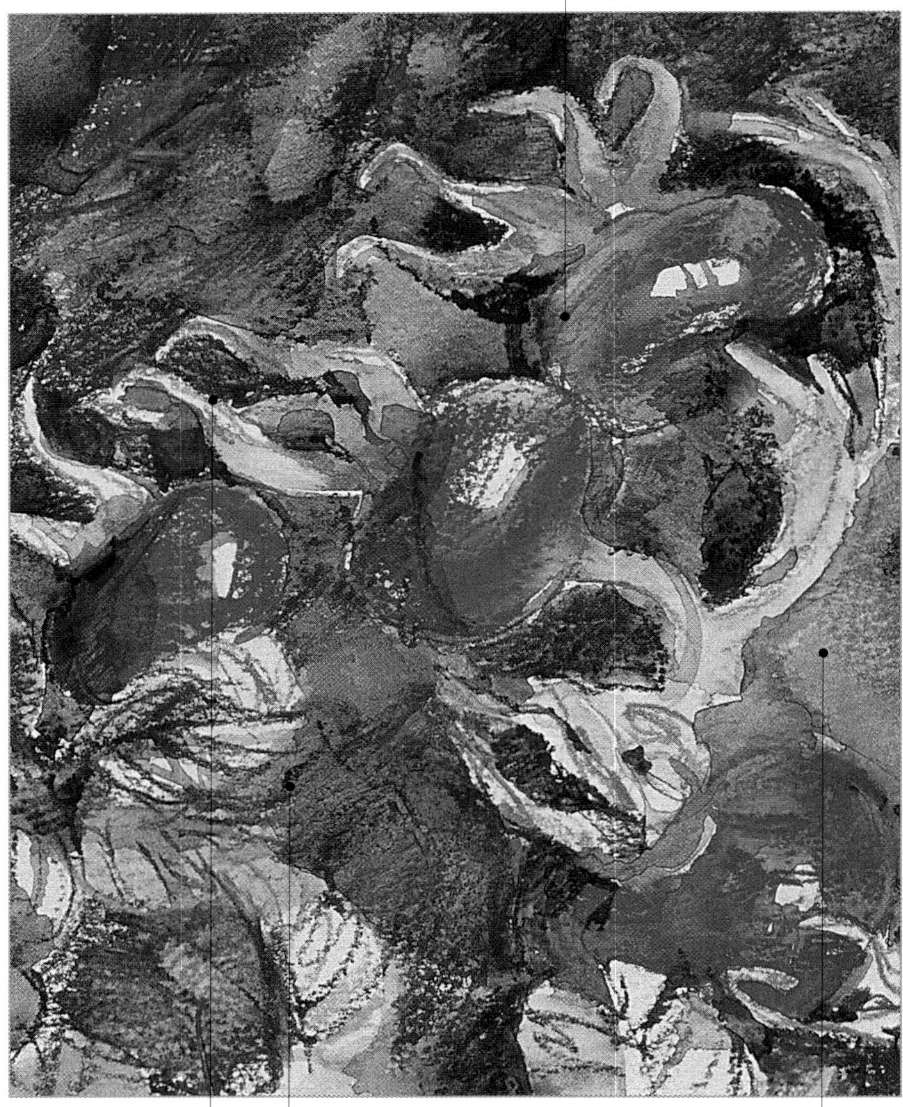

This area was washed, then left to dry, and when completely dry, some line was reapplied in pastel, which then was able to hold its edge

Water was added to areas of hatching in the shadows, washing away the pastel marks to various degrees.

Pastel marks were left unwashed, to keep the freshness of line against the white of the paper.

MAKING MARKS AND MIXING MEDIUMS

Using just a graphite pencil, the range of marks that you can experiment with is limitless. You can dot, dash, scribble, hatch, and crosshatch, blend carefully, run a constant line, vary the weight of line, erase, smudge—the list is endless.

Introduce water and you can flick, splash, run water down, puddle, drag a dry brush, and so on.

Mixing the mediums increases the possibilities, so try them out on samples or swatches of paper (or the back of unsuccessful efforts), and become more familiar with them. Finally, embrace mistakes, as they can often be a pleasant surprise or teach a valuable lesson.

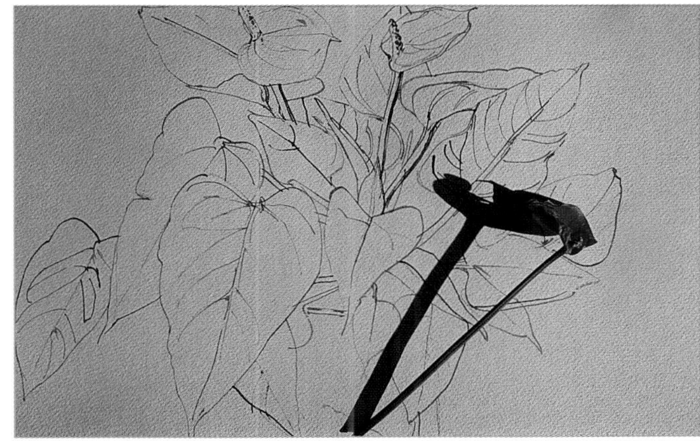

Making marks
The flower head on this lily was dying, so I used its stalk to dip in the ink for this linear drawing.

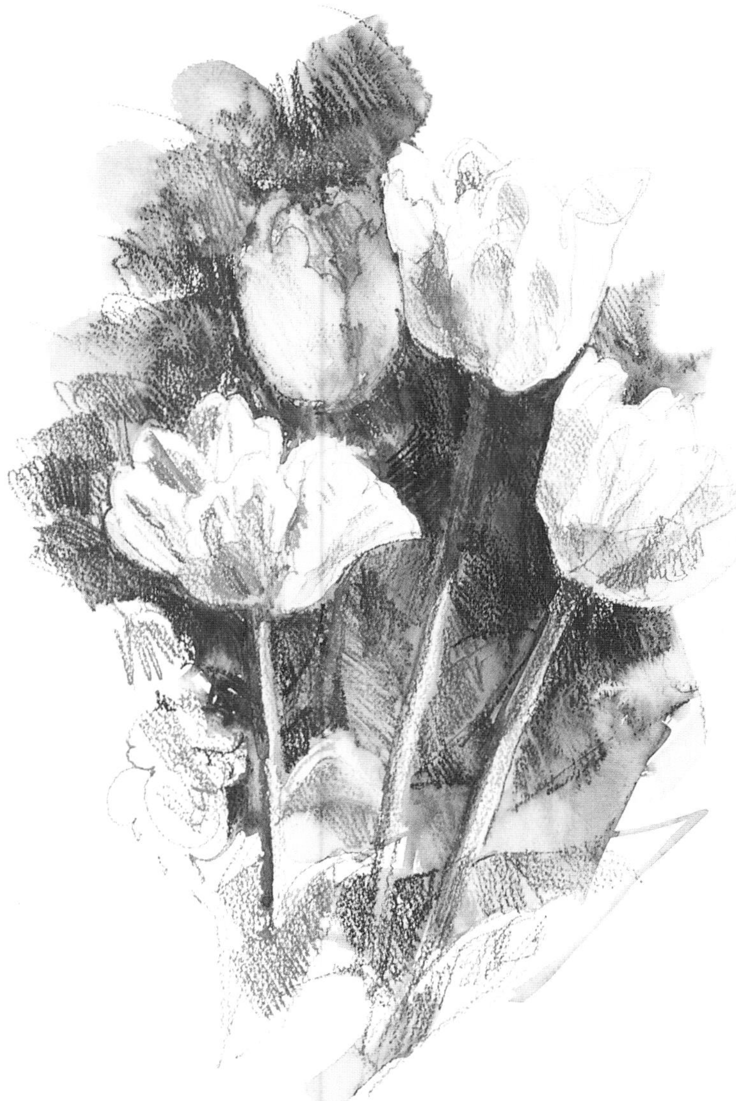

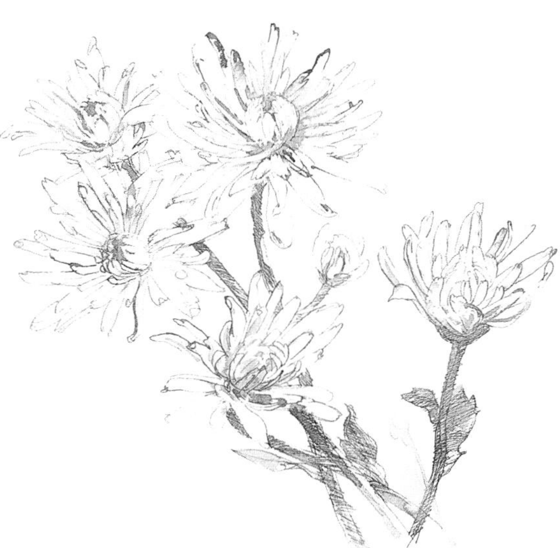

Mixing mediums
Using a light gray paper, I first drew with ink, added a little wash, then used white Conté to highlight the white petals on these daisies.

Tulips
The large range of available pastels enables you to use them for more delicate hues as well. Drawing these tulips, I still used the medium freely, but employed it to look for the light caught on these blooms.

Paper and sketchbooks

As mentioned previously, the choice you make from the wide variety of available papers can greatly affect the finished artwork, so it is worth taking time to find out what best suits your medium and style.

Generally speaking, a rough-textured surface works well with larger, or simpler, powerful images, but if you want to develop more detail, a finer, smooth surface is more in your favor.

Drawing paper is usually made of wood pulp that is treated with size to reduce the absorbency, so that a pen line or wash does not bleed into the paper. The weight of the paper also varies and can be affected by the medium. A lightweight 60lb (120gsm) paper can buckle badly if washes are laid on it. The heavier the weight (or higher the number), the less it will buckle, but for stability of working I would still recommend that you stretch the paper lightly (see page 30), unless you want to keep the deckle edges for more decorative, framing purposes.

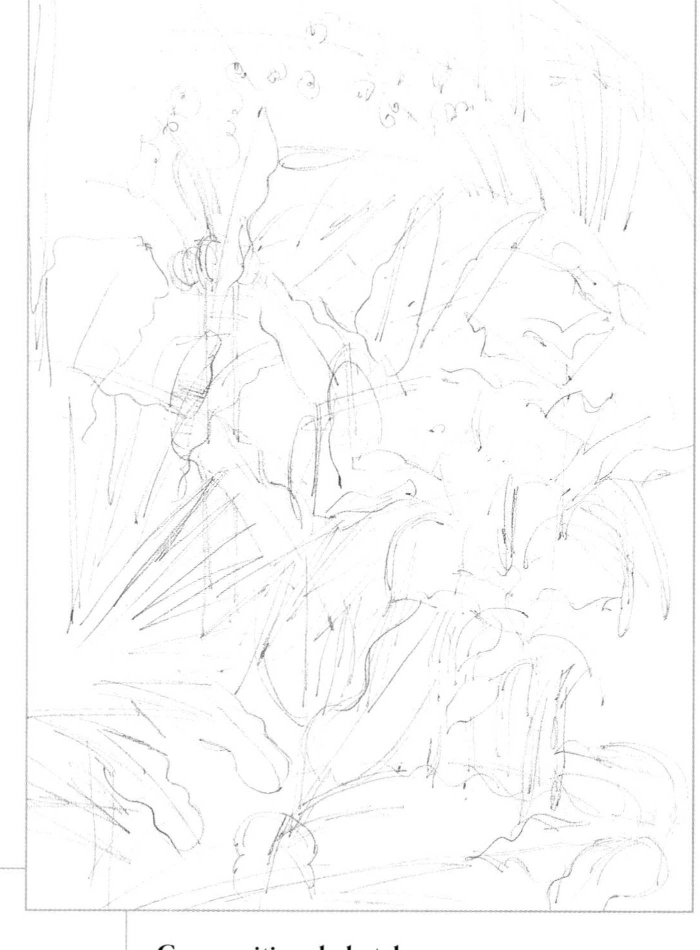

Compositional sketch
In this scene of complicated and intersecting elements, I sketched to feel my way into the image, which helped me to clarify the details and eliminate irrelevent areas.

Linear sketch
This sketchbook study explores the simple, abstract shapes of trees in winter.

Watercolor paper is sized and prepared so that it is perfect for large areas of wash. This is examined further on page 30, but it is a lovely paper to use for drawing, even in sketchbook form—it can bring out the quality of your line or wash, often making it a piece of artwork in its own right.

SKETCHBOOKS

Before buying a sketchbook, think hard about how you want to use it. Sketchbooks with mid-weight or fine-textured paper that is white or light cream in color are perfect for most uses. They can be pocket-size, suitable for thumbnail sketches, increasing to ones that just fit under your arm. The format can be portrait or landscape.

The larger sizes open up the possibilities of using different mediums, but are more cumbersome, and may be left behind for reasons of space. Watercolor sketchbooks are more expensive, but are worth thinking about if you want to develop watercolor artwork to a more finished state.

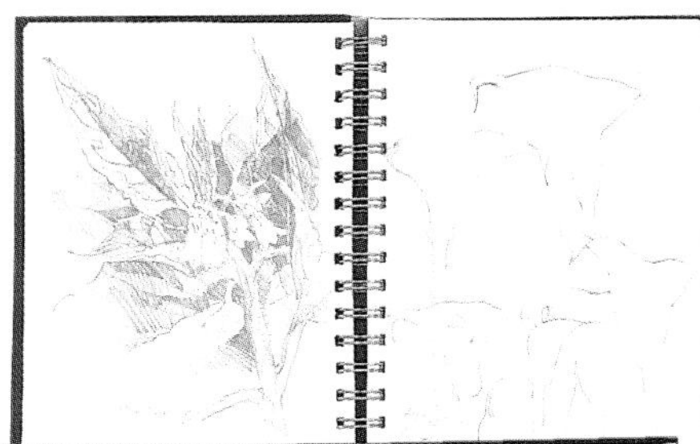

Spiral-bound sketchbook
These books are sturdy (glued spines can break apart), and you can remove pages if required.

Landscape sketchbook
A landscape format is perfect for just that very use—even a wide, linear landscape can be explored on a double spread.

Making a sketchbook

You can make books to suit your own requirements—this is fun, useful, very adaptable, and cheaper than buying sketchbooks from a store.

The simplest method is to just cut your own paper—of different colors and textures if you want—and card covers, then punch three or more holes along one side, and link the pages together loosely with ribbon or string. You can easily remove any sheets that need to dry—or perhaps to be framed.

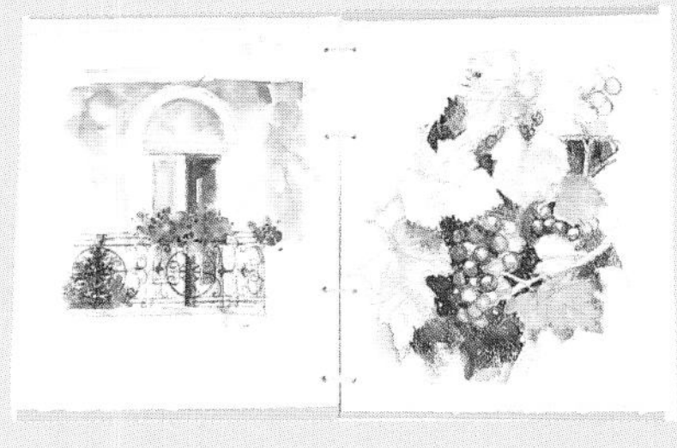

Location equipment

This can become as simple or as complicated as you want it to be, depending on how you want to work. Are you sketching quickly, moving around to try different angles and views–or have these decisions already been made, and a more finished painting is your objective?

Planning is crucial, specially if you are aiming to produce more finished artwork. A forgotten, important color or brush is frustrating, to say the least, and the light can change in an instant. I carry a very useful roll-up pouch with compartments for brushes, pencils, pens, erasers, etc. which are visible and easily checked. For short journeys I use a solid box for carrying materials, but it is lighter to use a soft bag for longer walks. I also have a bag that unfolds into a stool, which is very useful for longer studies and sketches.

A good drawing board, that can be purpose-made or a sheet of plywood, blockboard, or even thin MDF (medium-density fiberboard), is a must, because paper may need to be stretched, or just pinned, taped, or clipped, depending on your personal preference. The important thing is not to let the wind get the better of you! Even sketchbooks without clips can drive you to distraction in the wind.

The way you support the board can vary according to your method of work. For quick sketches, you will need only to hold it, or to lean it against a convenient wall or fence. A strap around your shoulders, attached to each side of the board, is very versatile when moving around, but if you are in one place for a while, a folding easel is a great asset. Comfort is important, as you don't want any extra distractions, so try a variety of equipment out from the many different designs on the market.

The choice of art materials is up to you, but consider the weight and safety and try to reduce the glass content—use plastic bottles for water and other liquids, and plastic palettes for mixing.

Anatomy

I do not intend to concentrate on the botanical study of flora in this book, but a basic knowledge of the structure and workings of a plant helps you to relax, and thus to produce a more convincing piece of work.

Absolute detail is not necessarily the point, but with odd angles or shaded light, for instance, a knowledge of the plant gives a confidence, fluidity and integrity to your work.

The drawing below shows the structure of some basic flowers, which are pretty well the same for most flower structures. The flower grows out from the central reproductive parts. These are basically symmetrical, either down the central line, like an iris; or radially from the center, like a daisy.

The outer calyx of sepals, which protects the flower bud, connects the flower to the stem. It can hold the head upright, or drop it downward like a snowdrop. Capturing details such as this really helps to characterize the habit of the plant, its weight, and its growth and movement.

Anatomy of a flower

Collectively, the stigma, style, and ovary are called the pistil. The anther and filament are the stamen, and where the sepals fuse as one, they become the calyx, joining the flower to the stem.

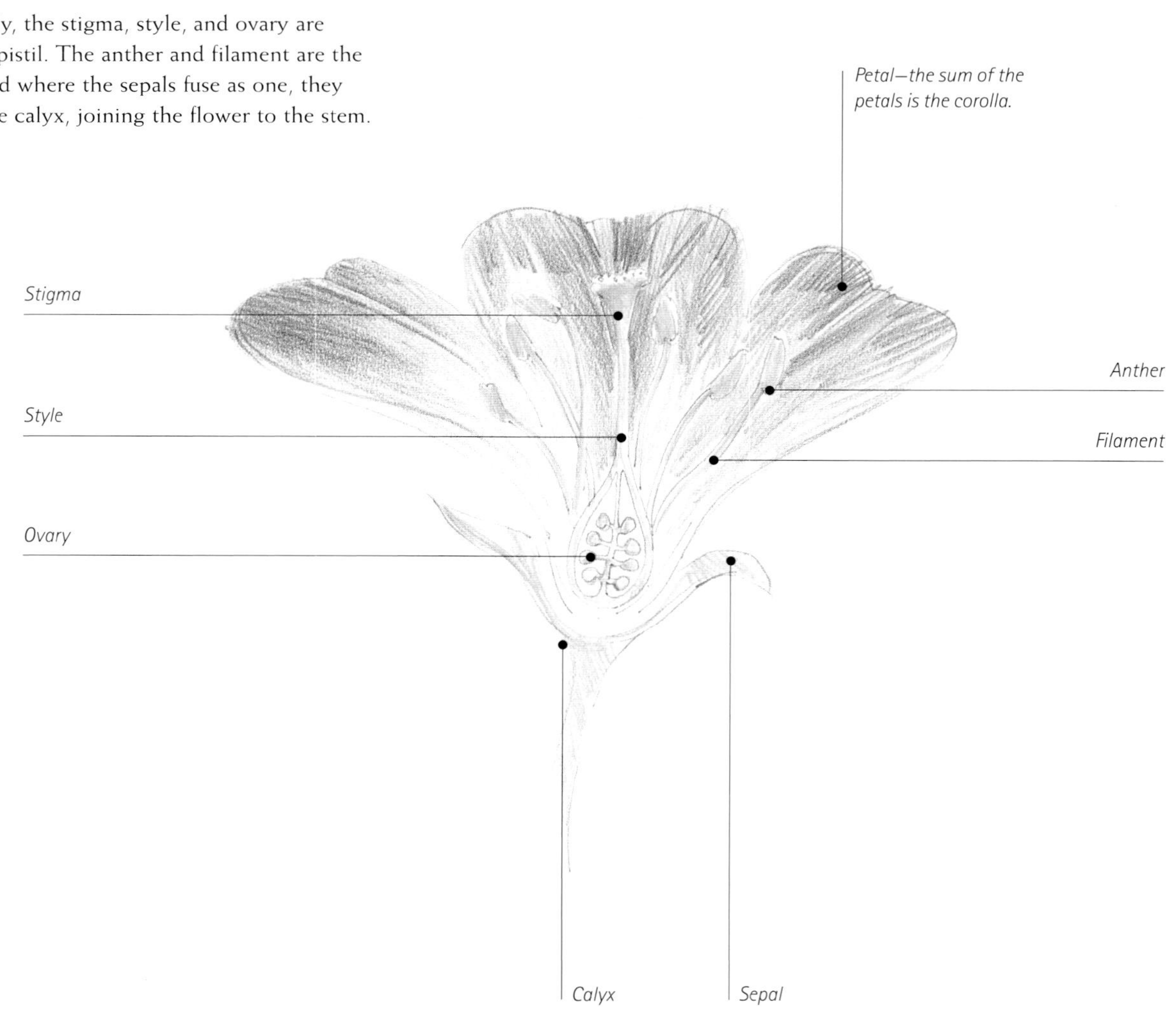

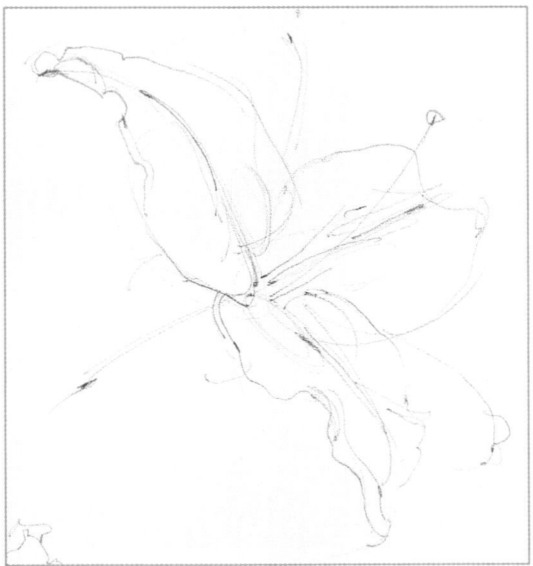

Developmental sketches
Above: *I first picked out the three primary petals of this lily.* **Below:** *From this I could determine the position of the second layer of petals (left). I was then confident to proceed with the tonal drawing (right).*

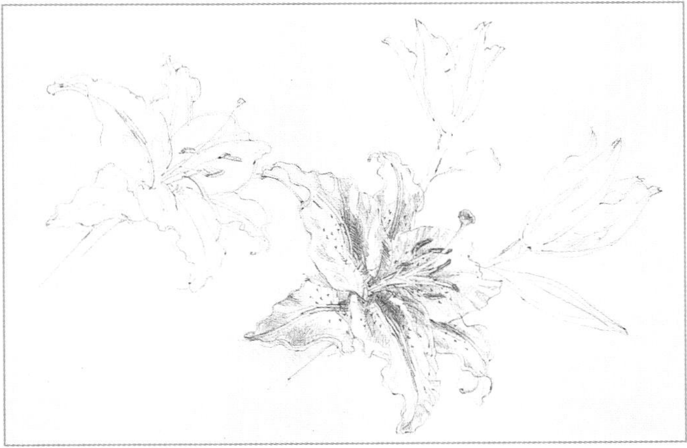

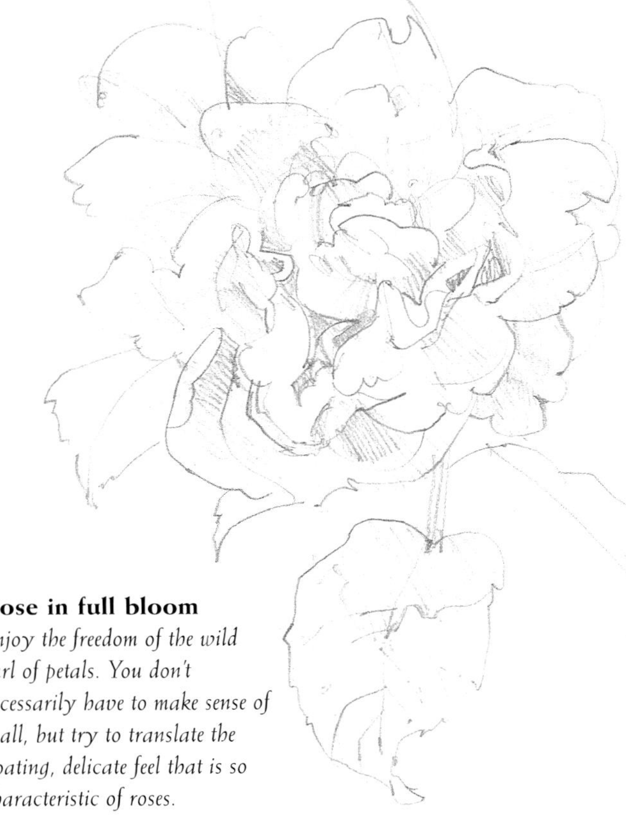

Rose in full bloom
Enjoy the freedom of the wild curl of petals. You don't necessarily have to make sense of it all, but try to translate the floating, delicate feel that is so characteristic of roses.

Leaves can be thin and delicate in their structure or solid and fleshy, smooth, shiny, matte, or hairy. All give hints of their character, which I believe is more important than always religiously recording every detail.

LEAVES

Moving down the stem, your next consideration is the formation of the leaves. The two main groups fall into the categories of opposite and alternate leaves. As you would expect, opposite leaves leave the same point of the stem in pairs, and alternate leaves are arranged along the stem individually.

Basal leaves occur at the base of the stem, most commonly rising from a bulb, or corm. Whorled leaves radiating out from the stem are less common.

Leaves can be very individual and recognizable—for example, oak leaves, with their "lobed" or wavy margins, are very obvious. The edges can be smooth or serrated, feathery, or have compound leaves made up of individual leaflets.

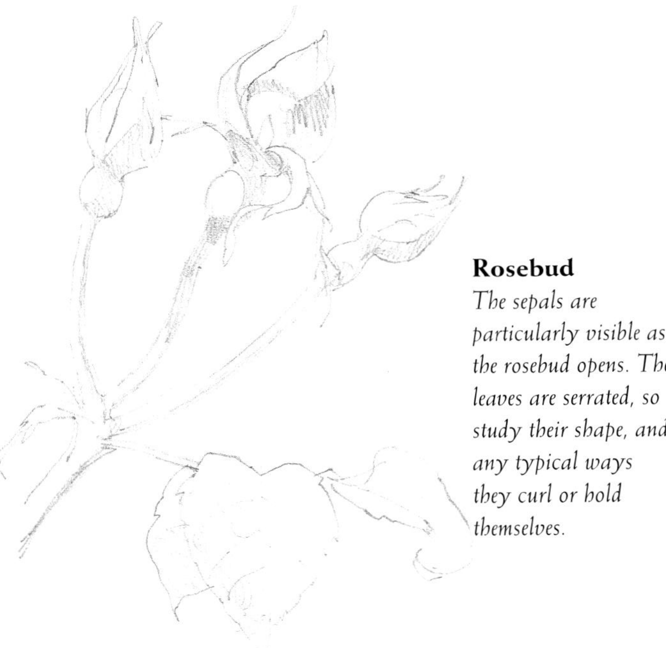

Rosebud
The sepals are particularly visible as the rosebud opens. The leaves are serrated, so study their shape, and any typical ways they curl or hold themselves.

Interior studies

It is often easiest to study a single flower or stem by cutting a good example to place in a controlled area—most probably your studio, or a well-lit room. This makes the environment more comfortable for you, there is more time to work than there is out of doors, and you have a variety of materials without the problems of transportation.

You can use natural light or supply yourself with a constant light source, even to the extent of spotlighting your subject artificially.

If you simply lay your specimen on a sheet or table, it may suffer from a lack of water within a few hours. Wrapping damp paper or cotton balls around the cut stem can help. I use a narrow vase to support my subjects, so they stay fresher, and keep their positions as in their natural habitats.

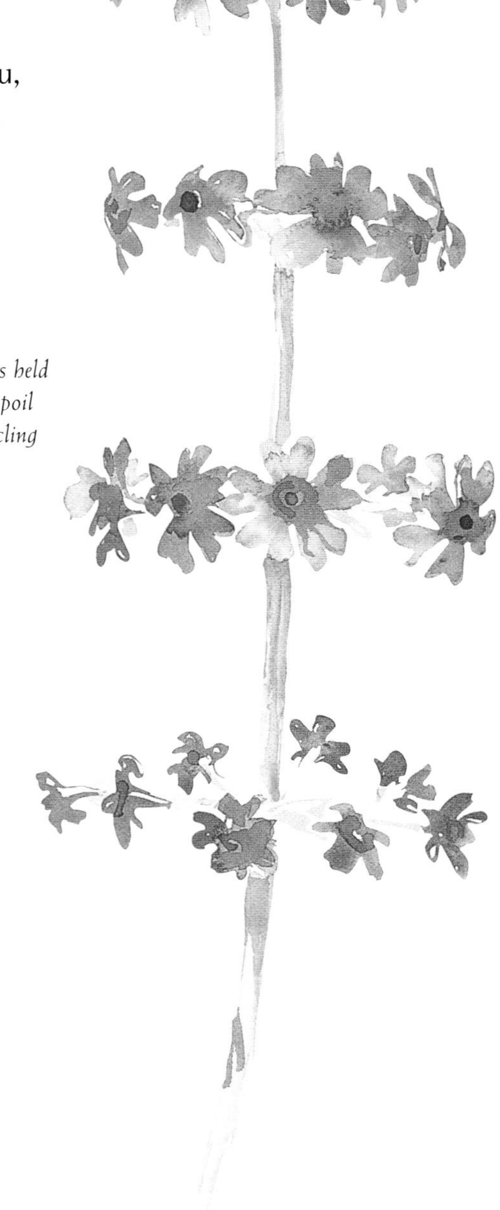

Concentrating on the subject
The single stem of this candelabra primula was held in a vase, so as not to spoil its tiers of flowers encircling the stem.

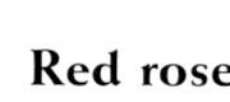

Red rose
This study shows the general shape and coloring of the leaf and flower, without drawing every vein on the leaf. The shadow shows that it is a cut specimen.

COMPOSITION AND BACKDROPS

Vases of flowers or potted plants can become quite involved, and often more preparation and time are needed. A simple bouquet can be far more effective than a huge, complicated arrangement because the flowers can be lost in a mass of detail.

You can choose to keep your subject isolated against a plain background—this certainly makes it easier to study the plant without the distractions of other details. On the other hand, a setting can sometimes help your

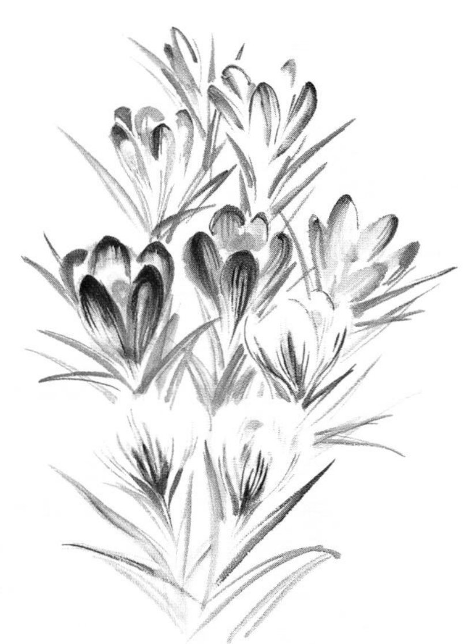

Crocuses
Light, airy brush-strokes can be particularly apt for capturing the delicate patterning on crocuses.

Caption head 18/2
Chinese white paint was used to bring these flowers to life on oriental paper. The simplicity of the the leaves echoes the oriental mood.

subject, especially if it is a simple shape. A shaded background can give strength to light and delicate blooms, so it is worth spending time setting up the positions.

BUILDING UP THE STUDY

At the early stages, remember to keep everything quite simple, and as you sketch you will become more familiar with the subject—your marks become more fluid, and the need to measure, check, and correct things decreases as confidence in your eye-and-hand coordination increases. This is not a botanical exercise in the strictest sense, and as long as you observe the basic form, structure and movement of a plant, you should have the essence, without needing everything to be scaled up and perfect in size with every detail included.

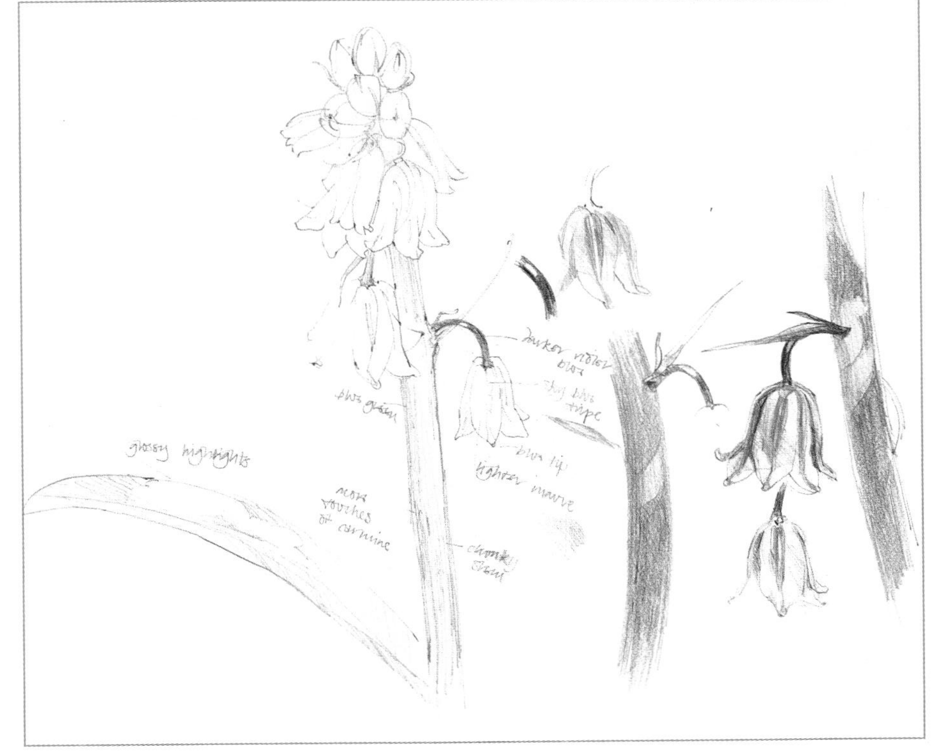

Bluebells
These studies were started with a B graphite pencil, but the amazing color change from stem to calyx and flower prompted the introduction of color, in note form and detailed examples.

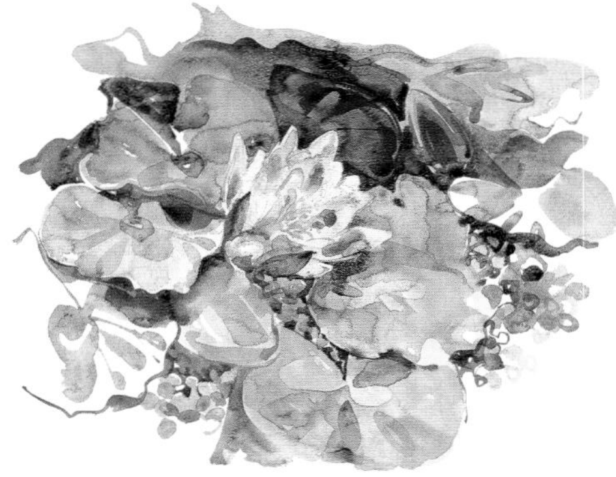

Water lilies
These lilies in my pond are a favorite subject, and watercolor seems to lend itself to this subject.

Exotic garden
Working directly in watercolor wash, the aim was to show the majestic, yet calming, atmosphere created when sitting among these columns of palm trees on the island of Madeira.

Exterior studies

It is true that sketching outside can be more uncomfortable than in your studio—the weather can be frustratingly windy or rainy, and carrying materials is awkward. However, the excuse to get out to enjoy the scent of a rose garden, find a quiet corner with a wonderful view, or simply escape and sit by a pond—all in the name of work!—is enough persuasion for me.

If you are farther afield than your own back yard, it is wise to prepare your materials carefully. Location equipment has already been discussed on page 17, but the important thing is to keep it light, compact, and suitable for the subject in mind. A quick sketch in pencil is always useful, and I often do a series of different views, where I invariably change my choice from the first view I had decided upon.

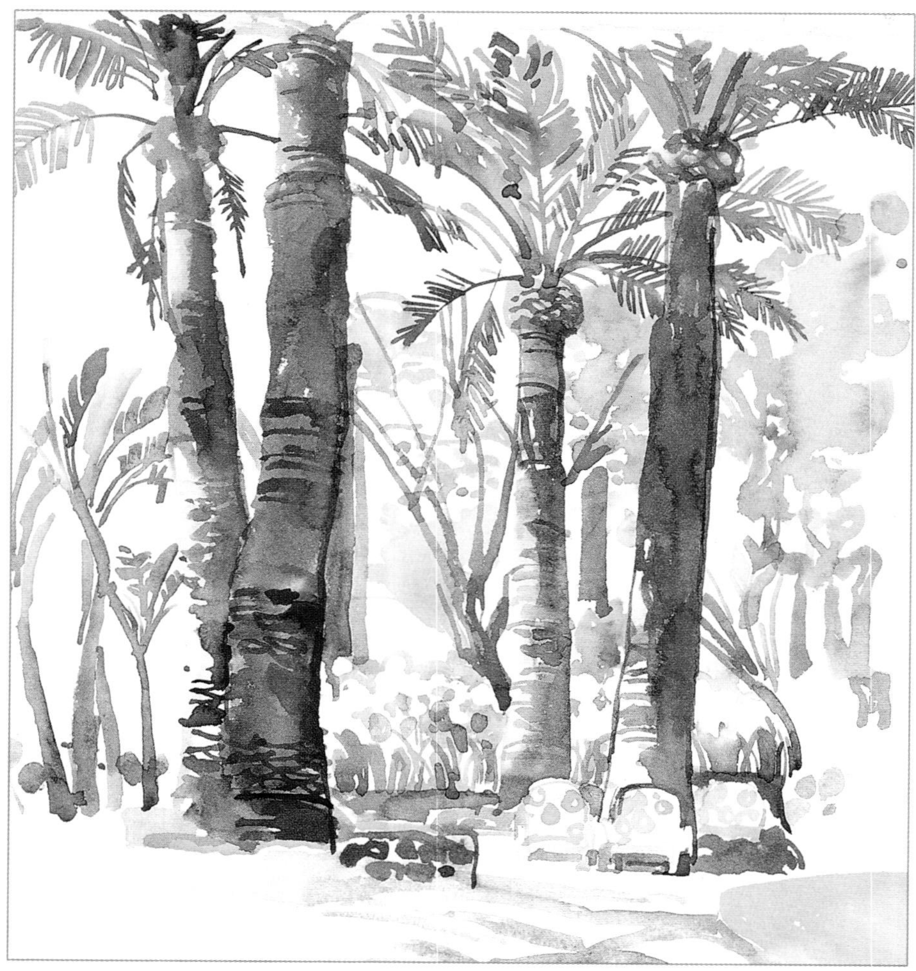

PAINTING STUDIES

In trying to keep a sense of freedom in my work, I regularly start immediately with paint, usually watercolor. I draw light washes with the brush, trying to keep to the basics to give a sense of light and structure. What happens next can vary—I might draw into the study with some other material, or leave it to start another version of the same or a similar view.

This particular approach comes only with practice and doesn't suit everybody, but it can work extremely well with strong, simple subjects. The ability to lay down areas of color and tone, to set up an immediate structure for the painting, counteracts the time required for it to dry—a sunny day helps too, of course.

DRAWING STUDIES

Detailed pencil studies are very useful, especially if you intend to gather together reference for developing a drawing or painting back in the studio. Do extra sketches of particular details with notes of color and tone, or maybe swatches of color added on. Get as much information as possible, recording shadow patterns, tonal values, and subtle changes of color. When you rely solely on your memory, the work can become labored and unconvincing. If you are not sure about any areas, keep them simple—you were probably not focusing on them in the first place. Photographs can be a useful memory aid, but don't rely on them. Rather use them as extra pieces of information.

Colored pencils are good for small-scale or detailed work; wax crayons and oil pastels are very practical; and pastel is a lovely medium, as long as you remember to fix it, or protect it with paper. Any of these mediums are useful, whether you are gleaning information or just enjoying the moment. I can't think of a better reason to get out.

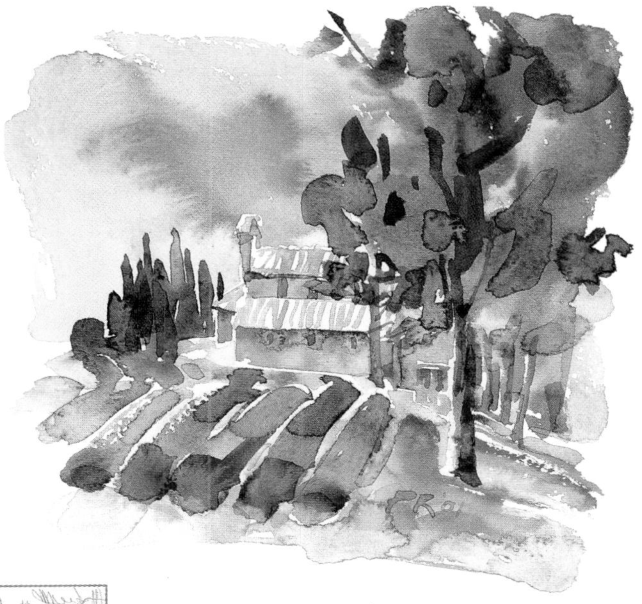

Reducing to basic shapes
The abstract patterning of these lavender beds needs only to be approached in a very simple, directional way.

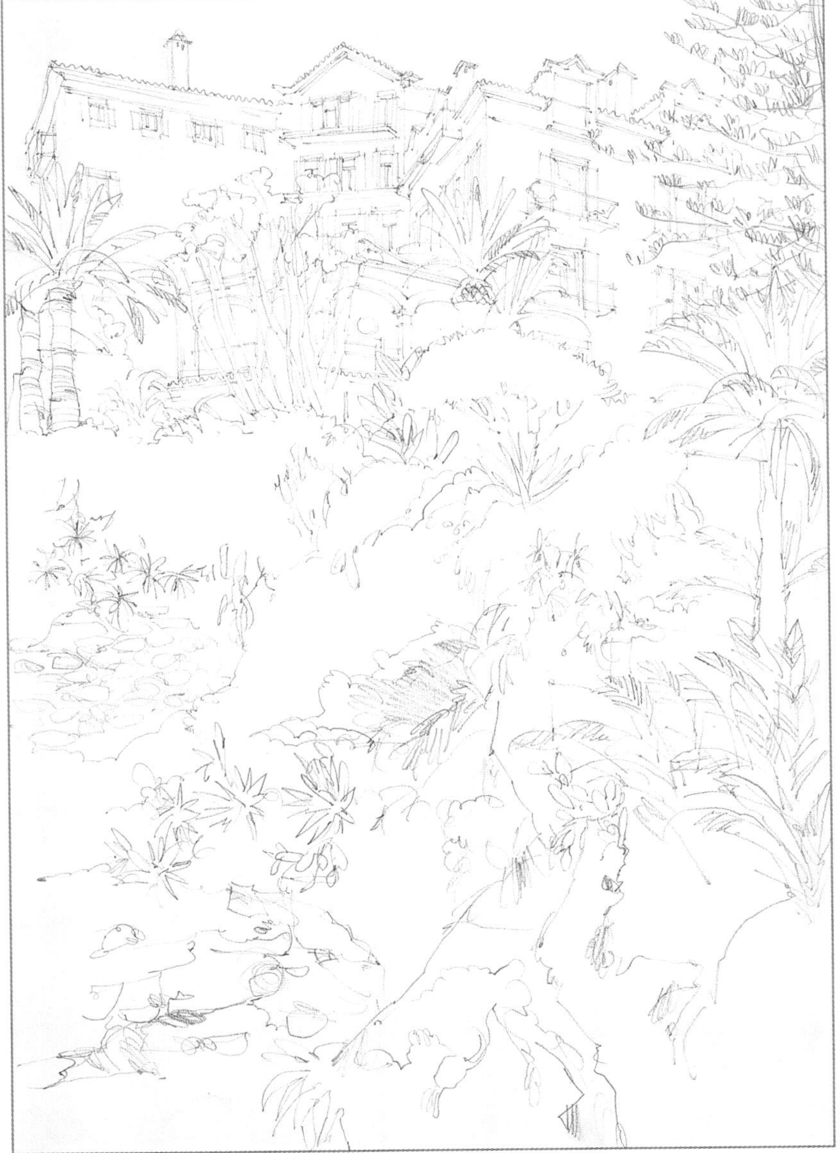

Cliff sketch, Madeira
This sketchbook study describes the wonderful, lush vegetation that clings to the cliff faces and tumbles to the garden below.

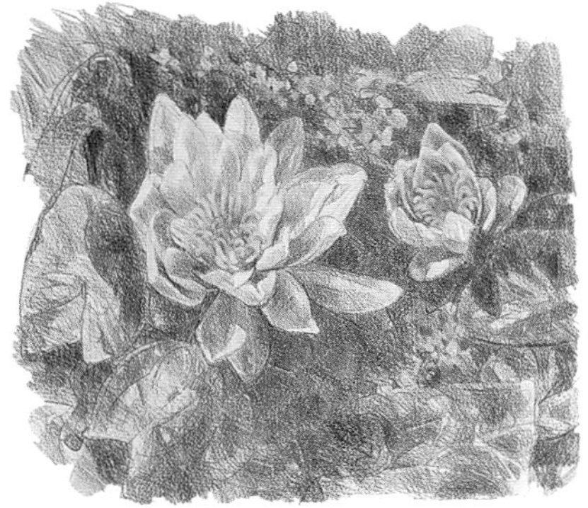

Wax crayons
Materials as simple as my daughter Lauren's wax crayons can be built up to achieve a wide range of tone, hue, and texture.

Developing your studies

Colored bars and sticks

The range of colored bars or sticks is huge. You can choose from chalk pastel, oil pastel, Conté sticks, water-soluble crayon, and wax crayon, not to mention the differing versions of each of these. Their common quality is their richer texture compared with colored pencils, which have more fineness of line.

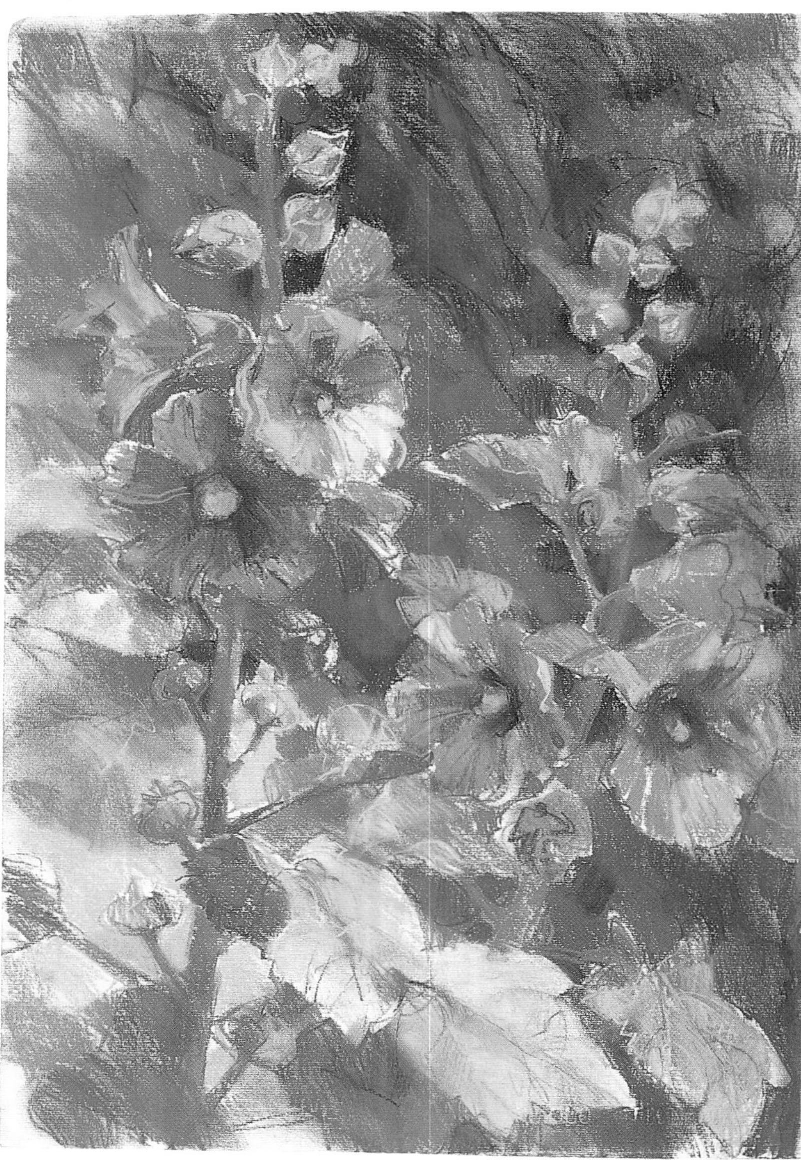

Chalk pastels
Great for larger, freer work, chalk pastels have wonderful softness, yet richness of color.

CHALK PASTELS

Generally, people think of chalk-based pastels as having a subtle, soft range of colors, yet most selections also include some wonderfully strong colors. The soft, powdery finish, however, can be a problem when working, as it is easily smudged. It is lovely to merge the powdery surface as an effect to soften texture, or mix colors, but mistakes can be made when leaning over the work. Regular fixing with a fixative spray can solve the problem, but overuse can alter the color of the pastels. The alternative is to put protective paper over the areas you wish to shield.

Look after your pastels, preferably in a box. They are delicate, and can crumble apart if not protected. It is worth the effort, as pastels have wonderful qualities—they are fresh, and the effect is spontaneous, you can work light pastel on top of dark, brush back where you want changes, and spray-fix areas that you want to develop.

Conté pastels are a more compressed and therefore hardened form of pastel stick, and are very useful for finer lines, or smaller-scale work.

WAX CRAYONS

Wax crayons have a richer line that can be used for broader, expressive marks, or when trimmed with a blade to produce a chiseled edge, can make quite fine lines. They resist water, and can be used with water-based paints for interesting results.

The picture [directional] shows the subtlety and depth of color that can be achieved using only my daughter's wax crayons. By hatching in different colors you can build up the layers, although, like watercolor, you have to leave the whites and light areas light and clean, as white wax crayons are not opaque and don't cover dark areas.

Water-soluble color crayons, or watercolor pencils, briefly mentioned on page 13, are a wonderful addition to your art materials. They have a wonderful range of colors that are rich in texture, and the simple addition of a brush and water can gives you smooth washes, making them incredibly versatile, both in the studio and out on location.

OIL PASTELS

Oil pastels have a similar intensity of color to wax crayons, with great texture in their broad marks, which work well for expressive, large works that benefit from the power of these pastels. You can scratch back for added texture, or to expose the colors that lie below the top layer or layers.

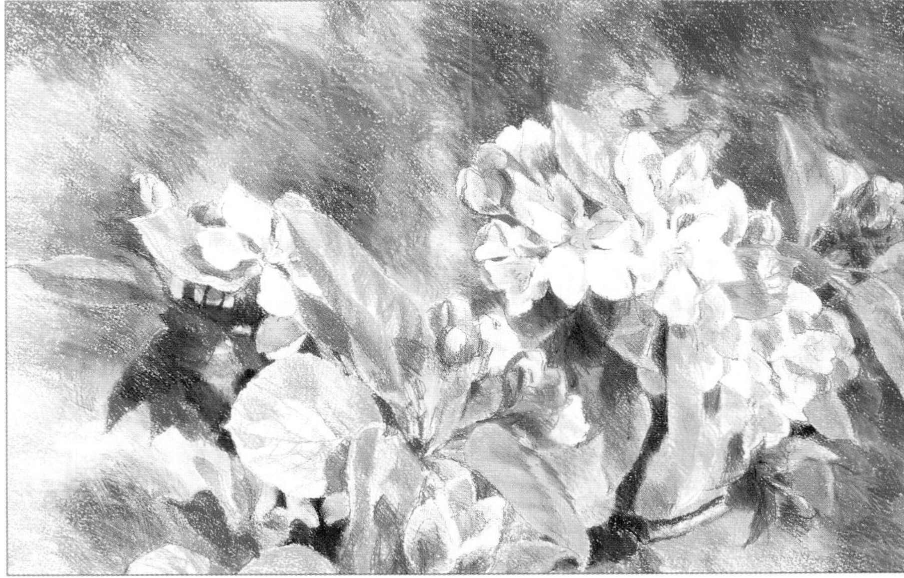

Oil pastel
You can vary the texture of oil pastel, from line reacting with the tooth of the paper, to subtle smudging. Scraping back reveals the colors below, and adds to the texture of the surface.

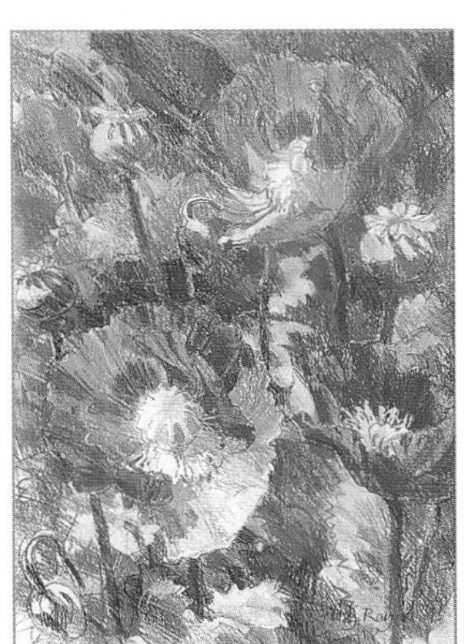

Chalk pastel
For the papery texture of poppy leaves, the linear strokes have been left fairly visible, to emphasize the freshness of the image.

Pond in chalk
Using chalk pastels, the deep shadows of a pond can be richly layered, with lighter highlights and reflections brought back at later stages.

SURFACES

The range of papers or boards suitable for pastel and crayon work is wide and varied, but generally has to have some kind of "tooth" or texture to it. If it is too smooth, the pastel tends to skid across without adhering too well.

Look at the scale in which you want to work, what your subject is, and how much detail you want to include. Heavier-texture paper is powerful, but used on a small scale it can lose the content of the subject, because details become too crude.

An interesting way to approach these mediums is to use a colored pastel paper from the large range available in art stores. A midtone, neutral paper can give a nice base to work from, but also try some of the more vibrant colors. Perhaps pick a color that complements your subject—for instance, a rich green for a green-dominant composition—or do the opposite by using a rich, red paper that will bring the green to life as the complementary colors react to each other.

I like to use watercolor paper with a medium texture, and if I wash it roughly with color (see page 31) I can achieve a more varied textured ground from which to work and apply other mediums.

Watercolors

Watercolor has often been seen as a gentle, old-fashioned way of working, with pretty, pale washes and delicate line. It does indeed work beautifully in this way, but it has so much more to offer, whether used on its own or mixed with other mediums.

Watercolor is what it says—water mixed with pigment, with the addition of glycerine or gum, which holds the pigment to the paper when the water has dried. This produces a transparent color that allows the whiteness of the paper to come through to give light to the pigment. If you paint on a dark surface, your color will hardly show—unlike working with pastels, acrylics, or oils. This translucent color gives a wonderfully fresh feel to a painting, producing pigment that glows, and rich, dark shades of tone that put to shame anyone who says that watercolor is only weak and washy.

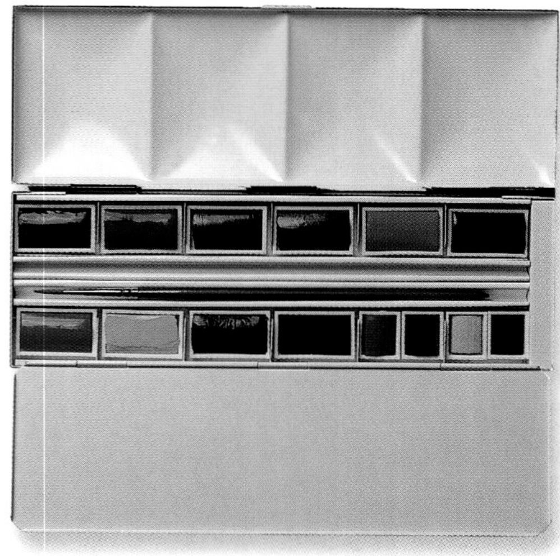

Portable pans
Watercolor pans in a box combine palette, paint, brush holder, and traveling box—excellent for outside work as well as inside.

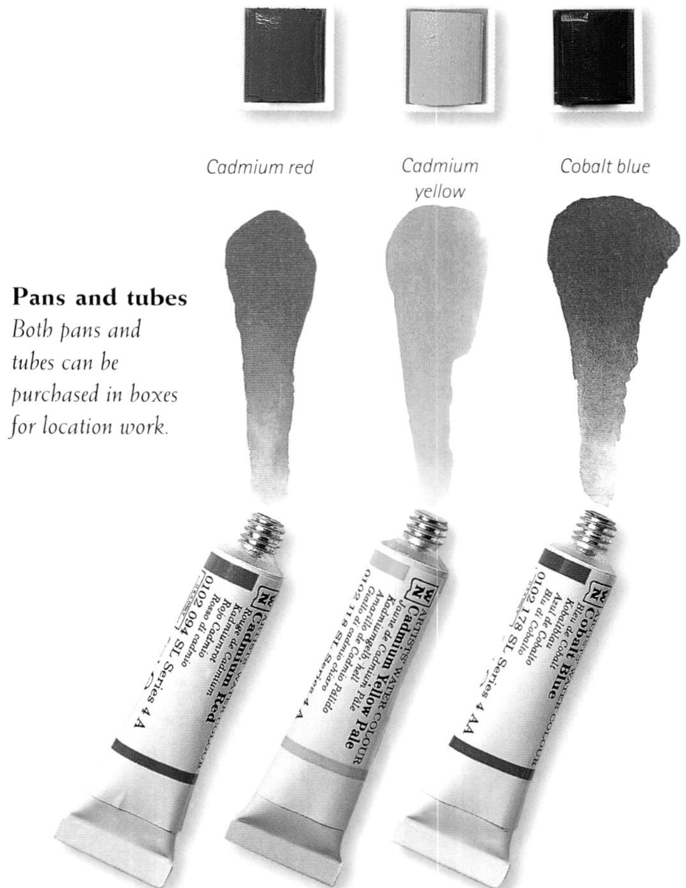

Pans and tubes
Both pans and tubes can be purchased in boxes for location work.

WATERCOLOR PAINTS

To a degree, success in watercolor does depend on the quality of paint that you choose to buy. I'm afraid that the more that you pay, the better the result. You will get better pigment, less filler to pad out the paint, and pure, clean color with no chalky residues in it.

A more personal choice is whether you want to use tubes or pans of paint. Tubes are great for large, strong, or dark washes, as the paint is already moist and easily mixed. Pans, on the other hand, are conveniently packaged to fit into a paint box, perfect for transporting.

I tend to use a little of both. I have a box with pans with which I do the majority of my work, but sometimes, even with the best of intentions, some colors get dirty, and when I need a really clean pure yellow or magenta, it can be disappointing. Color throughout the tube is always perfectly clean, so I have a limited selection of bright, primary colors in tubes, enabling me to use pure color when I need it.

Watercolor can also be bought as a liquid in bottles that have a superb color range, but do check their lightfastness. No pigment will last forever, but some are better than others. I have found that some liquid colors are particularly disappointing, because they fade both badly and quickly. Tubes often have an indication of the permanence of the paint, but if not, ask the store or supplier because as much permanence as possible is important if you want to hang a piece of work.

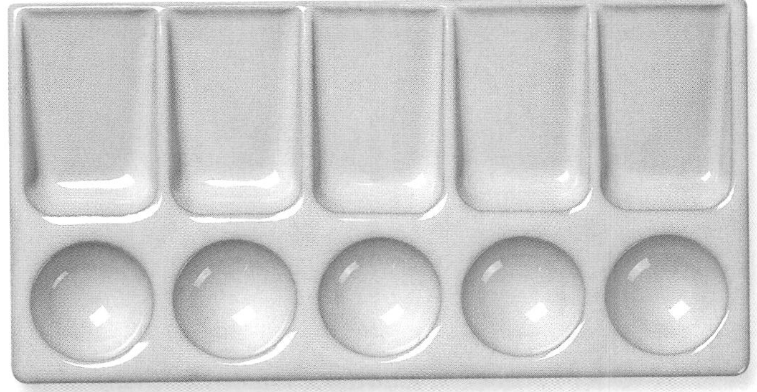

Ceramic palettes
Ceramic dishes are heavy, but great in the studio. They do not stain, and their various sizes are good for large or small washes of color wash.

PALETTES
If you have your paint in pan form, you already have a palette of some sort as part of your box. Additional pans can be useful, especially when making up large washes. These can be metal, ceramic, or plastic, but they should be white so you can assess your hue and tone properly before putting the paint to your paper. Ceramic is lovely but heavy. Plastic is light and great for transporting, but it can stain. Again, look at your situation to decide what is best for you.

BRUSHES
Although watercolor is simple, convenient, and relatively clean to use, the few materials that you do need should be good-quality. This applies just as much to the brushes and paper as it does to the paint mentioned above.

Sable brushes are the best, and of course are also the most expensive, but if looked after, they can last a long time. A cheaper and very acceptable alternative is the range of good synthetic brushes that, although they don't hold the paint quite as well as sable, can keep a nice point.

As logic would tell you, large brushes are recommended for large washes, with smaller ones useful for detail. When their point has gone, keep them for mixing and that will save your newer brushes. There is a huge range to look at, so ask and try.

I love using oriental brushes because they are so versatile. They hold a lot of paint for large washes, but in the same brushstroke you can finish with a fine line or point. The fine brushes are also useful for free, fine lines of color, whether straight, curved, or jagged.

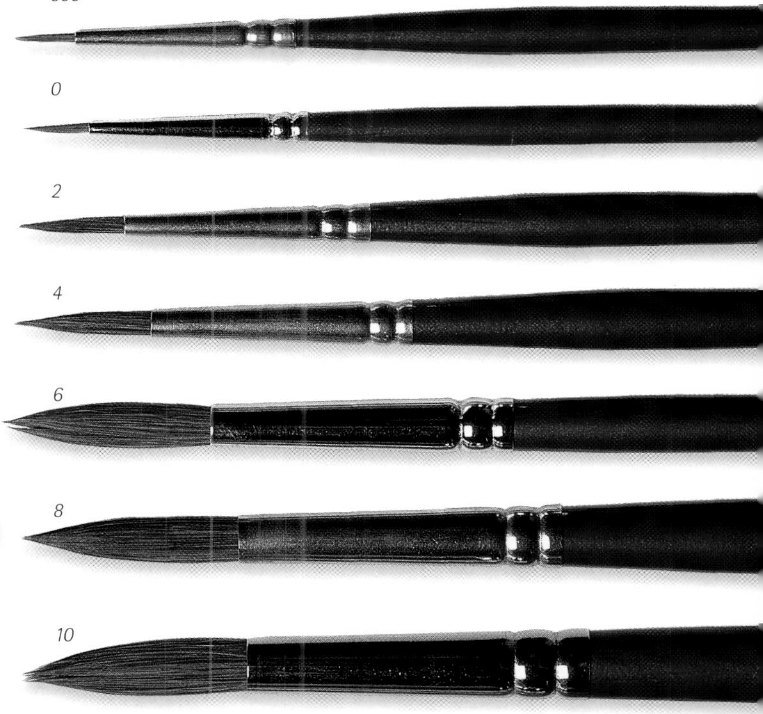

000

0

2

4

6

8

10

No.3 sable brush

Oriental brush

Flat brush

Mop brush

Brushes
A selection of different-size brushes is always useful to have at hand. Sable brushes (above) are especially worth protecting to preserve their points.

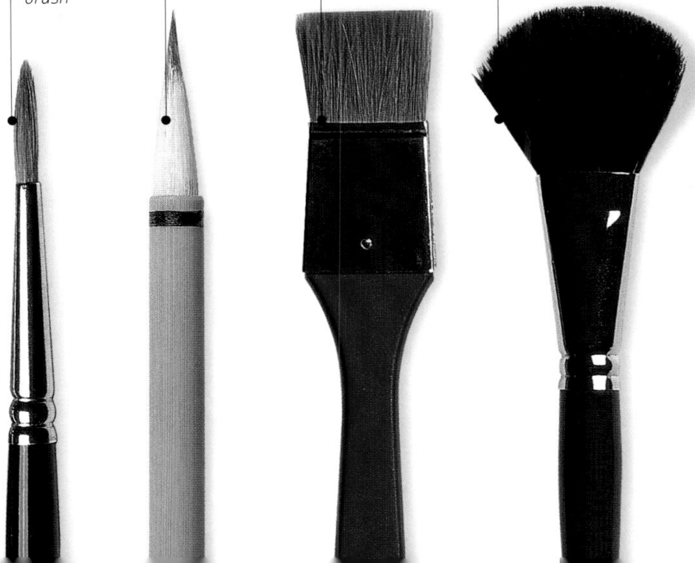

LIQUID FRISKET

Applying watercolor is a matter of careful construction. You can use white paint for highlights, but the freshest way, in my view, is to leave the white paper clear to make your highlights and then develop your washes around them, "carving" the color to make your shadows, almost like taking stone away from a sculpture.

Liquid frisket can be used for intricate areas of highlight. Paint it on with a fine brush or pen to the areas that you want to stay white. Be warned, though—wash liquid frisket out of your brush immediately, otherwise the bristles will be destroyed. Let it dry, and then continue painting over the area, developing your washes. When you are ready, peel off the liquid frisket, and either leave the paper white or tint it with your chosen color.

Don't think that this primary effect is liquid frisket's only use, as it can be applied much more freely with different implements for a looser affect. Otherwise, try using a color shaper—the soft, rubberized tip is smooth to draw with, and you simply wipe the fluid off after use.

Different applied textures

From left to right: Scoring with the back end of a paintbrush when the wash is still wet; bamboo pen drawn in when wash is still wet; scraping back with a knife when wash has dried.

In the latter stages of a painting you can create rough highlights by scratching back with a blade edge, but do this carefully, as the roughened paper is there for good. Dry brushwork can look similar, but can be washed over and flattened if needed.

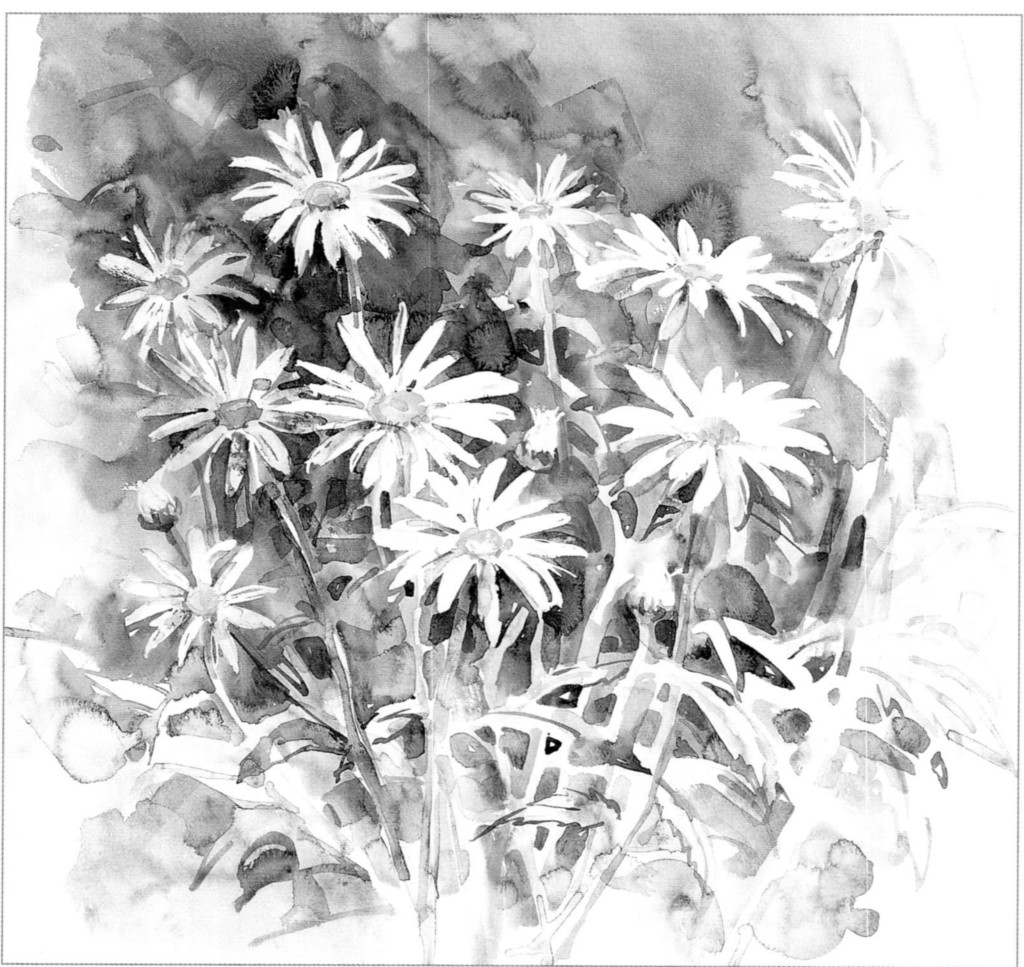

OTHER ACCESSORIES

You may need nothing else, but there are some accessories that can be useful to try. Small, natural sponges make a dappled texture, as can old toothbrushes for flicking color, and bamboo pens for drawing line. Rags, paper towels, cotton balls, or swabs are all very useful tools for mopping up, drawing out excess paint, smudging, and correcting any mistakes.

Additives to your water

White daisies

Liquid frisket was painted very loosely to indicate the patals of these daisies. Free washes formed the background. After removing the dried frisket, only minimal shading was needed to complete the picture.

Lilies

"Cropping in" to a collection of blooms enables you to concentrate on the textures and forms of the flowers.

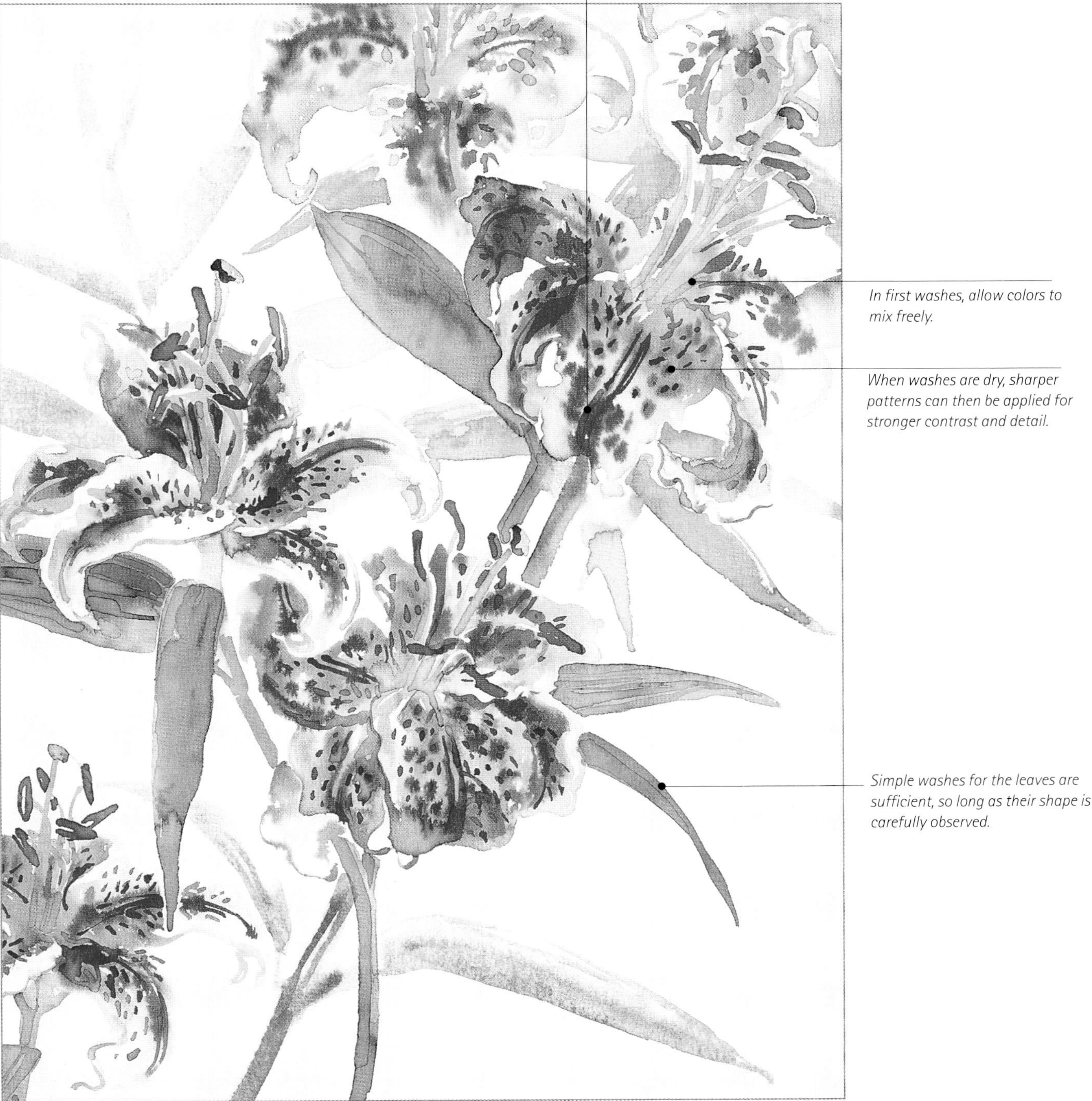

Gum arabic is added to the wash to suppress too much spreading of color. Drops of deeper color are added while the wash is still wet, to create blurred effects

In first washes, allow colors to mix freely.

When washes are dry, sharper patterns can then be applied for stronger contrast and detail.

Simple washes for the leaves are sufficient, so long as their shape is carefully observed.

and paint can also be useful. Gum arabic has a variety of uses—a little added to the water glass gives an extra glow and transparency to your colors, and if added to a wet-in-wet wash, discourages too much movement of the merged colors. When such a wash is dry, you can also wet areas and draw the color out of the paper for glowing highlights.

Ox gall liquid works in the opposite way—by adding it to a wash you get a more even mixture of color that produces a smoother effect.

PAPER

Because of the nature of watercolor, paper has to be light in color, as already mentioned. Handmade watercolor paper can be very expensive, and starting to paint on such a surface can be quite nerve-racking.

Good-quality, machine-made paper is a very good alternative. It is usually made of cotton or rag, and varies in weight, color, and texture. HP paper is "hot pressed" to give a smooth surface. CP, "cold pressed," or NOT (for "not hot-pressed") paper has a light texture, and "rough" paper is, as it says, heavily textured.

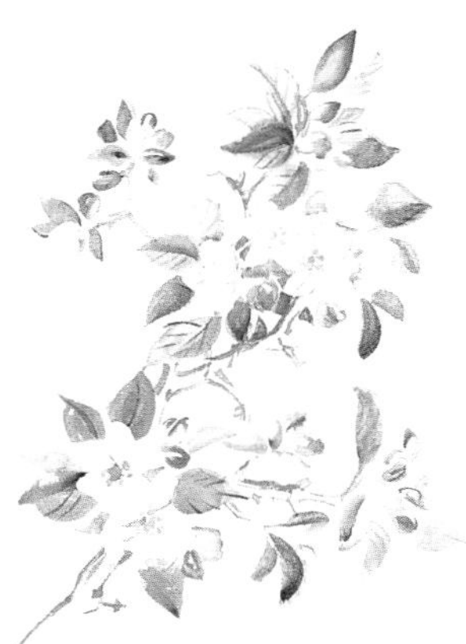

The quantity of size applied also varies, so that some papers are more absorbent than others. Some papers are slightly creamy, or you might prefer a pure, white paper for your highlights.

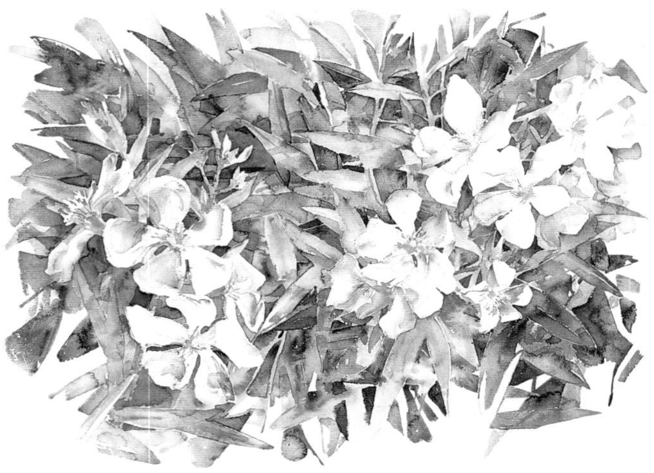

Textured paper
Because the paper is slightly absorbent, keep washes simple and decorative, and let colors merge for good results.

Last, the weight of paper does not necessarily affect the quality of your work, but it does mean that you might have to stretch your paper. Lightweight paper—i.e. 60lb (120gsm)—won't take a lot of scratching back or rubbing, and watermarks from buckling during large washes may be more prominent.

STRETCHING PAPER

My way of stretching paper is a little different from the standard method. Most demonstrations show the whole of the paper being dipped into water to soak, then excess water is drained off, and the paper is laid flat and taped down. With the problem of the paper's surface suffering from multiple washes, I started to wet only the back surface of the paper.

I like well-sized paper, and by not soaking the whole paper I find that the surface is not spoiled or the size washed out. This is a personal development, and if you are at all sceptical, the traditional way is recommended.

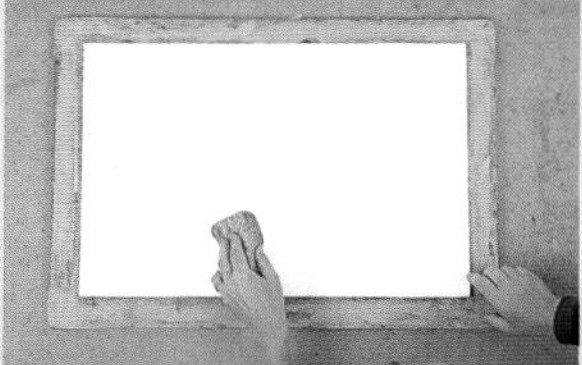

This probably takes longer, but I lay water on with a sponge, let it soak in, and then apply more until the paper has stopped cockling and is laying flat. This can take 15 minutes or so, depending on the paper. Try not to let water run off the edge and soak the front edge of the paper.

When the paper lies flat and is fully soaked, turn it over and you are ready to tape it down. Cut gum strip 4" (10cm) or so longer than your paper, wet it, and lay it down. Because your paper is only slightly damp on the front edge, the tape sticks really well, and I never have had the need to secure the corners with thumbtacks.

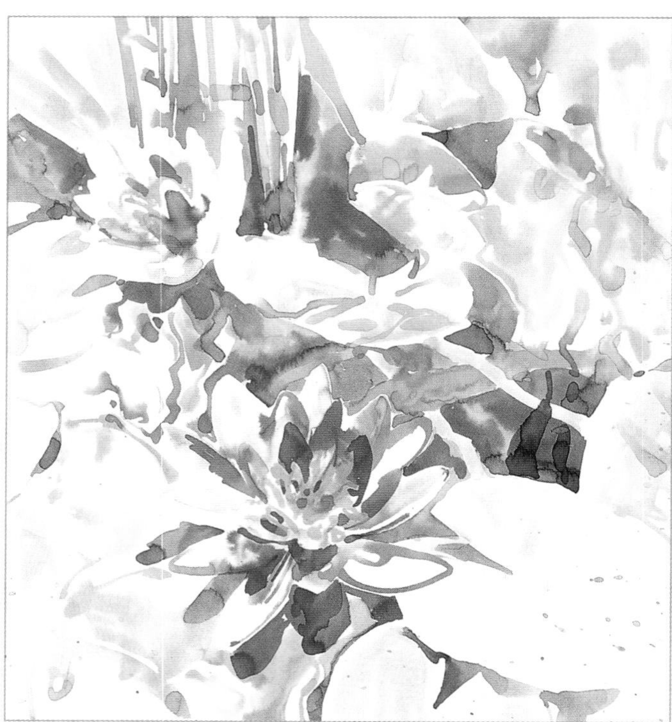

Smooth paper
The brush glides smoothly, and sometimes washes can puddle, creating their own patterns. If this happens, use this to your advantage.

Washes

Left to right: A gradated wash demonstrates the process of running from dark down to light; a drier brush gives a more broken wash—aided, perhaps, by a more textured paper;a variegated wash incorporates two hues merging together.

APPLYING WASHES

Watercolors are a huge favorite of mine, but sometimes they can be the most frustrating, exasperating medium. They have by their nature a wonderful translucency, but for this very reason they can easily be overused, leaving a muddied mess.

You can often see when someone is unsure about a detail or is trying to remember something that has moved—the marks are hesitant, overlaid, and changed repeatedly. A sense of movement can be fun with overlaid washes like this, but when a clear, concise simplicity is needed, it pays to plan and practice.

Laying a flat wash is the basis to many techniques. Mix up a large amount of your desired color, move the board slightly towards you and work with a broad brush, left and then right, across and down the paper. You can dampen the paper before you start for a smooth wash, or drag the brush if you want a broken wash, like a sky. Adding more water fades the wash down to white if desired, or subtle additions of different color change the tint to give a variegated wash.

MORE TECHNIQUES

Dab on cotton balls or a sponge to pull highlights out, or drip stronger or different colors into the wash, and let it merge and spread in its own direction. This wet-in-wet technique can be very unpredictable, but the effect is to be embraced, as interesting effects can come from it. Don't be tempted to fiddle too much.

If a wash is blatantly wrong, try to remove it as quickly as possible with, say, paper towels, but otherwise, maybe leave the vicinity to give it a chance to dry without you being tempted to interfere. Subsequent washes can adapt and correct areas that you are not happy with.

Hard edges or darker color around a wash is something that I like to use in a painting, but again if you don't want this effect, make the wash less wet, and perhaps merge the edges with a sponge or cotton ball.

These techniques are important because with watercolor mistakes cannot be easily covered up. They may seem complicated, but with practice you will gain confidence.

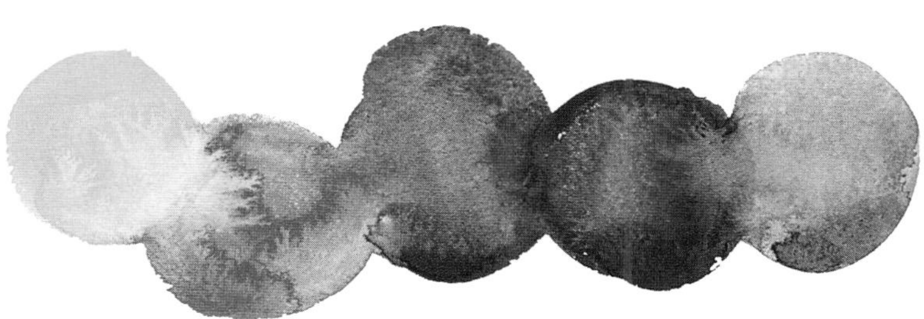

Wet-in-wet

When keeping the wash fresh, you can let the color bleed from one area into another. When dry the edges will remain, but the color will build up, demonstrating its translucency.

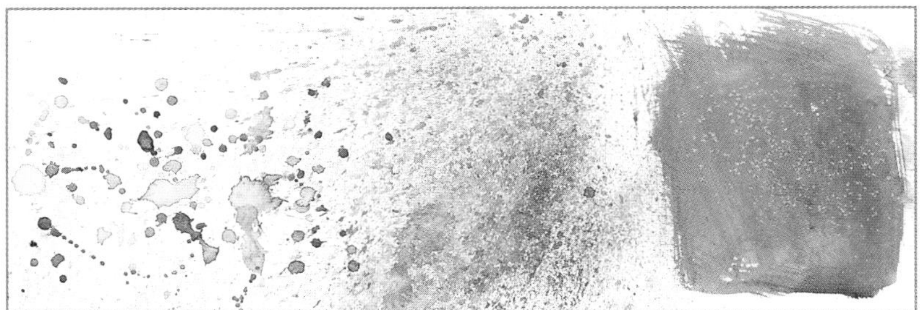

Applied textures

From left to right: Spattering with a paintbrush. Finer drops sprayed with a toothbrush. Adding salt produces a speckled effect, as the salt rejects the color.

Acrylics

Acrylics are robust—strong in color and flexible, with amazing, adhesive properties that can be manipulated for various approaches.

Pastels, watercolor, gouache, oils, and tempera paints all use the same pigments as those of acrylic paint. The exciting difference is the binder. For hundreds of years the painting mediums listed above were used in a variety of ways, mixing natural binders such as gum, egg, linseed oil, and wax, to hold the pigments in place, whether on wood, canvas, plaster, or paper. Often primers had to be used, the mixing of paint took time, and there was constant experimentation to improve the stability, purity, range, and longevity of color.

The binder for acrylic paint was new, man-made specifically for the job and based on a polymer resin similar to Perspex. Polymer resins are milk-white, plastic emulsions that dilute with water, but dry quickly and

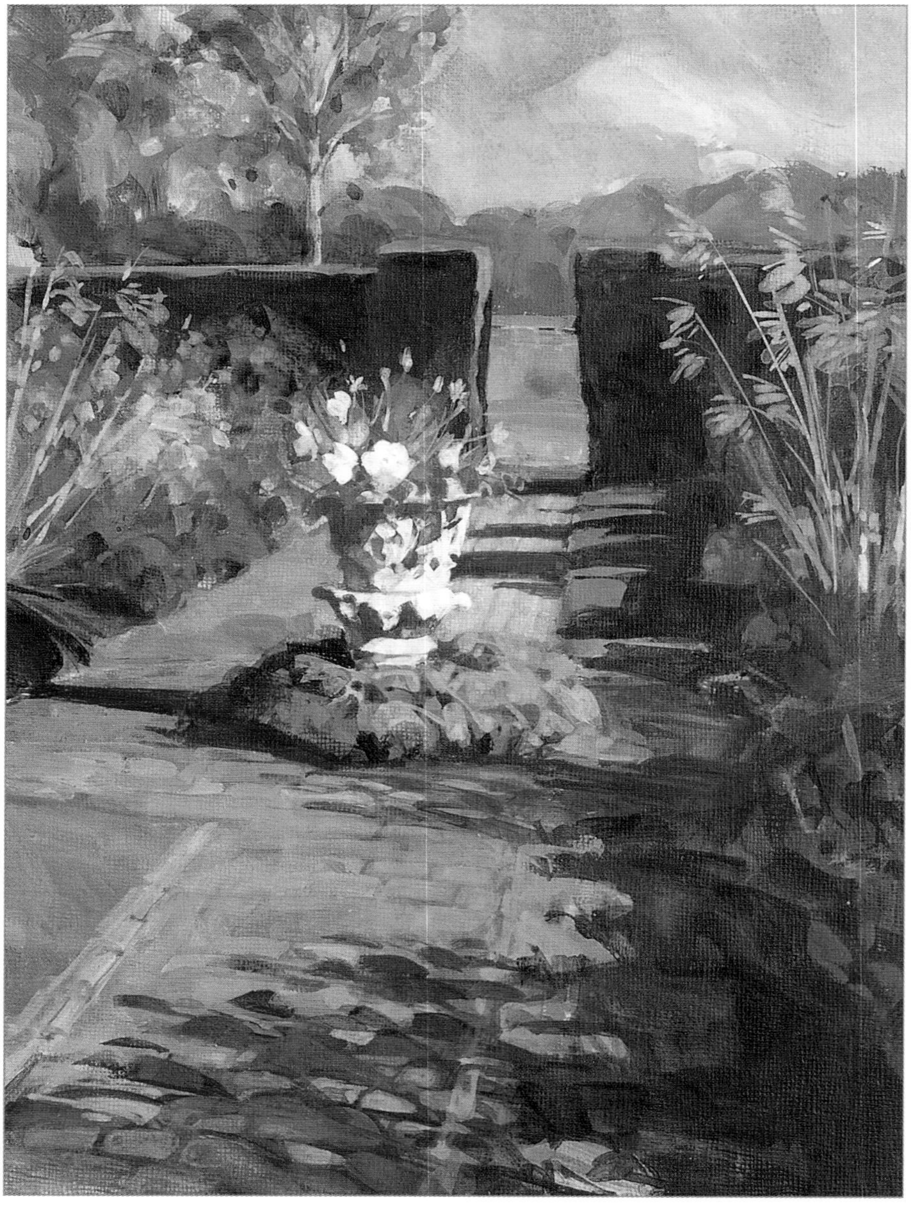

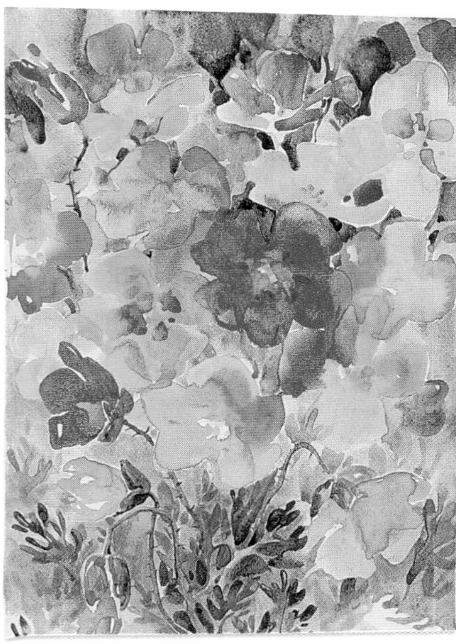

Liquid acrylics
Liquid acrylics create a translucent wash, useful for fresh images. Their advantage over watercolor is that when they dry, the wash is totally fixed, so subsequent layers stay pure.

Building up color
In this garden in late light, the blue/violet underpainting, or ground, was a strong base for the subsequent layers of color. The path, in complementary contrast, glows, picking up the highlights of the ornamental grasses.

clear. The paint is totally waterproof, though flexible, and its strong adhesive properties mean that it can be directly applied to any surface.

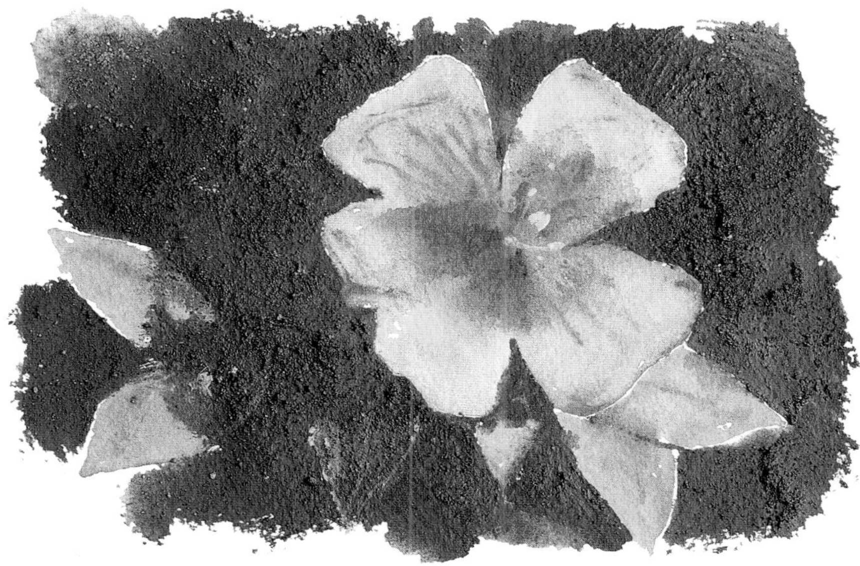

Adding texture
Sand mixed with paint adds to the density of the shade enveloping this delicate bloom.

MEDIUMS AND ADDITIVES

Different mediums, retarders, and solvents can be easily mixed with acrylics to expand the range of possibilities of this modern paint. You might want to increase the translucency, increase or decrease paint flow, create a thicker paint, add texture, or slow the drying process. There are many additives to chose from, any of which may or may not be applicable for your approach; but experiment a little, as this really can open up the possibilities.

Gloss medium increases the translucency of the paint, and keeps the brilliance of the color. It dries quickly, and enables multiple layers of glazes to be applied. Each glaze is waterproof when dry, so that no lifting of paint occurs when subsequent layers of glaze are laid. Matte medium achieves much the same as gloss, but, as you would expect, it is in more of a matte finish. Gel medium is thicker, and therefore does not flow or run. It can be used for textured impasto, or thinned down for translucent glazes—the intensity of hue is not impaired with either technique.

Thick, textured paste is used for modeling areas of texture, usually with a brush or palette knife, although any implement can be used. It can be mixed with the paint, or applied in advance to dry and subsequently overpainted. Because of its very strong, adhesive power, string and other textures can be embossed or added, to increase your range of possible textures.

Thin layers of glazed color applied over textural work can heighten the effect, whereas thick, opaque paint gives the more traditional effect of impasto. This thick, textured form of painting can substitute for oils but with the advantage of much quicker drying times.

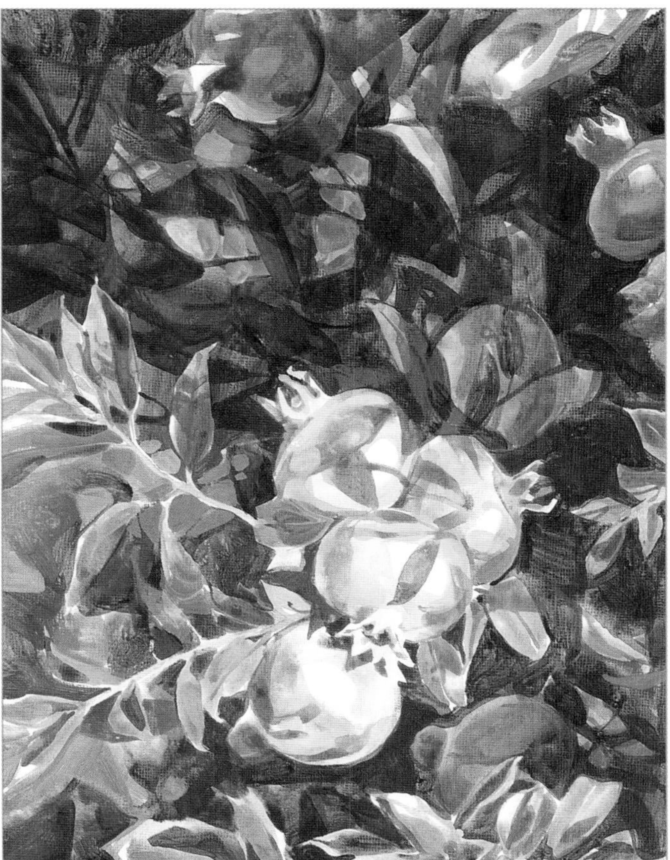

Pomegranates
The acrylic paint was used here in the same way as watercolors are used, with the white paper showing through as highlights. Darker layers built up in the shadows, and then opaque midtones were added.

Mixing mediums

You can either plan deliberately to mix mediums, or let the work begin and decide as it develops where and when a different texture or medium should be introduced. If you are using the resist of wax crayon, this has to be decided beforehand, but adding colored pencil or Conté to a watercolor can be a last-minute decision, made as the work progresses.

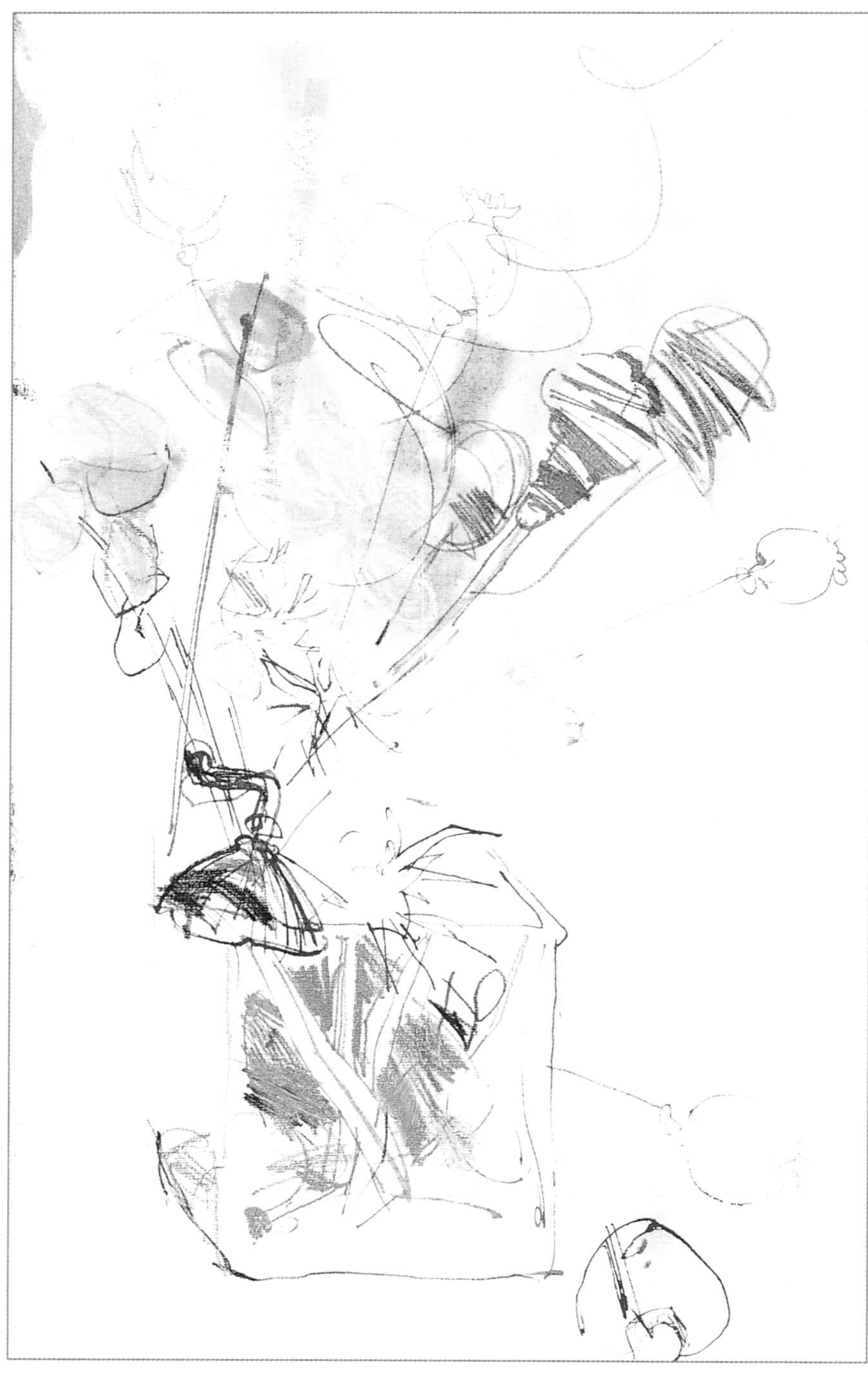

Even with the simplest of sketches, you can use the contrasting qualities of different materials, such as pen and ink highlighted with chalk, for good effects. It is very useful to introduce, for instance, pastel, acrylic, or pen work to rescue a piece of work. Watercolor is renowned for its difficulty because it is easy to overdo, and thus lose the freshness of the painting, but it can make a very nice underpainting for further development with pastel, however unplanned!

Pastel work can sometimes need a little detail, and Conté sticks or colored pencils can produce a finer line for those areas that require it. Pen work can sharpen a pencil drawing, and wash can be added to produce large areas of simple tone.

Some combinations work better than others, so experiment in sample form on scrap paper or on the back of unsuccessful work—for instance, oil-based materials generally react better over water-based work than over other work, unless you are using a paint-resist technique.

Making marks
Rough, textural samples are invaluable when exploring the reaction of different materials to each other. Here, oil pastel, soft pencil, ink, and wash were all integrated.

Florence square

This view of a shaded square in Florence appealed to me. I wanted to express the relief that we felt when we found this cool, shaded, peaceful garden in the heat of the day.

Verticals and horizontals give feeling of stillness.

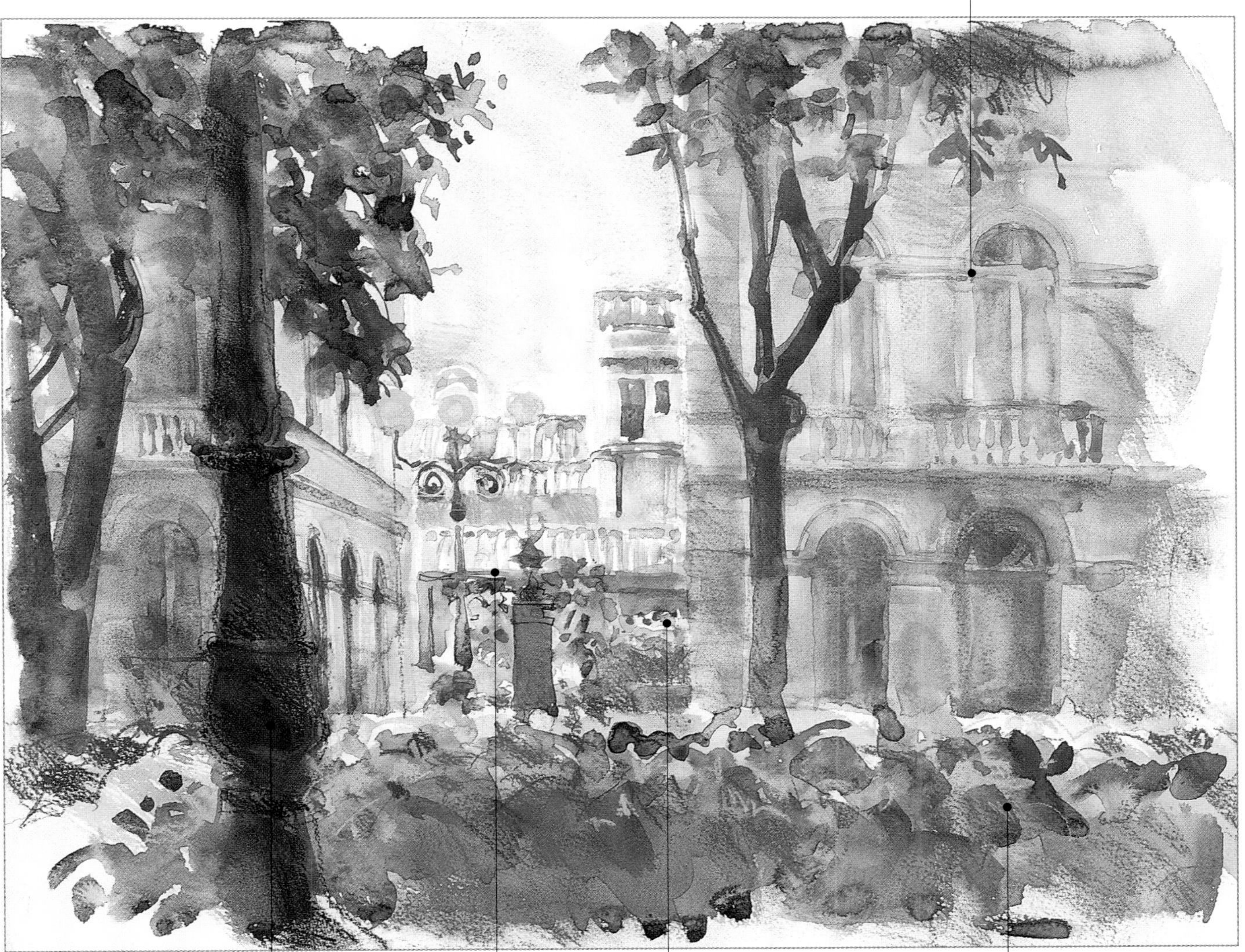

Silhouetted trees and lampposts in foreground contrast strongly with the distant courtyard ablaze in sun.

Conté and colored pencil pull out tonal contrasts and detail, bringing attention to the focal point.

Warm colors of flowers and roofs emphasize heat.

The strong texture of pastels gives power to cool shadows, and eliminates detail.

Composition

Composition is how you consider what you put where in your picture space. You will have already thought of the subject you want to paint, but what is the next most important consideration?

Naturally we tend to look around a scene, and then eliminate the surroundings to concentrate on the main point of interest, the focal point. Placing this point centrally has a tendency to leave your work static, but placing it too close to the edge of your composition has the danger of leading your eye off the picture. This, however, is only a general rule, and sometimes when the balance is carefully made to deviate from the norm, it can produce interesting tension.

THE GOLDEN RULE

A traditional way of creating pleasing compositions often is referred to as the Golden Rule; it refers to the division of your picture into thirds. By positioning the main point of interest in any one of these three areas, you create a comfortable basis for the composition. Verticals and horizontals intersecting at these points give a calm structure to the work, then curves lead you in, and diagonals give energy and movement.

Secluded French square
Strong verticals and diagonals, created by the shadows, direct the eye around and across this painting. The focal position of the majestic doorway leads you past the heat of the flowers to the diminutive figure.

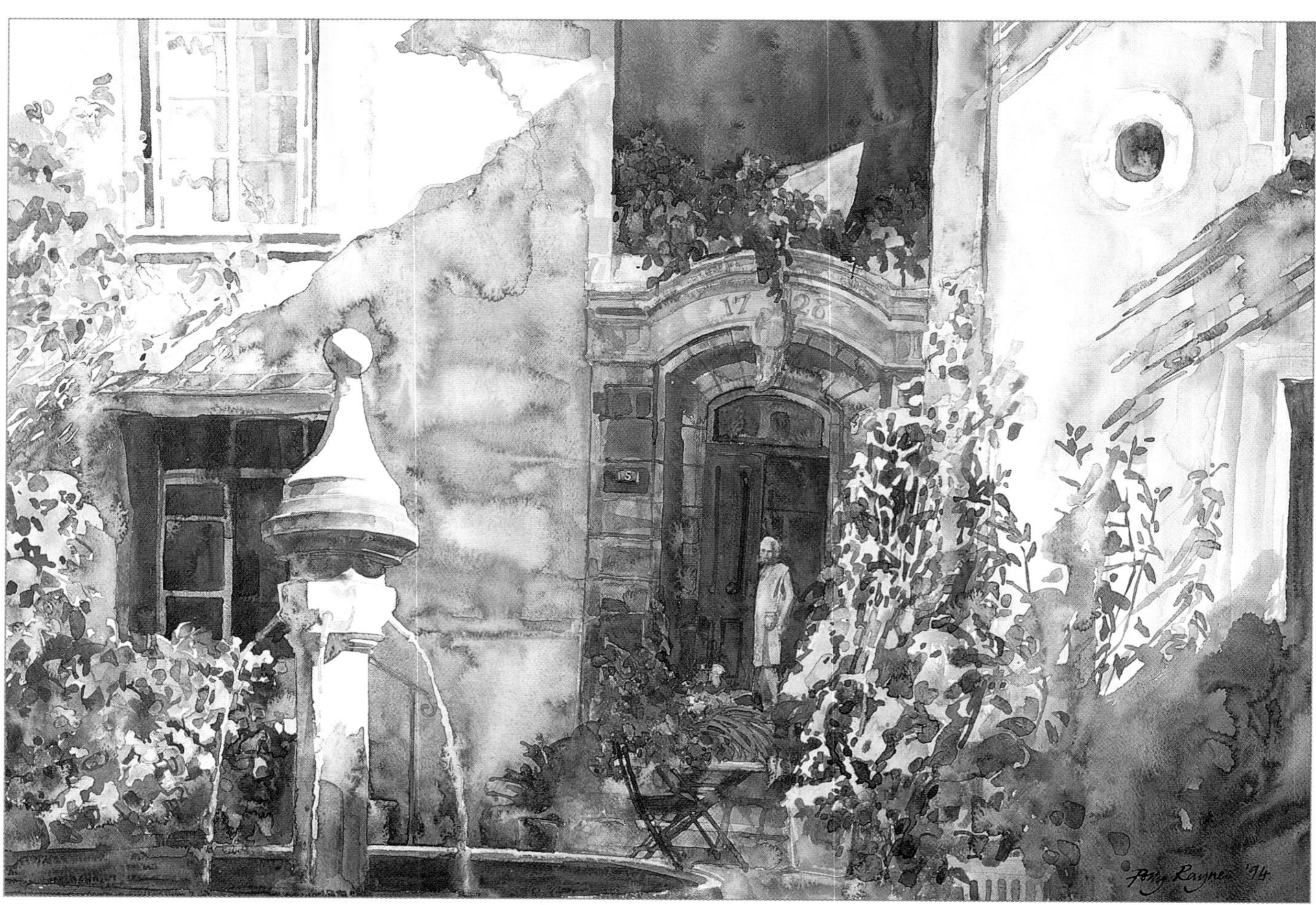

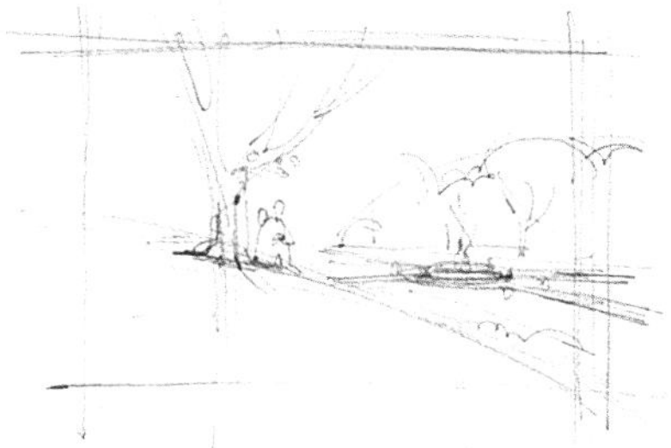

THE IMPORTANCE OF PREPARATION

Too busy a picture can be confusing, so consider where you concentrate your details. Strong, warm colors hold your attention, as do strong contrasts. All these elements are important, and the best way to assess how a picture balances is to sketch quick variations before you embark on a more involved piece of work.

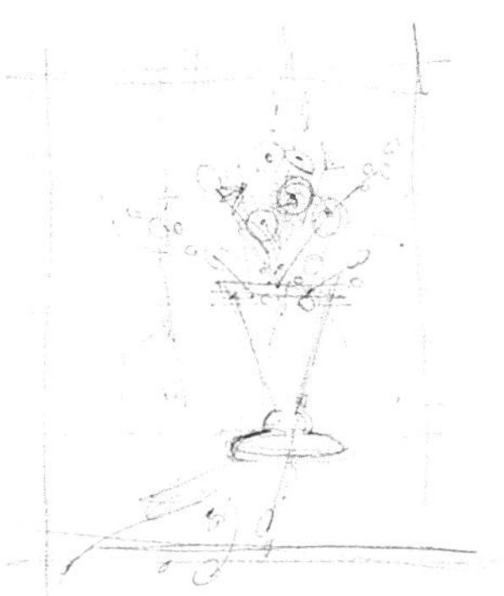

Thumbnail sketches
Two-minute sketches can help to clarify ideas for a larger composition.

STILL LIFE BY FIREPLACE

Initially the focal point might seem too centrally positioned, but the strength of the top right-hand plant pulls the eye up and around.

Echoing the rich textures of the fireplace, the potted plant draws the eye up, helping to balance the composition.

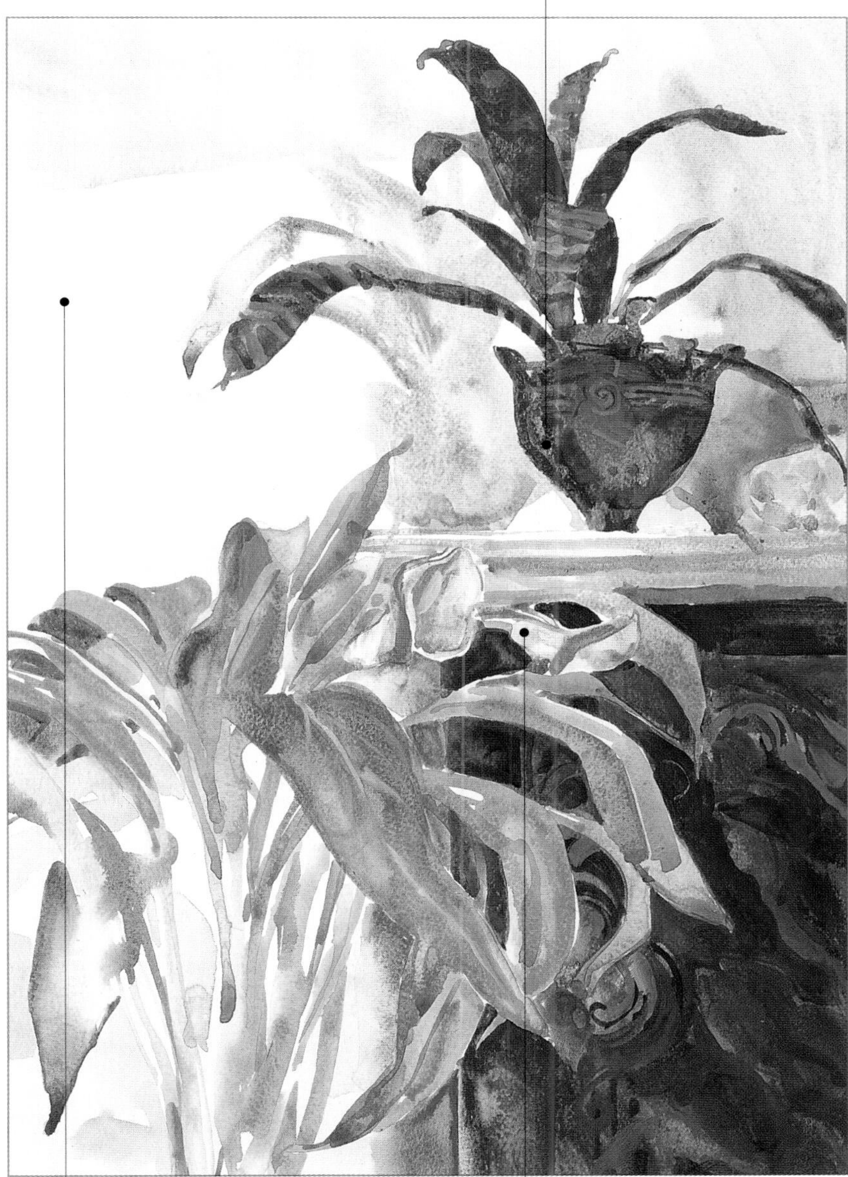

The light and simplicity of the top area contrast strongly with the diagonally opposite corner, where the dense detail of the fireplace gives weight to the composition.

The two pink flowers curl away from the central position.

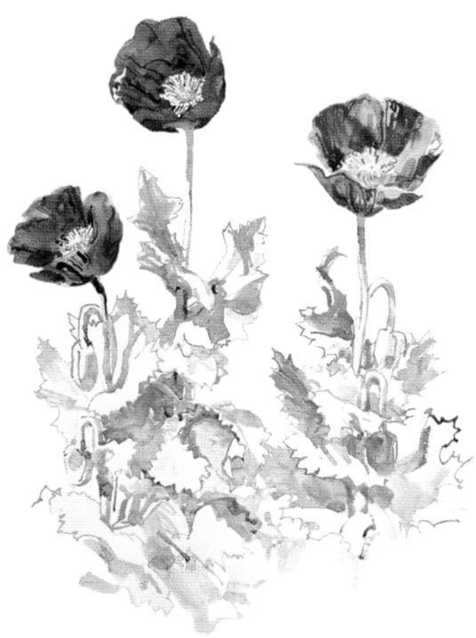

Poppies in full sun
Determine whether a background helps your composition, or distracts the eye in a confusion of color or detail.

Indoor composition

How you compose your space is totally personal. A single flower can be viewed, cropped, and lit in many different ways alone, and vases, mixed bouquets, or potted plants in an interior setting give you unlimited choices.

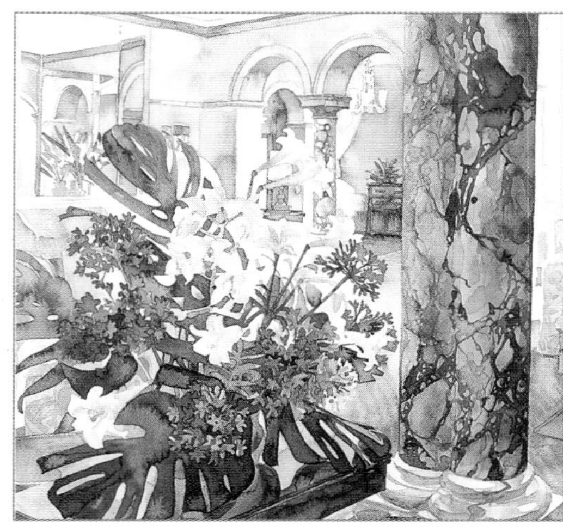

Atmospheric setting
The grandeur of this magnificent drawing room works as an atmospheric backdrop to the sumptuous arrangement of flowers.

Use the balance between the subject matter and the background space to unify the composition. Negative space is just as important as are positive shapes, particularly if you approach the subject in the traditional way, with the background space white. Awkward, large shapes created by leaves or petals can create holes that distract the eye. Use curves and directional stems to lead you in and around comfortably towards a focal point that produces a harmonious balance.

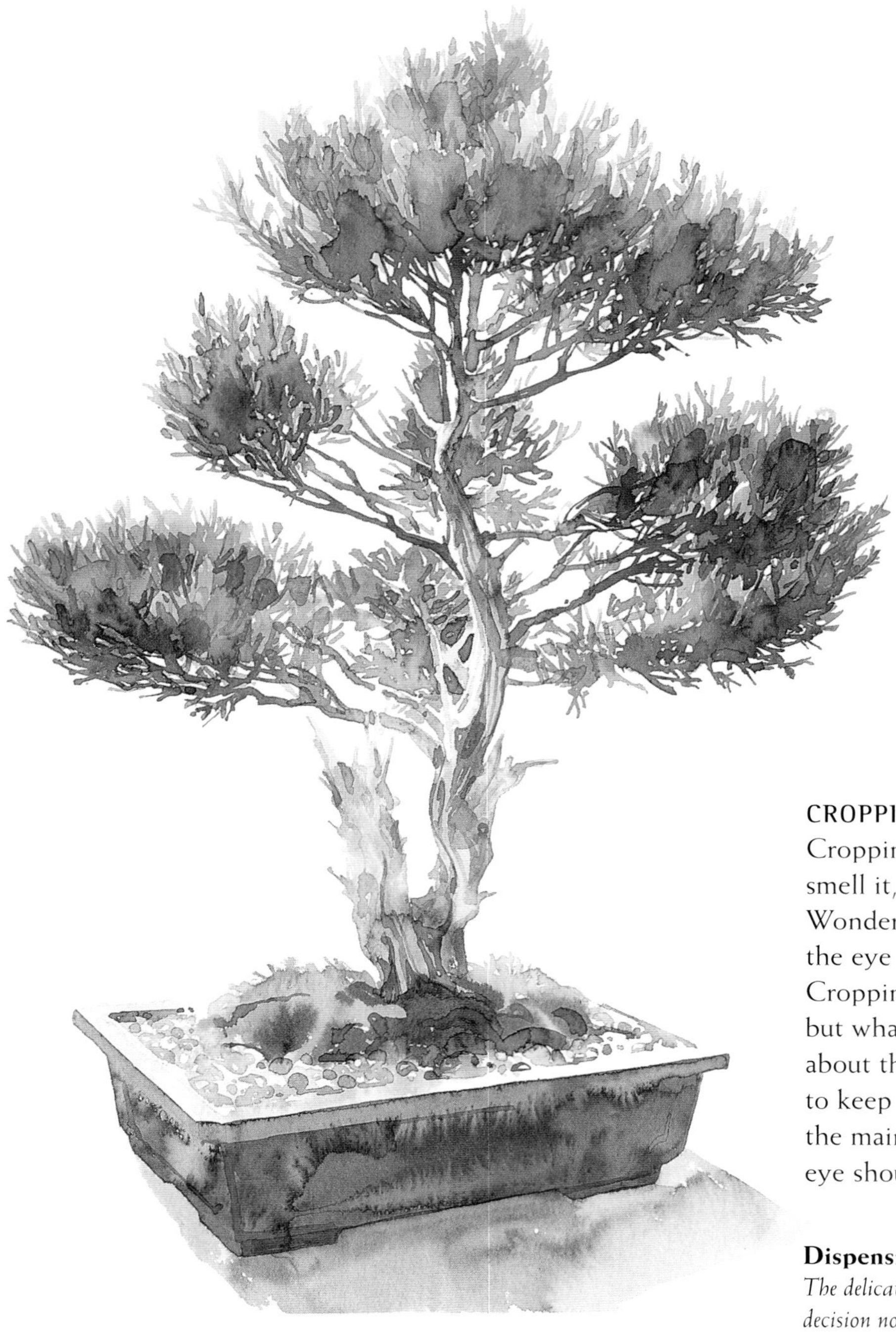

CROPPING

Cropping into the flower really closely, as if to smell it, conveys a sense of being immersed in it. Wonderfully abstract patterns create a rhythm, and the eye is absorbed in the dance of light and shade. Cropping can make a fun, strong, or serene image, but whatever the effect, it helps you learn more about the plant. You might want to trim the stalks to keep them within the composition. As long as the main flowers are within the composition, the eye should not be pulled off the page.

Dispensing with the background
The delicate detail reflecting the nature of this bonsai led to the decision not to complicate the painting with a background.

PLANES AND HORIZONS

As soon as you include a vase or vessel of some kind in a composition, a horizon or surface is formed. Be conscious of how this affects the balance—does it give a comfortable base to the composition, or just divide it? Strong contrasts along this line might be too distracting, and sometimes vertical planes, such as a doorframe or window, can help to balance because they draw the eye back and form a grid within which the main subject can sit, creating a calm, cool atmosphere. Classic lines and curves often fit within the Golden Rule (see page 36), while diagonal lines and curves define power and movement for a more dynamic composition.

LIGHT

Lighting is important, especially if you are using cast shadows as part of your composition. You can concentrate on using natural light if this is of the essence, but the real advantage of working indoors is that you can control the position of the light source or sources to achieve a constant, predictable still life.

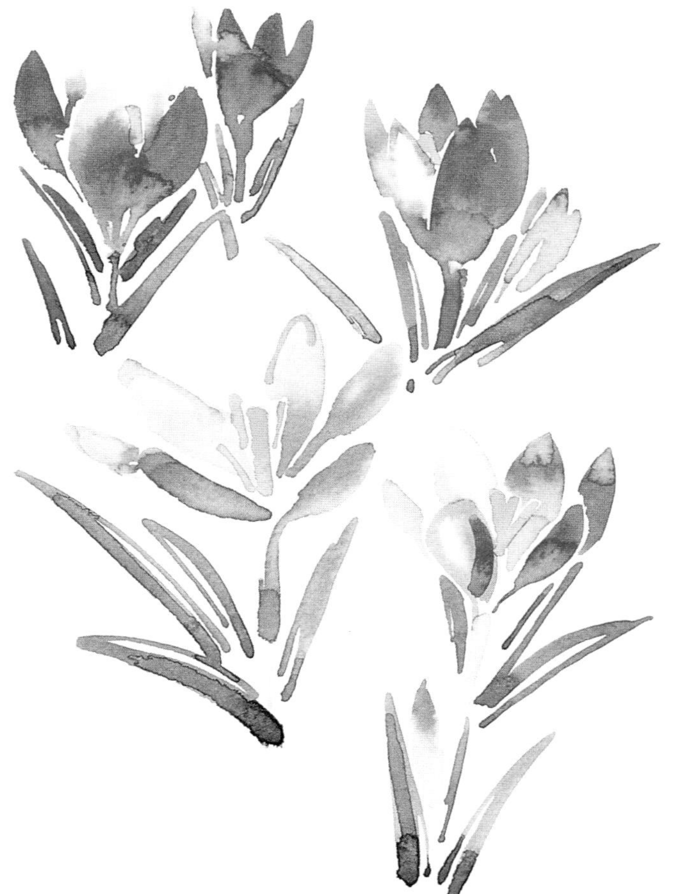

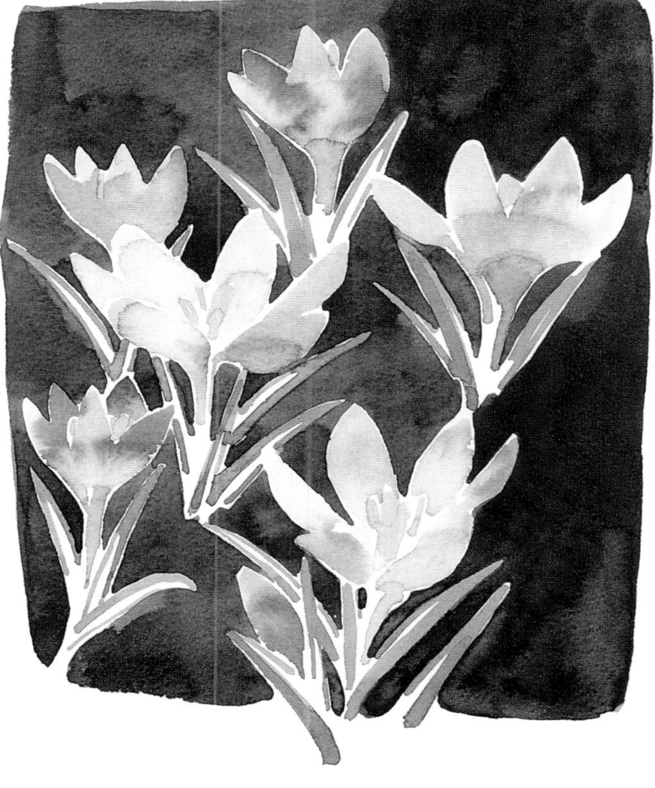

"Breakthrough crocus"

This cancer charity picture was commissioned with the crocus as a symbol of hope. Two simple ideas developed—(left) the image peeping up through the snow against the adversity of the cold, and (right) the image standing strong and bright in the darkness. The second image was used for a variety of publicity material. These two approaches show how differently an image can be adapted to communicate different messages.

Outdoor composition

The general guidelines from the previous pages apply in many cases when tackling an exterior subject. Your reaction to a plant or view is so personal that the suggestions given here are not meant to be followed slavishly. Trial and error is the key to finding your own methods and techniques.

Whether you are concentrating on one plant, even one flower, or an intricate garden scene, try a series of very rough sketches beforehand. A viewfinder is often useful—cut card stock to the proportions of your paper, then view through it to gauge how much of your subject you actually want to include. Check your eye line—do you want background, and if so, how much? Where is the structure? Where are the horizontals and verticals? Do you need to move your position? Do you need to change your paper format? These are just a few of the questions that you might ask yourself to plan the composition.

Sometimes you know immediately—you feel comfortable, and can almost walk into the composition. Other times, however, something in the foreground may be distracting. You can move your position, or even be prepared to eliminate the object entirely from your composition if it interrupts the flow and rhythm of your work.

USING COLOR IN COMPOSITION

As already mentioned, central focal points can be static and uncomfortable to the eye. See where the image takes you.

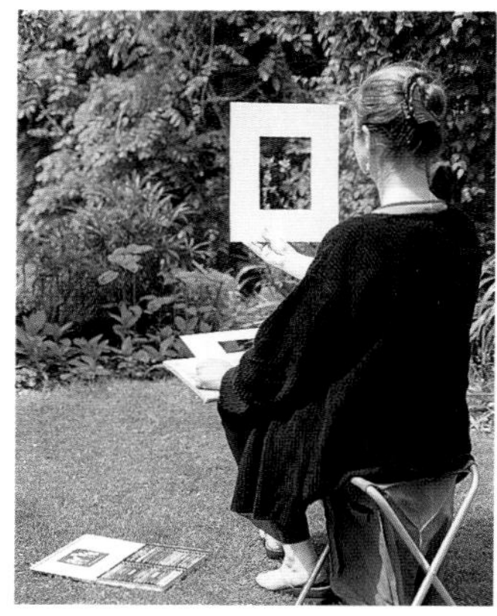

Viewfinders
Square and rectangular viewfinders can be useful when considering your compositional content.

Glyndebourne Lake
Using the horizontals of the lake and the verticals of the trees, and their reflections, this painting has an air of calm and tranquility. Even the color is subdued and restful.

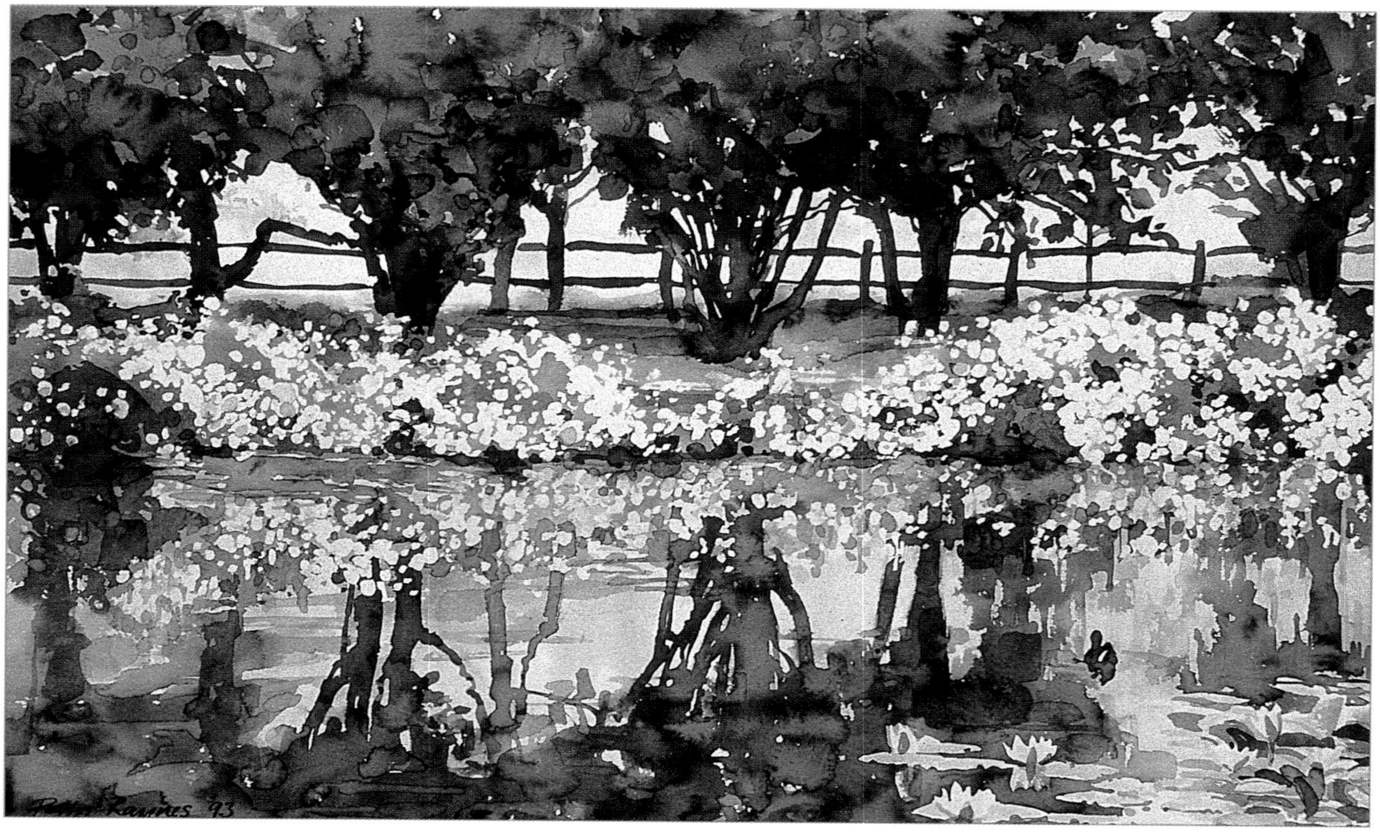

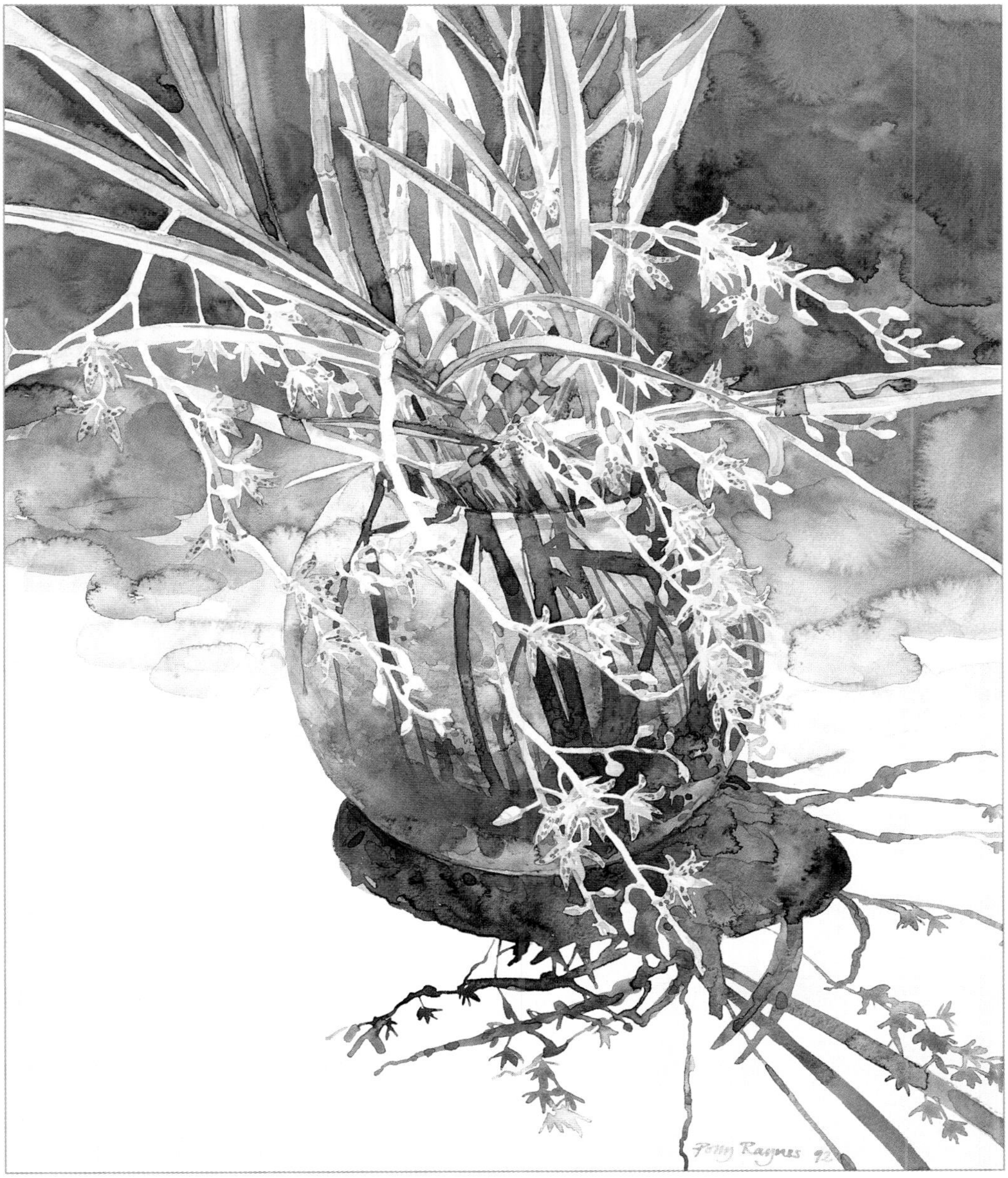

African orchid
The spikiness of this potted African orchid is exaggerated by its sharp, cast shadow. The local, earthenware pot is simple, as is the background—only the shadows bring out the strength of the sunlit plant.

Tropical garden
The path leads strongly up into the composition. Curved walls, arching banana leaves, and lush plants catch the eye as you walk into the garden.

Hotter colors draw the eye, so too much red, for instance, on the edge of a painting is distracting. Touches of repeated color drawing you into the composition can link different elements and create a balance. Strong contrasts of dark and light again draw the eye and pull the image towards the foreground. If you want something to recede, the general rule is to make the hue cooler and the tone more subtle.

Directional shadows, together with the visual elements, all combine to give structure to the composition. Then use your color, tone, and detail to develop your focal areas, leaving other areas simpler to rest the eye.

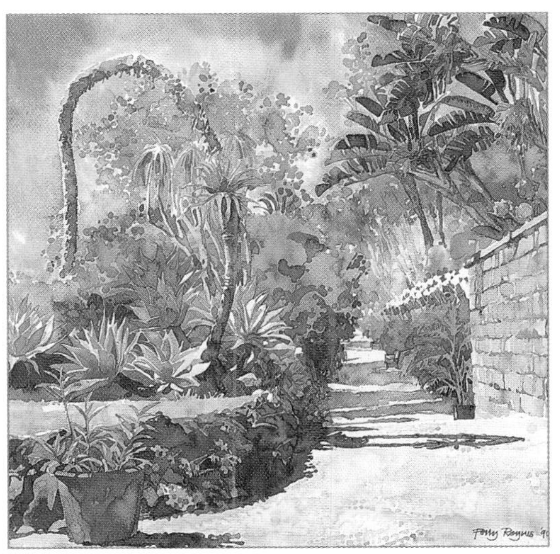

Perspective

When considering a composition for a painting of flowers, or even a garden or yard, perspective may not seem to be immediately important.

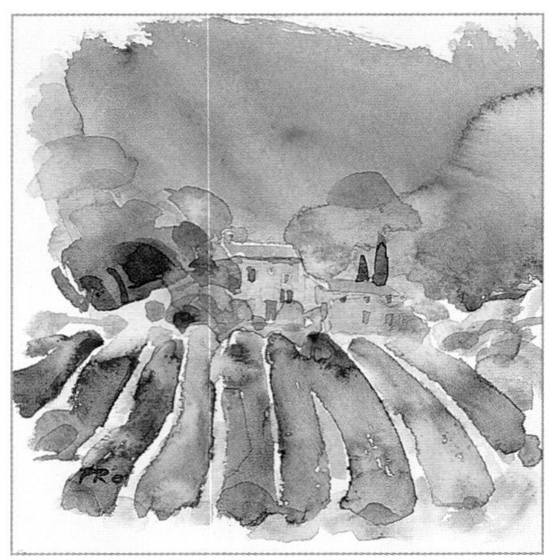

Recession
Sometimes visual tools, like rows of flowers or trees, aid your sense of receding space. Look carefully at the angles, and hold out a pencil or brush vertically for a more accurate perception of an angle.

It is true that when studying an individual plant specimen, careful measuring and study of form, color, and texture are of primary importance. Nevertheless, as soon as you include a vase, interior, or structural landscape, a basic knowledge of perspective is useful to balance structure, give three-dimensional objects solidity, and make individual elements sit comfortably together on the same plane.

You can, of course, achieve this through accurate measuring and careful study of the angles of receding planes, but this can be tedious and time-consuming. Angles can be surprisingly steep and mistakes can be uncomfortable to the eye, but checking is easy with the confidence of quickly being able to mentally calculate where the vanishing point lies.

Combinations of the simple constructions shown on this page can be used in conjunction to make sense of complicated views. By reducing subjects to their basic structure, the fundamental form is easier to place within the composition, and you can then embellish it with detail, tone, texture, and color.

One-point perspective
This is a simple way of establishing the basic form of an object, or an avenue view. The bare necessities to consider are the ground or base plain and vertical surfaces, whether facing the viewer or receding into the distance. The height above the ground plain from which the viewer sees the object or vista establishes the horizon line. As long as the ground plain or plains are horizontal, i.e. not running up- or downhill, all vertical and horizontal surfaces or same-size objects recede in size until they disappear at a pointon the horizon line—the vanishing point.

Shallow box
A simple shallow box shape can be easily formed by first establishing your horizon line and vanishing point. Two lines extend out away from the point, and horizontal lines intersect these to form a square shape receding into the distance. Drop vertical lines away from the corners, and another square is formed beneath, by the same process to the square above. By running lines across to join the diagonal corners, the point at which they cross establishes the center and halfway point. This helps if you want to divide the space up equally, or extend it accurately.

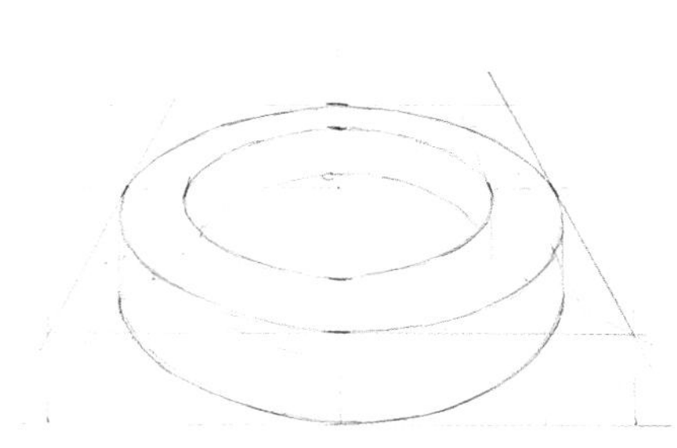

Circular hedge
To create a circular shape, use the central spot to find the halfway point on each of the square's edges. The ellipse touches those four points. Unless you have a huge array of ellipse stencils of different sizes and depths, you have to hand-draw between these points, which can take a little practice. Again dropping verticals down from the ellipse, you can start to form a tube to the depth you desire.

Two-point perspective

Depending on your position in relation to the object, you may have a two-point perspective. If you do not stand squarely in front of an object, you have two receding planes—one to one vanishing point, and the other to a second.

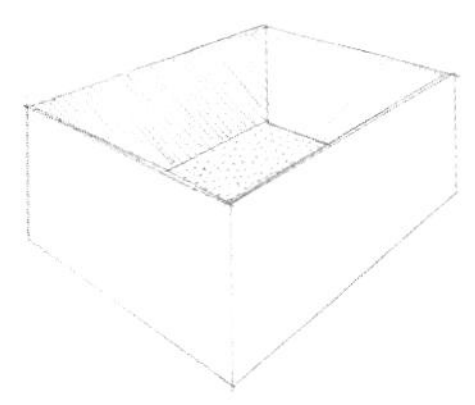

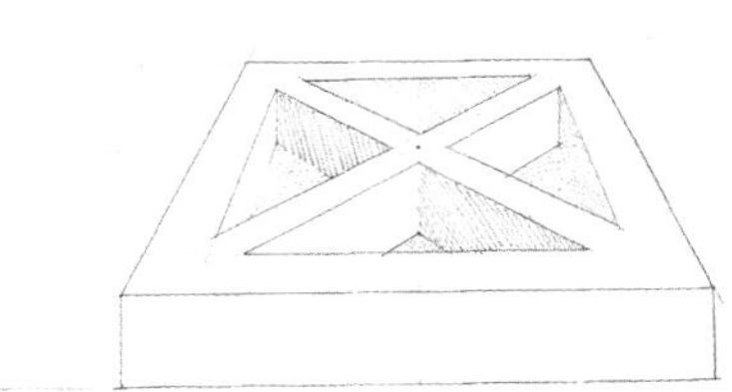

Extra vanishing points

If the surfaces, fences, paths, and walls are not parallel to each other, they will not disappear back to the same vanishing point. Different angles, for instance the diagonal patterning of the box hedging here, disappear back to different points on the horizon line. If they go off the edge of your paper, lining up to the vanishing point can be difficult. If you need to be accurate, you can add paper to continue your vanishing line to the desired length.

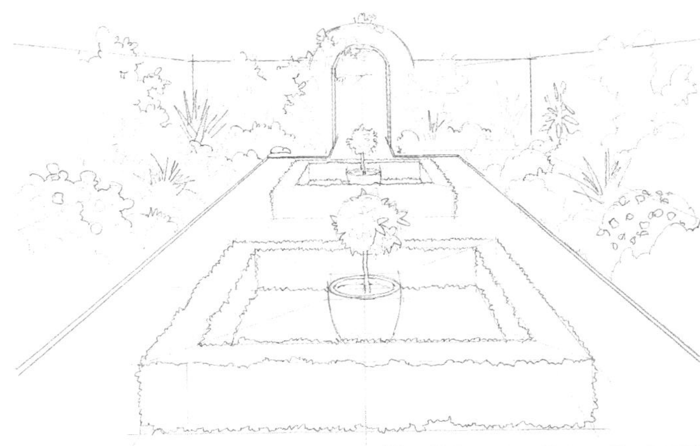

Using combinations

Combinations of the simple constructions shown on this page can be used in conjunction to make sense of complicated views. By reducing subjects to their basic structure, the fundamental form is easier to place within the composition, and then embellish with detail, tone, texture, and color.

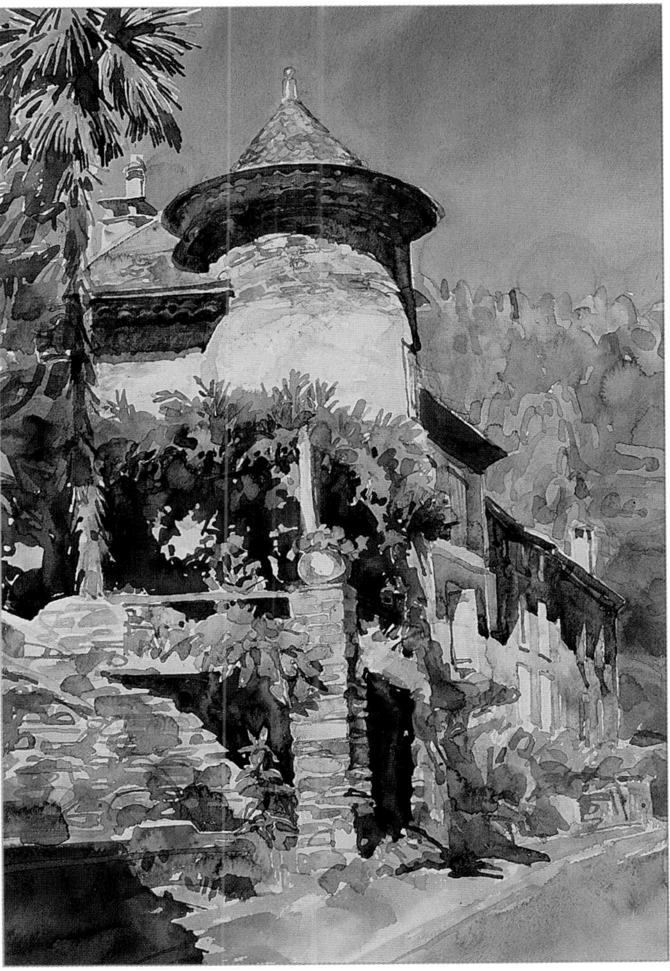

Turreted house

This French house is viewed from nearly a side view. The frontage recedes rapidly, with the steep angles lining up with the vanishing point, not far off the right-hand side of the painting.

Color

When considering floral subjects, I find that color is impossible to disregard. Although a black-and-white image can work wonderfully to produce dramatic effect, the color, whether it is bold and strong, or subtle and delicate, is of huge importance.

There are a few words that help to categorize a color. Hue is the basic color, the part or parts of the spectrum that we view. Each hue has a tonal value that is affected by how light or dark it is—yellow has a high tonal value, as it is quite close in tone to white, whereas violet has a low tonal value, being much nearer to the tonal value of black.

The saturation or intensity of color refers to the amount of pigment in the paint, and tints are produced by adding either varying amounts of white to opaque colors, or water in transparent washes.

Botanical painters study color very closely, testing colors against the subject to obtain their exact hue and tonal value. This can often be a useful exercise to do, and a clear understanding of color is absolutely essential to artists of all disciplines.

THE COLOR WHEEL

A good starting point is the color wheel. This shows the full spectrum of color as we see it in the rainbow, but turned around into a wheel shape. The basic principle is that there are three primary colors—yellow, blue, and red—that cannot be made by mixing other colors. From these three colors, in theory, all other colors can be made. When mixed with their neighbors, these primary colors produce secondary colors—green, orange, and

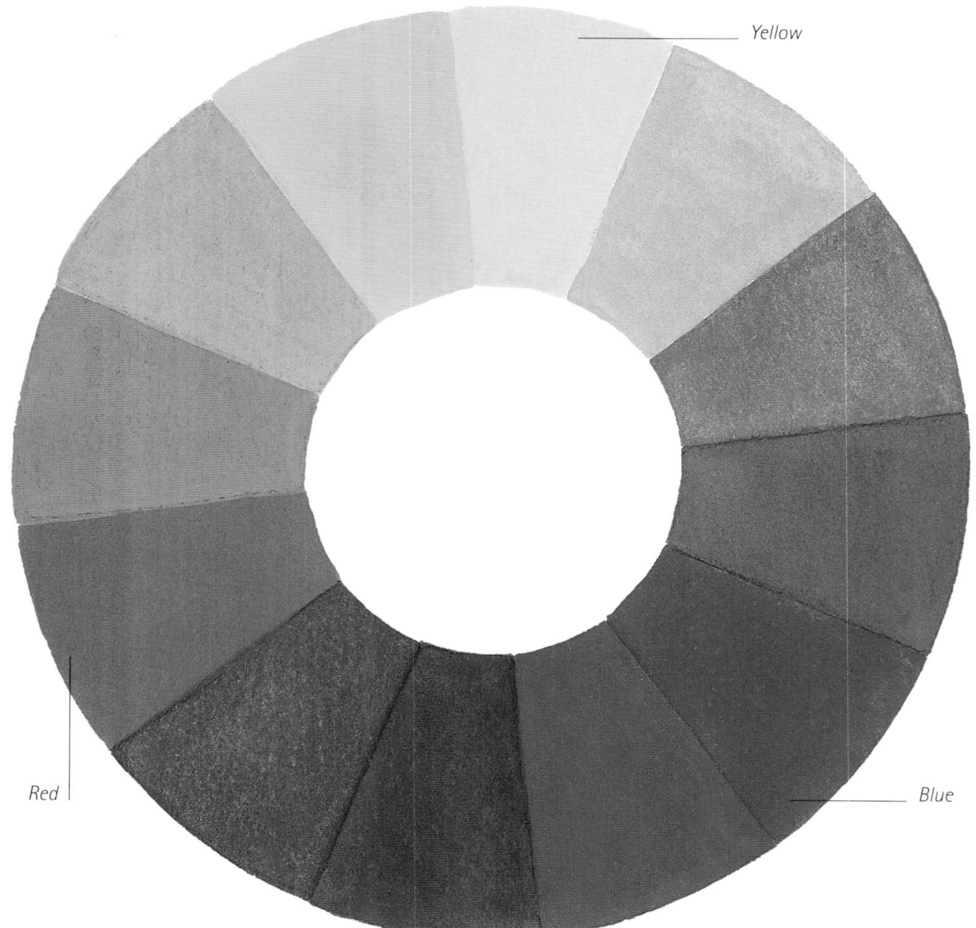

Color wheel
The three primary colors are yellow, blue, and red. Mixing these colors produces secondary colors, green, purple, and orange. When mixing adjacent colors, the wheel breaks down into a rainbow range, encompassing all the colors of white light. The color directly across on the other side of the wheel are a color's complementary color—yellow/purple, green/red, and blue/orange.

Reaction of color to color
Yellow is tonally the lightest color, so when surrounded by other colors, it always looks bright to some degree. Purple, being the darkest, always looks dark, especially against its complement yellow. The other colors vary in tone, and it is interesting to see how they react to different surroundings—sometimes calmly, and sometimes violently; the latter is usually its complementary opposite.

purple—and variations of mixtures then will produce an infinite range of these six basic colors.

COMPLEMENTARY COLORS

Pairing up the colors on opposite sides of the color wheel, such as yellow and purple, or red and green, produces what are termed complementary colors. These colors contrast strongly with each other, and if the pigments used to manufacture them were totally pure, both colors would contain the total range of the spectrum. When mixed, they would produce black or neutral gray.

Complementary colors can be useful for mixing neutral tones without using black, or, when used in their pure form next to each other, to create a strong reaction that draws the eye.

Mixing complementary colors
An interesting exercise is to pick, for instance, a yellow, and stick to it, then choose a purple/violet that you think is its complement. If, with gradual mixing, the hue becomes gray, it is the opposite color in the spectrum, but if it is warm in tone, your purple is too red. Experimenting is fun and shows you what a wonderful mixture of subtle colors you can achieve with so few pure colors.

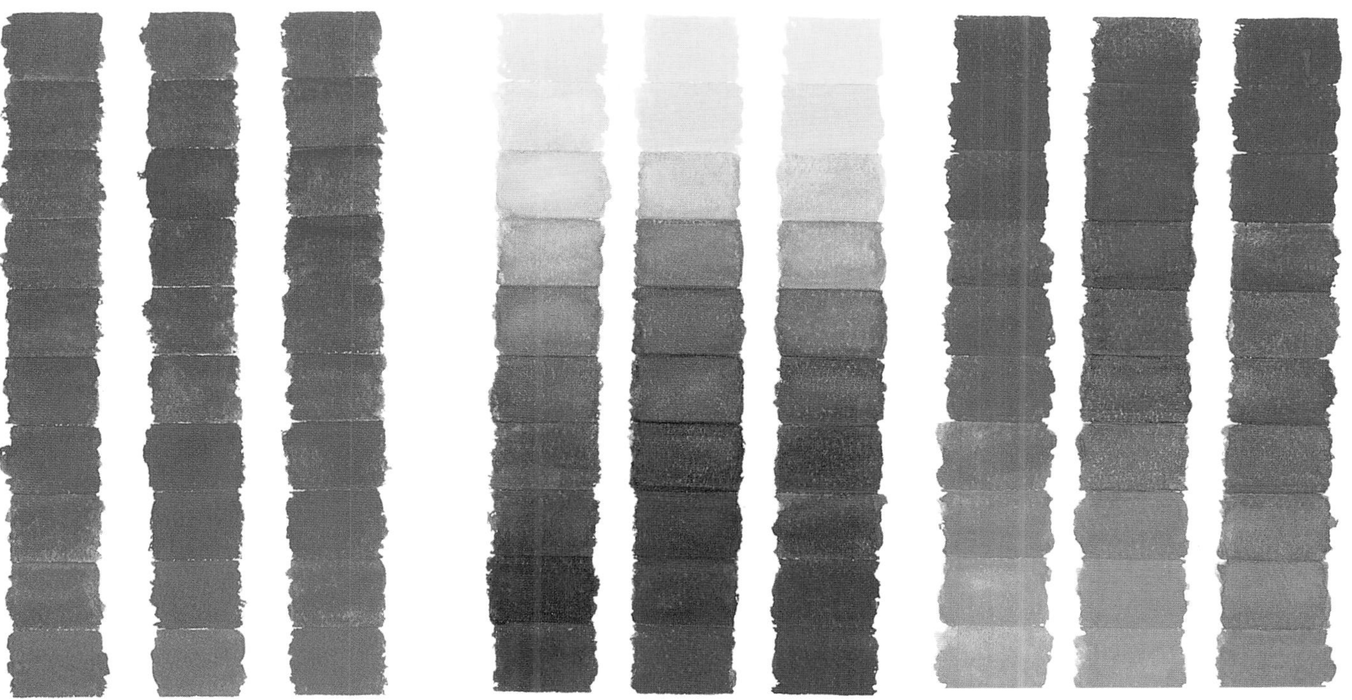

USING COLORS

With the confidence of being able to mix your colors, you next have to consider the location of colors to each other, the lighting, and the atmospheric conditions that affect your chosen subject.

Color can be very fickle—different light will make the same object appear a different color. A pure red against green can almost vibrate with intensity, or the same color can look dark against yellow, and light against violet. Light reflecting off a green surface can backlight a red object with a green shadow.

LIGHT

The apparent color of an object is the part of the spectrum that is not absorbed by that object. If the light is not pure white, i.e. containing the whole of the spectrum range, then the apparent color that it gives off will be different. Think of the sense of light at sunset. The absence of blue tones in the light gives an absence of blue in what we see—for instance, the lovely, coppery tones of a garden at sunset.

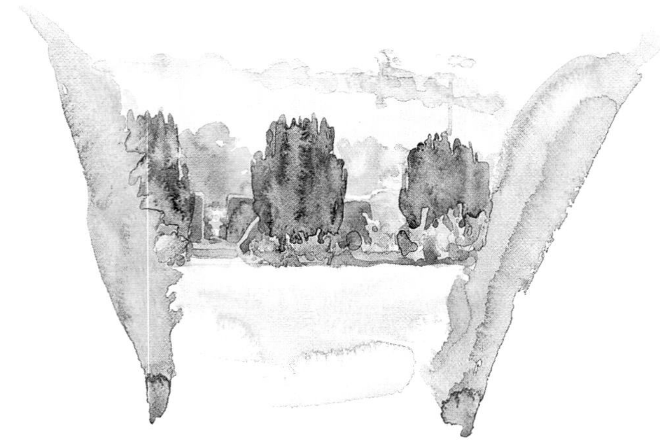

Evergreen gardens
Mixtures of greens in structural gardens make a wonderful subject, and become an exercise in color mixing.

If you are looking at a general view, your distance from the subject affects the tone and color, as well as the proportions or dimensions. As an object or view recedes we see it through more "air," which in turn is filled with moisture and dust particles of all kinds. This dulls our vision and so reduces the intensity of color and strength of tone—warm colors gradually disappear to make images appear more "blue" and faint. This can be useful to remember if you want to enhance the effect of distance, or pull out a foreground for greater attention.

Strong light can give the effect of bleaching the color out of a flower through our optical response to the extreme tones of light and shadow, so sometimes a duller day can be more appropriate for painting.

COLOR AND EMOTIONS

Our interpretation of color can be subjective; our emotional response to a flower or view will often depend on the

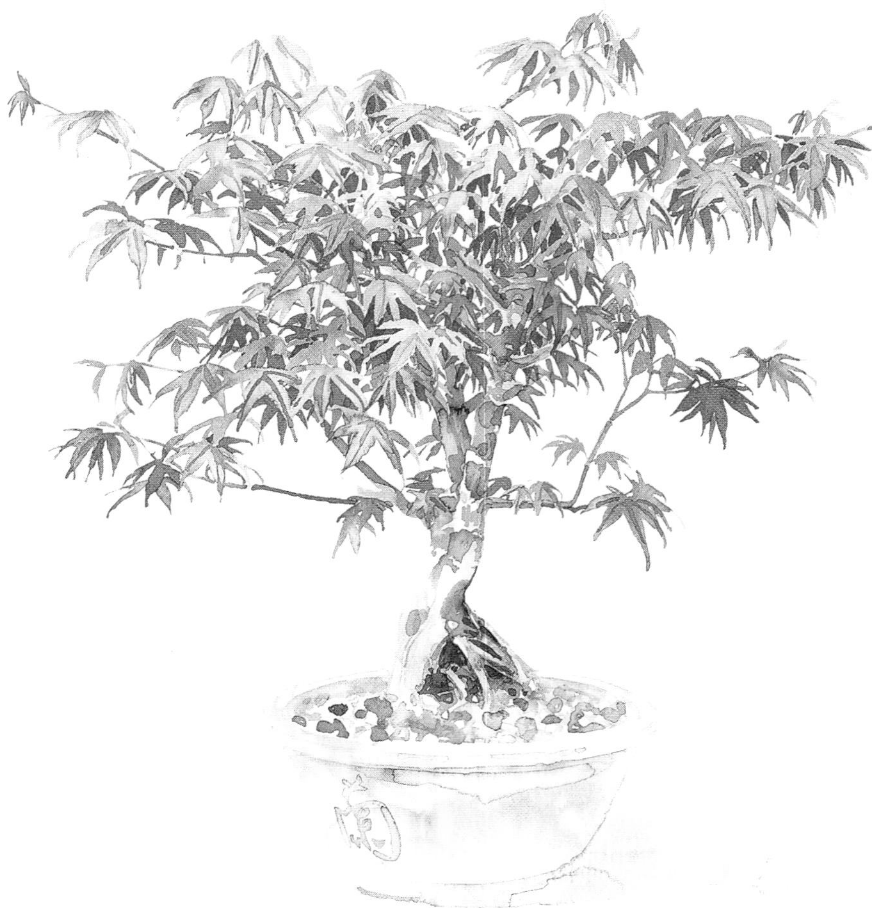

Maple bonsai
With color as stunning as this, a background is not needed—the color says it all, together with the delicate structure of the foliage.

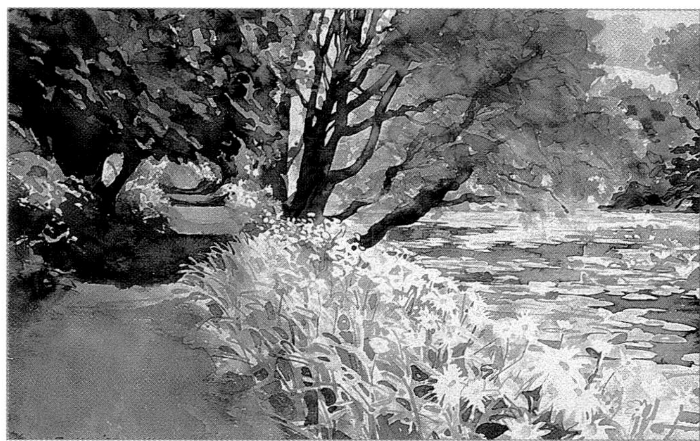

Tranquil garden
In this painting, the meandering path and calm lake are complemented by the gentle hues and tones.

associations certain colors have and can affect our vision of the subject. Rich, exotic flowers somehow need strong, deep colors to sing with the sunshine of their native lands. Pure, cool, architectural flowers, on the other hand, often are enhanced with crisp, fresh colors. History and literature infiltrate our thoughts—white flowers for purity, purple for royalty, red for love.

The colors of the seasons are so evocative that it is not surprising how much flowers and plants have influenced us. Spring and summer have an explosion of color, when the abundance of pattern can challenge the painter. Fall, in contrast, often feels to me like I am wearing tinted glasses while a richness fills the air—and winter rests the eye with a monochrome view, whether this be cool, sleepy, or stormy.

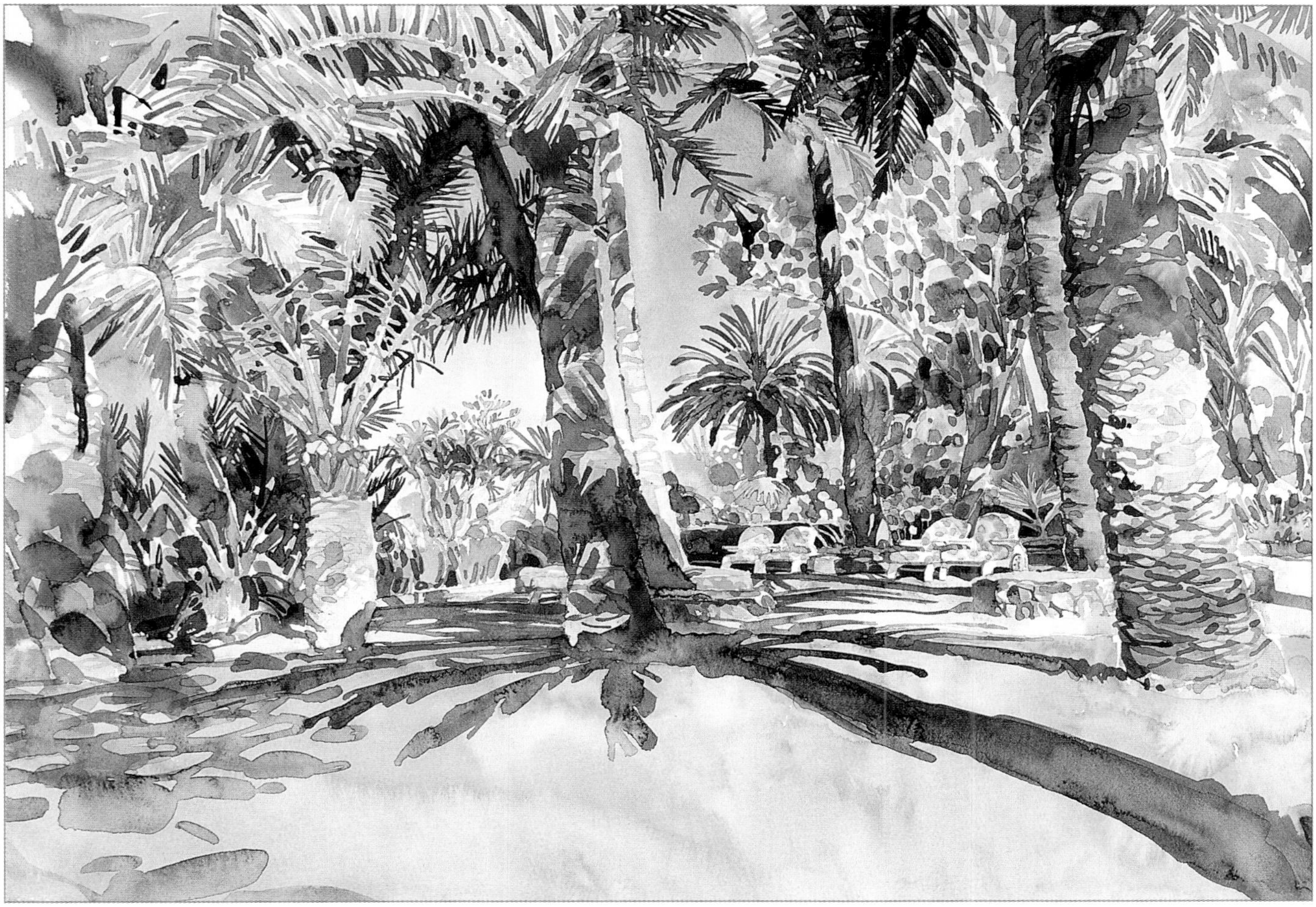

Colonnaded palms
The strong color and movement created by the arched palms express this exotic setting well. The blue sky enriches the golden hues on the palm tree trunks, with cast shadows emphasizing heat and sunlight.

Putting it all together

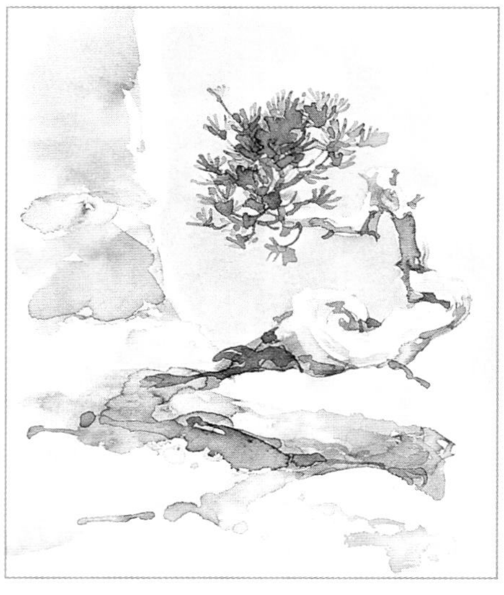

Cliff edge

Sometimes a particular situation really gives the essence of a painting. Here, a bonsai exists in the barren soil where these plants first originated.

With all these considerations, I feel that we have come full circle. I can only repeat what was said at the beginning—a drawing or painting can be as simple as one flower or leaf, or as monumental as a large, intricate landscape. Use as little or as much as you need to convey what you want to say—your view is personal to you.

Use structure and composition to set the scene, balance, and mood, and use color, texture, and tonal contrast to lead the eye and help balance the composition. The addition of more detail to certain areas can also help draw the eye to rest at focal points, so if your composition has both foreground and background, for instance, think about how you want to approach it. If the foreground is of primary interest, keep the stronger color and contrast there and let the distant view recede with more gentle hues. If the background is your focal point, make the foreground a loose frame that can lead you into the main area of your composition.

MATERIALS AND TECHNIQUES

The choice of materials, or the combination of them, and how you use them, can really help you to express the weight, texture, delicacy, or atmosphere of the subject or scene, but I mention this with a word of caution. Experimentation is fun and valuable for keeping your approach fresh, but using too much technique can become an end in itself. If it takes over, you can end up looking at the effects and losing the picture as a whole. Use different techniques and textures judiciously, and remember to stand back, take a minute's rest, and check the balance. Sometimes facing away from a picture and using a mirror to view your work can give you a renewed perspective, as well as reveal structural and tonal inbalances.

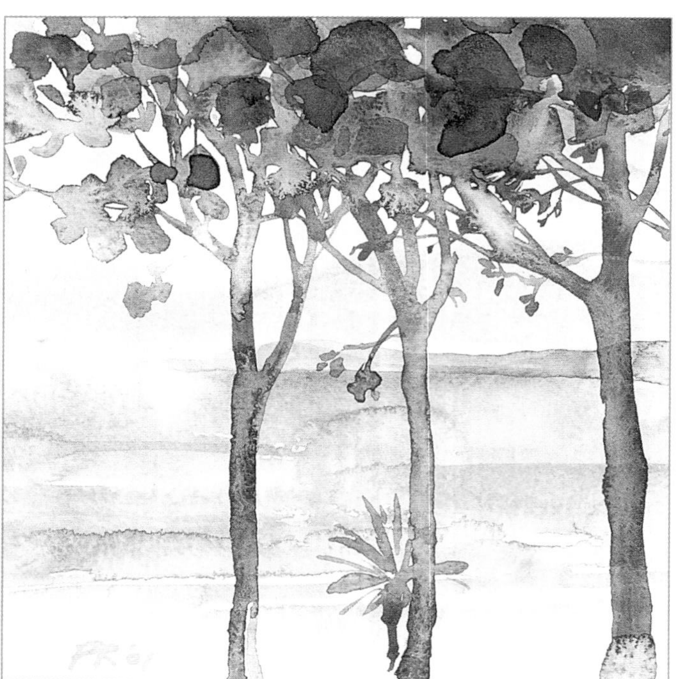

MAKING DECISIONS

The decisions that you make can be instinctive or consciously planned, or perhaps a bit of both. Personally, I find that rough sketches to loosely determine the feel and structure of the composition are sufficient preparation, as I usually enjoy exploring the painting as I go. Without planning everything, you can and do have failures, but I regard these as part of the learning process. These unsuccessful pictures can in turn be revived by introducing another medium that can knock back overworked areas, and develop new textures and details.

Mediterranean coast

These trees in semi-silhouette convey everything about the welcome shade they provide along the hot coast in summer.

I sometimes try the same subject again in a different medium, which can totally change the atmosphere.

You will find out what approaches best suit you. Different compositions will need varying degrees of preparation, so keep your options open, be bold, and try different techniques or combinations of materials.

Think of the appropriate situation for a particular plant—which medium expresses it best? What light shows the character of a flower? What eye level describes its size? The emotional response that we have affects the way that we want to view it, so use this to your advantage.

The most important thing is to enjoy your subject. Painting and drawing can be wonderfully therapeutic, and plants and flowers make it even more so. Have fun—this is a fantastic subject to explore.

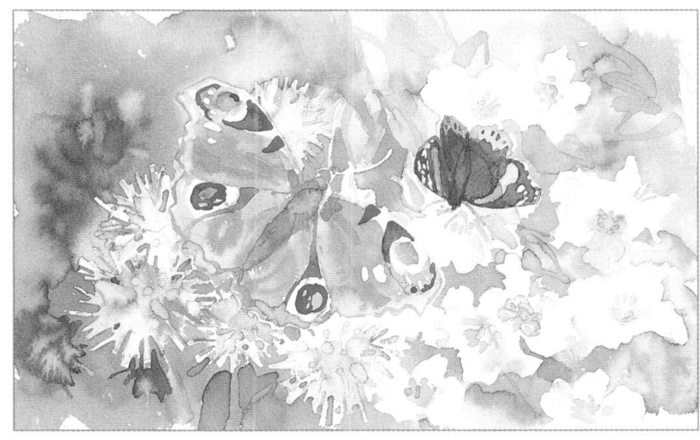

Fragrant flowers
In addition to their beauty, these butterflies convey a message of fragrance and warmth in the flowers on which they are sitting.

THE STUNNING COLORS OF FALL

Fall color can be dramatic, and the hues quite vivid. This acrylic painting celebrates those colors.

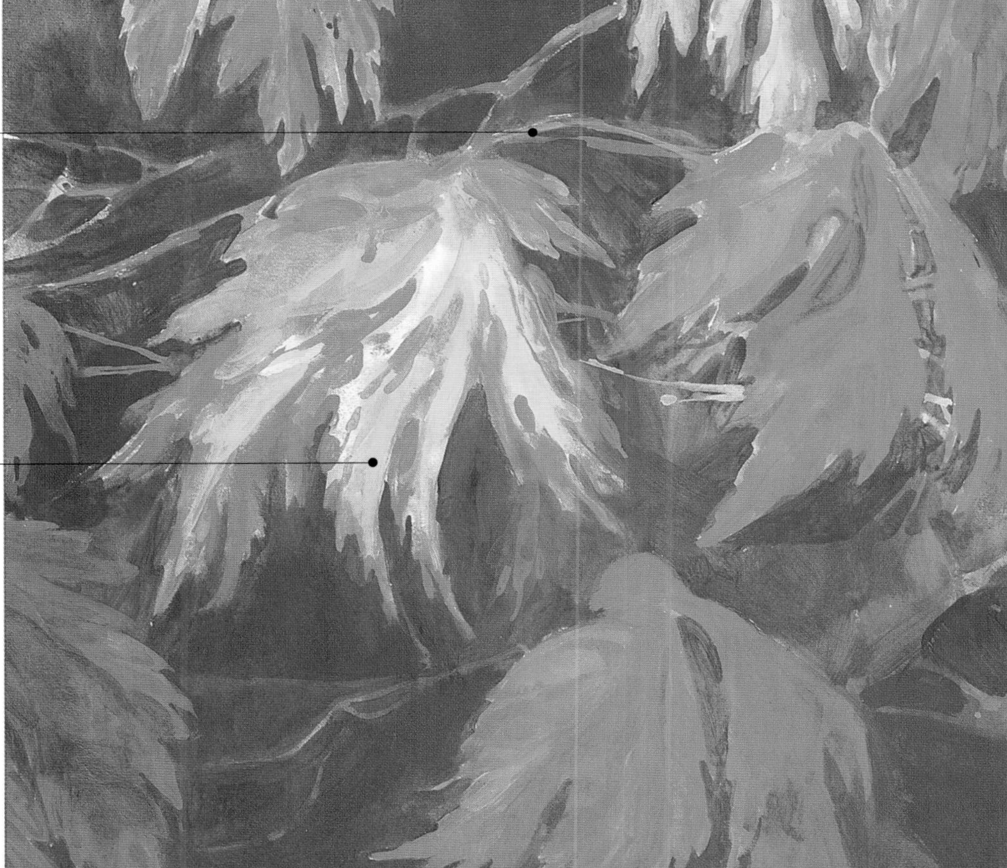

To keep the freshness of the scene, some twigs were overlaid with body color, while others kept their washed appearance.

The first light washes of the leaves are kept simple, to keep the leaves translucenct.

Violet shadows enhance the fiery colors.

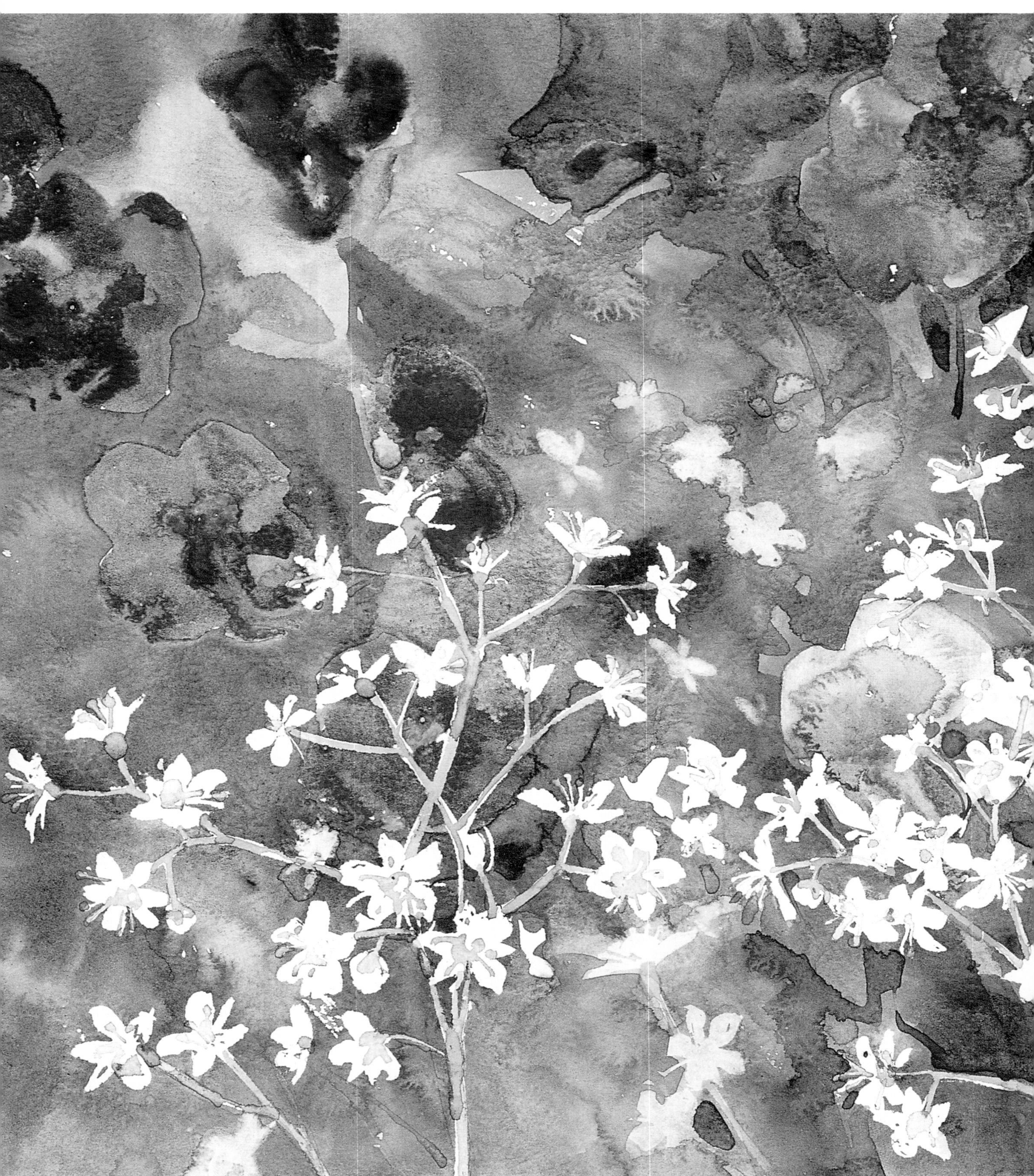

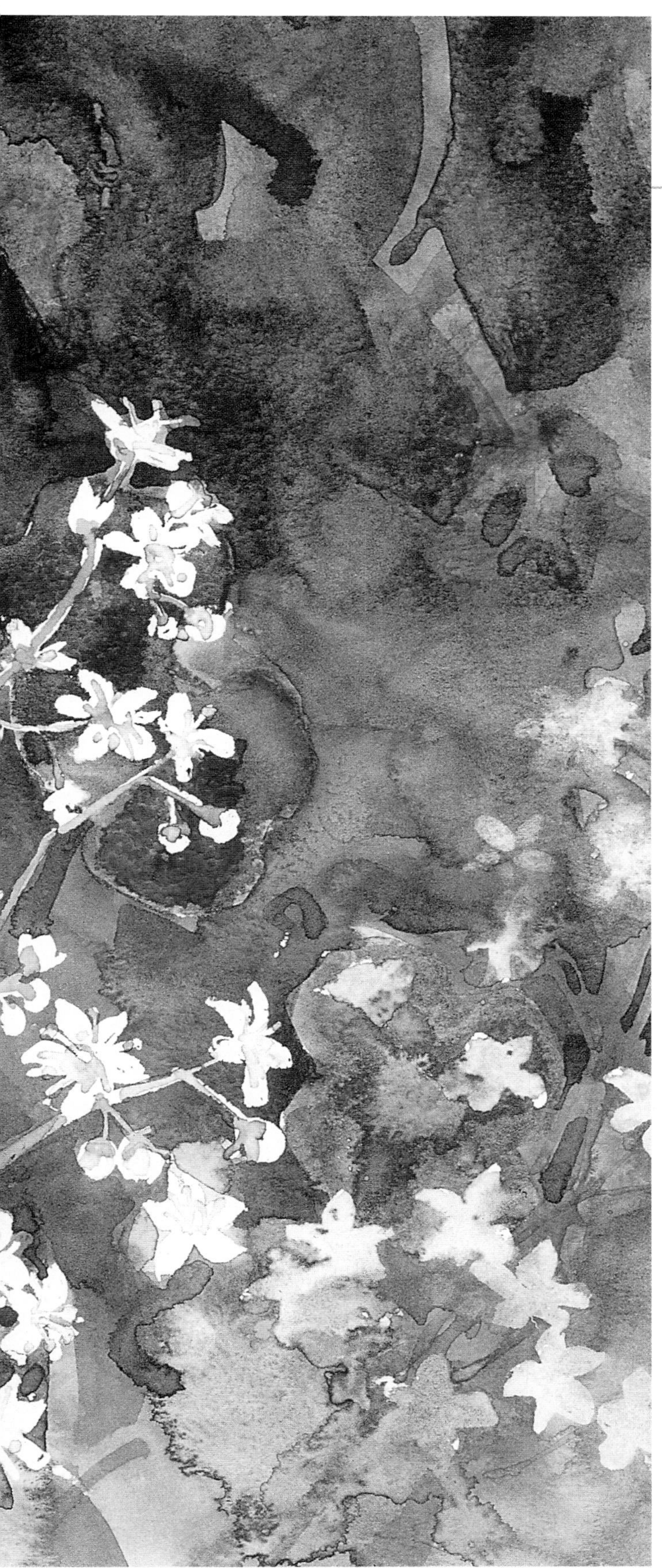

PART 2

In practice

On THE FACE OF IT, FLOWER and plant painting might appear to be a rather narrow, specialized field, but when you consider the range of approaches and include "gardenscapes," be they small and secluded, or grand vistas, the subject is immense.

The following section introduces a selection of possible views, varying techniques, and mixtures of art materials to explore. They vary in the time taken to complete, with some projects retaining their sketch quality. The ever-changing seasons are considered, as they are crucial to the well-being of our gardens, and signal the progression of sprouting plants as the growing season develops. A garden or yard under a blanket of snow has such a tranquil feel compared to the vibrant explosion of color that can dominate the same garden in high summer.

Hopefully, seeing the stages developing will take the mystery out of techniques that seem difficult. You will find that although some vivid stages can seem complex on first view, by developing them through to the final stage the elements will come together.

The projects are to serve merely as guidelines, so take from them as much as you need. Utilize a detail from one project, a technique from another, and then put together your own interpretation of your subject.

Public garden: watercolor on semi-rough watercolor paper

In this exuberant composition, oriental brushes can accentuate the free, calligraphic feel. The painting of the topiary has been kept deliberately simple, to give the eye some relief from the jumble of brightly colored flowers in the herbaceous borders. Remember to keep your washes light—they can always be strengthened later.

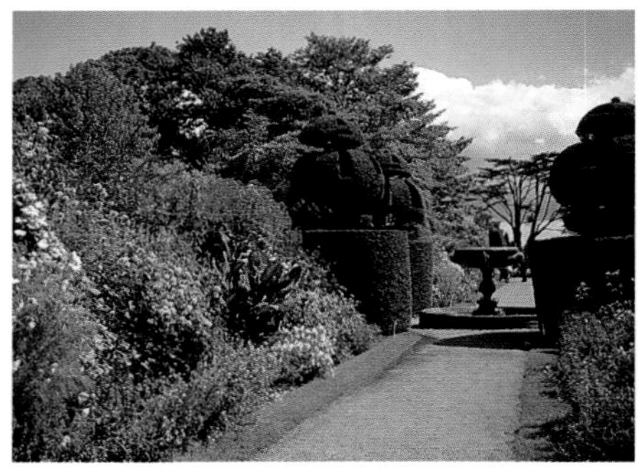

MATERIALS

- Semi-rough watercolor paper
- 3B pencil
- Large and medium oriental brushes
- No. 2 and fine long-hair sable brushes
- Watercolor paints
- Masking fluid
- Clean water

1 Sketch the overall composition with a 3B pencil. Using the large oriental brush, lay down a loose, wet wash for the sky with a warm tone of light blue, then a cooler hue of blue for the shadow area of the clouds above the horizon. Using a drier mixture of dull yellow to emphasize texture, lay down a light broken wash over the path area.

2 Using the medium oriental brush, draw in a number of the white flowers with masking fluid. Make this selection fairly random to avoid too mechanical a look when the masking fluid is removed. Allow the fluid to dry thoroughly.

3 Using the no. 2 sable brush and a pale wash of yellow-gold, paint in the highlights on the fountain, and add some detail of the red flowers in the borders. Keep the drawing loose and free, and try not to make it appear too labored.

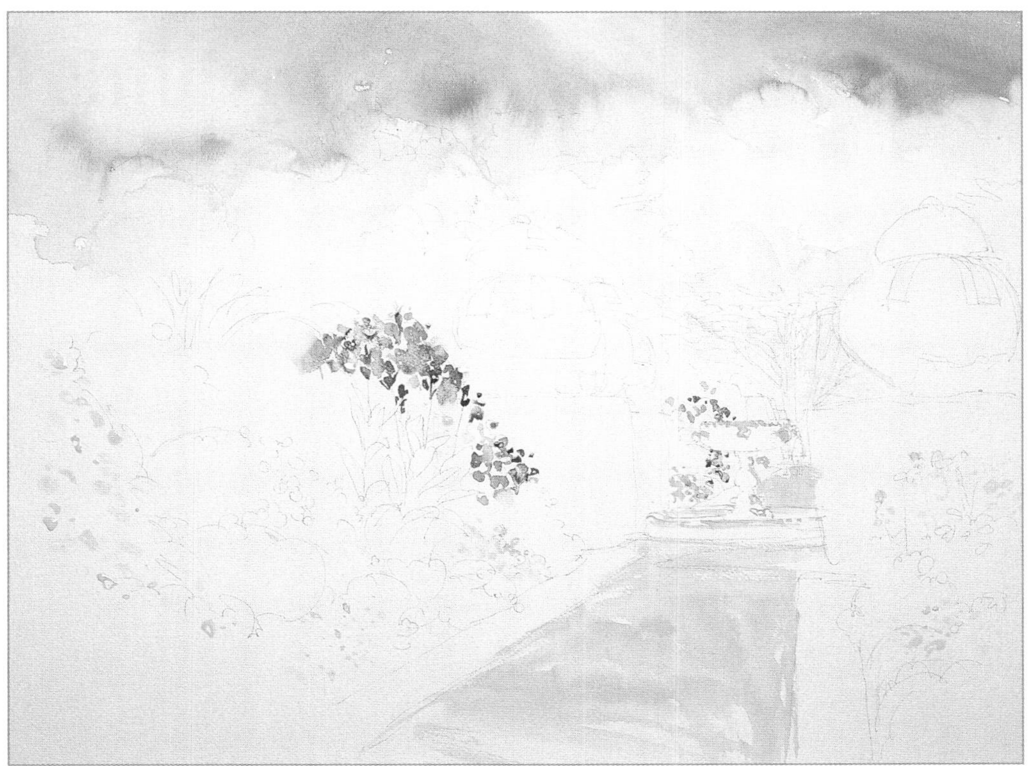

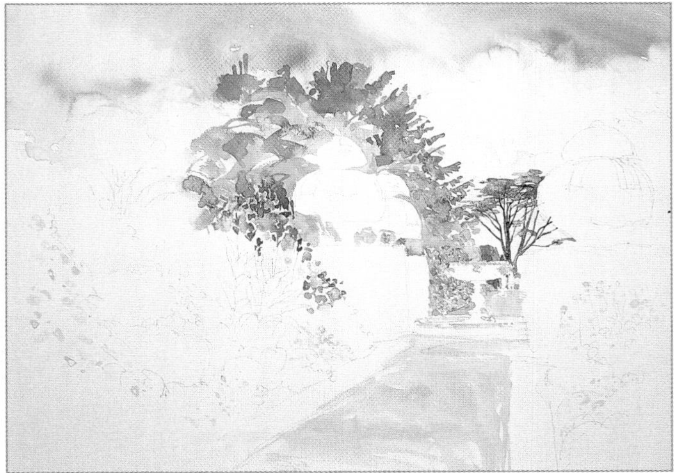

4 With the medium brush and a light green wash paint the distant foliage, drawing around the red flowers but covering the masking fluid. Repeat for a loose impression of the foliage of the distant trees. Work over the first wash with a darker one, building up the foliage effect. Draw in the distant tree using the long-hair brush.

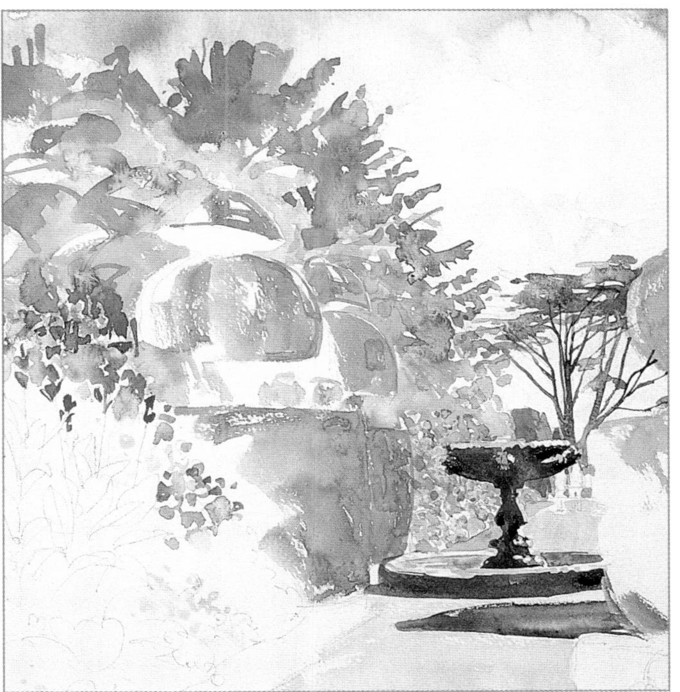

5 The topiary and fountain are near-silhouettes against the bright sunlight. Start with a midtone, some of which can be later left as highlights. Carefully define the detail of the fountain because this will be the most "finished" area of the composition—paint around the golden highlights.

6 Using a wash of darker green, build the strong, architectural form of the topiary's extensive shadow areas. Paint into the right-hand foliage bed, washing over the masked areas but working around the remaining flowers, which are either left white or have color added later.

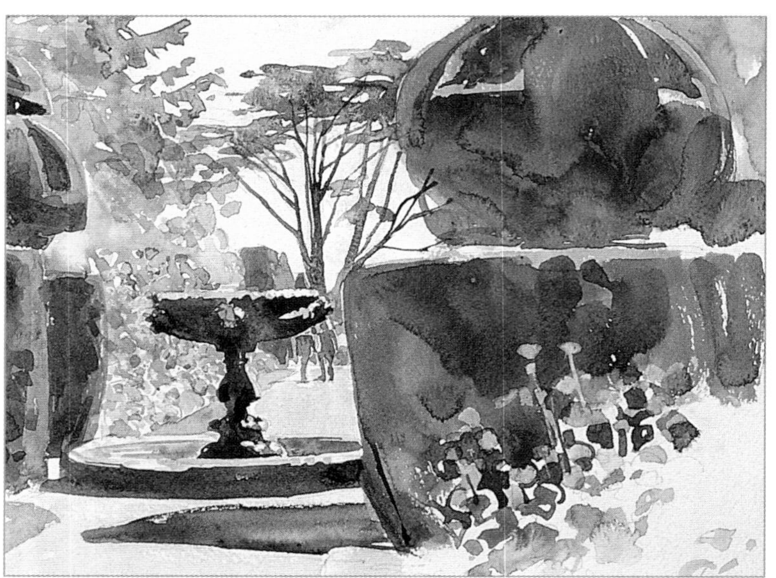

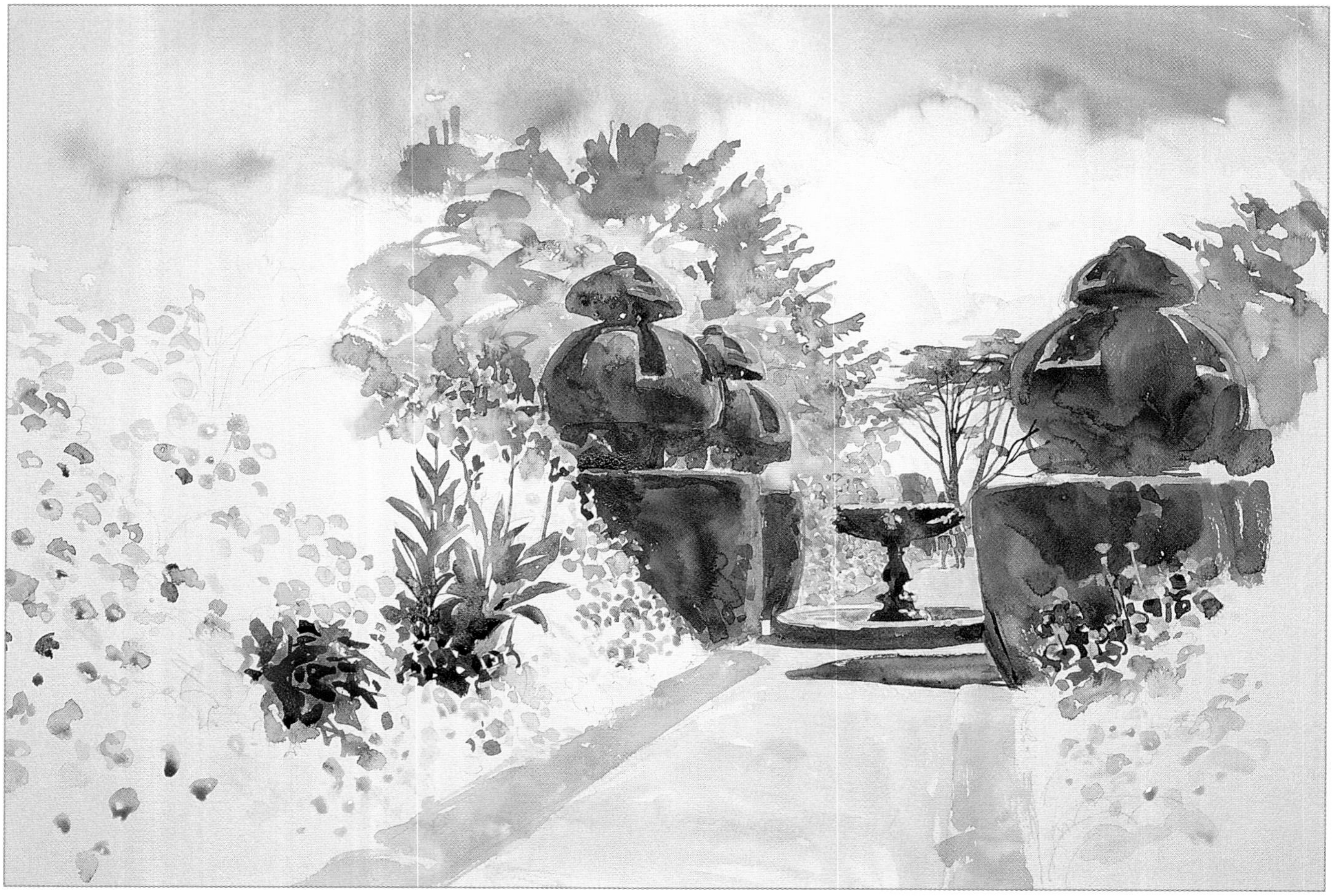

7 On the main flowerbed freely draw the pattern of flowers using a range of lilacs, mauves, reds, and yellows. Establish the shapes of some of the more architectural plants, such as the crane flower in the middle ground, that give form overall.

8 Working carefully around the individual flower patterns, wash in further areas of foliage. Vary the tones and hues of the greens. Look and draw constantly, and avoid simply filling in color areas. Add cool hues of green to the background trees to give a feeling of recession. Using a watery mixture of this same wash, knock back some of the brighter flowers.

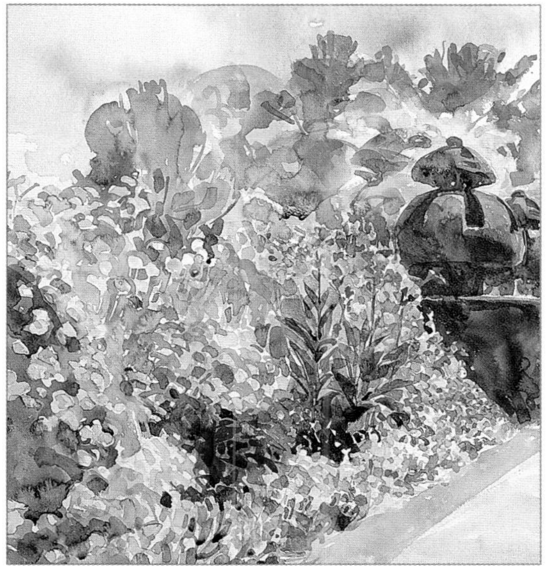

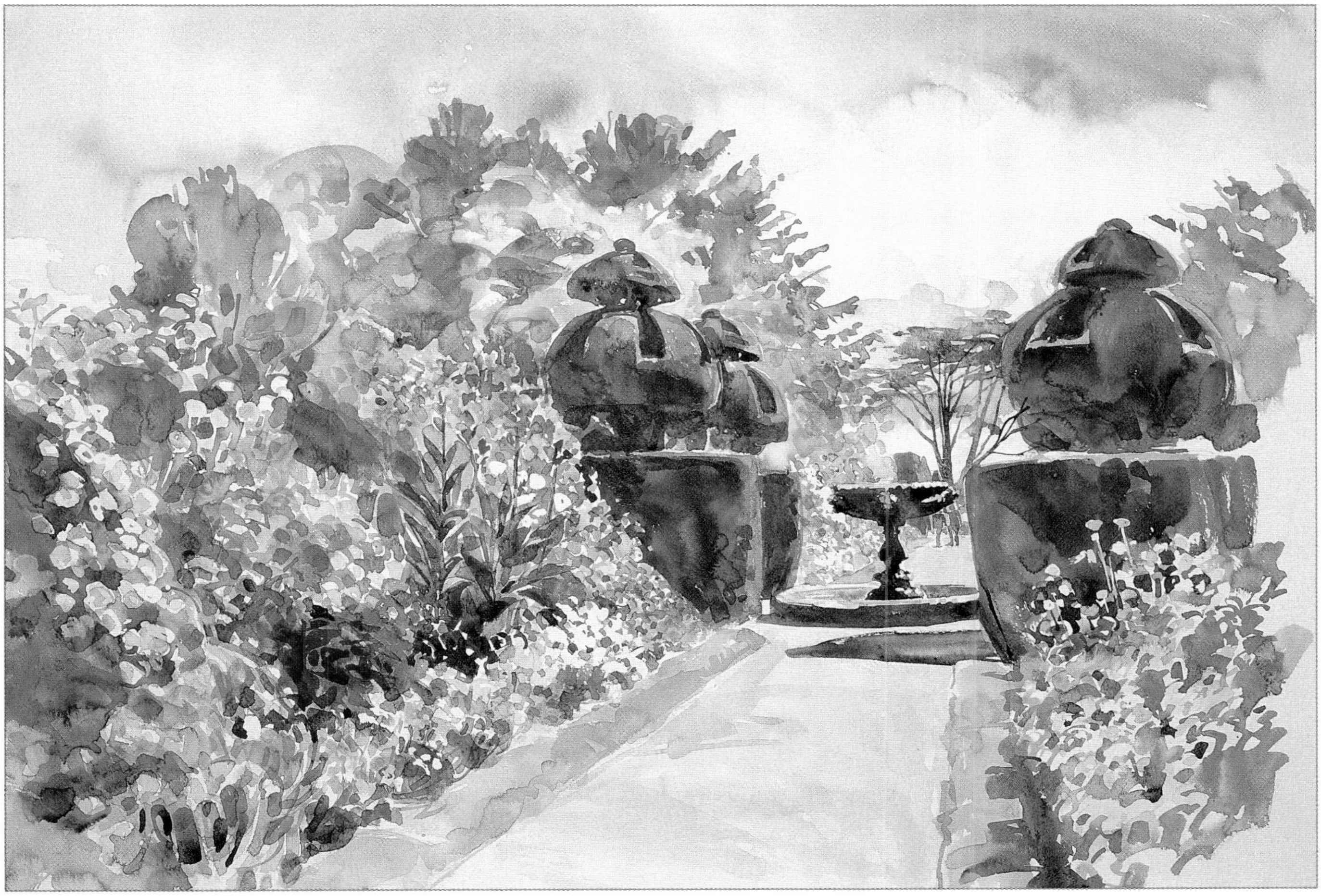

9 Finish the painting by adding more foliage detail to the right-hand border, and observe how the more extreme foreshortening on this side simplifies the detail. Finally, when the painting is thoroughly dry, remove the masking fluid gently with a fingertip to give white highlights.

Wild plants: acrylics on gessoed masonite

In a summer meadow or field, wildflowers grow in profusion, and choosing what to leave out of a particular view can be as important as what to include. Using acrylics gives you the option of being able to knock back any areas that aren't working, and to revise or repeat them without too much effort.

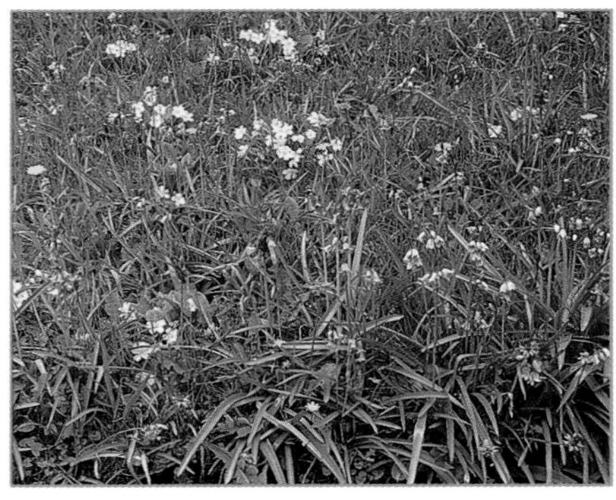

MATERIALS

- Gessoed masonite
- Sable brushes
- Acrylic paints
- Clean water

1 Using a sable brush, lay down the basic colors of the grasses, mixing and blending greens, yellows, and whites as required—this will act as an underpainting for subsequent layers. Paint freely to catch the directions of the leaves of grass, especially in the foreground.

2 Block in the top of the leaves with wash-like applications of diluted paint, then use blues, browns and crimsons for the foreground. These shapes help to find the darkest tones. Use thin glazes on top of wet strokes to blend and unify the patterns. Look to use both the positive and negative shapes.

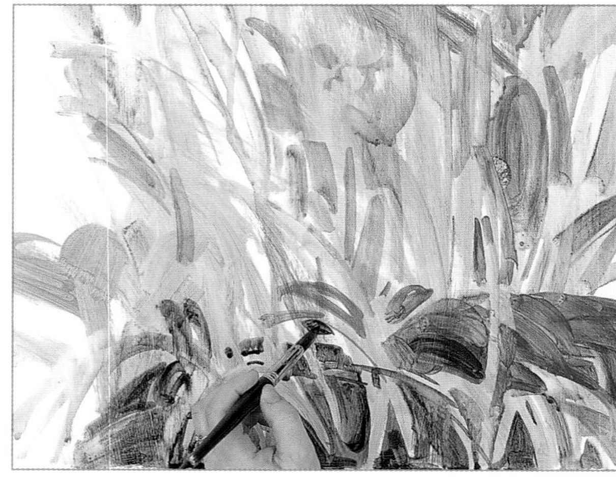

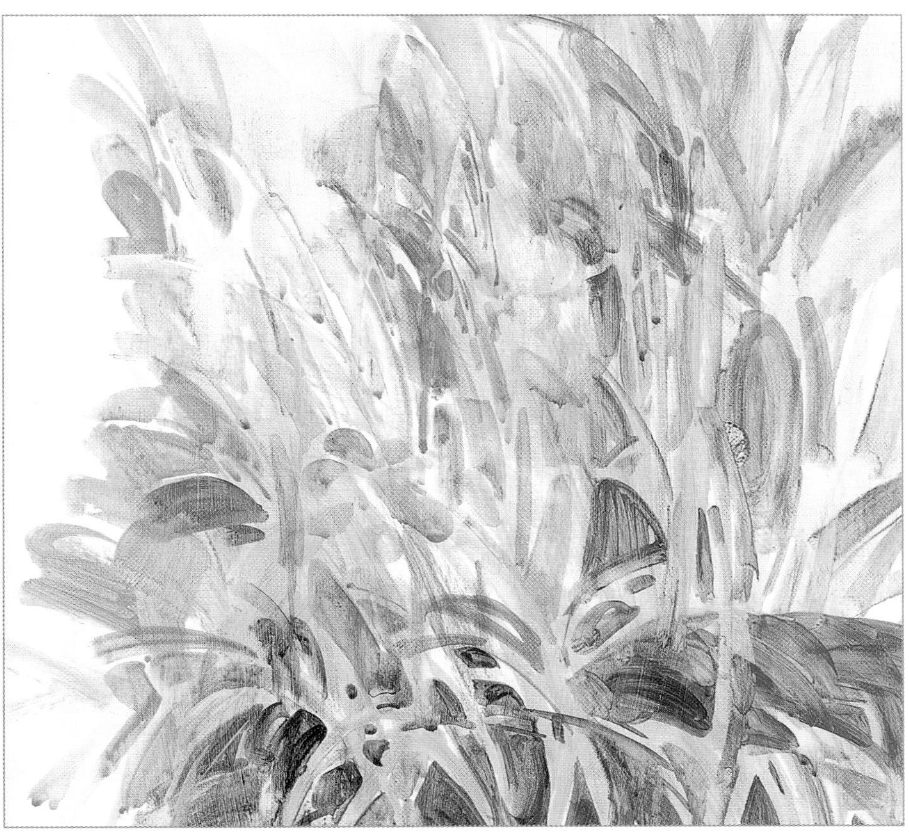

3 To give the impression of more depth in the center, switch to a smaller sable brush and add detailed blue-green lines. Work more finely to show the sense of scale on the stalks and leaves in the central and background areas. You can use a hair dryer to dry the paint thoroughly, or alternatively, let it air-dry.

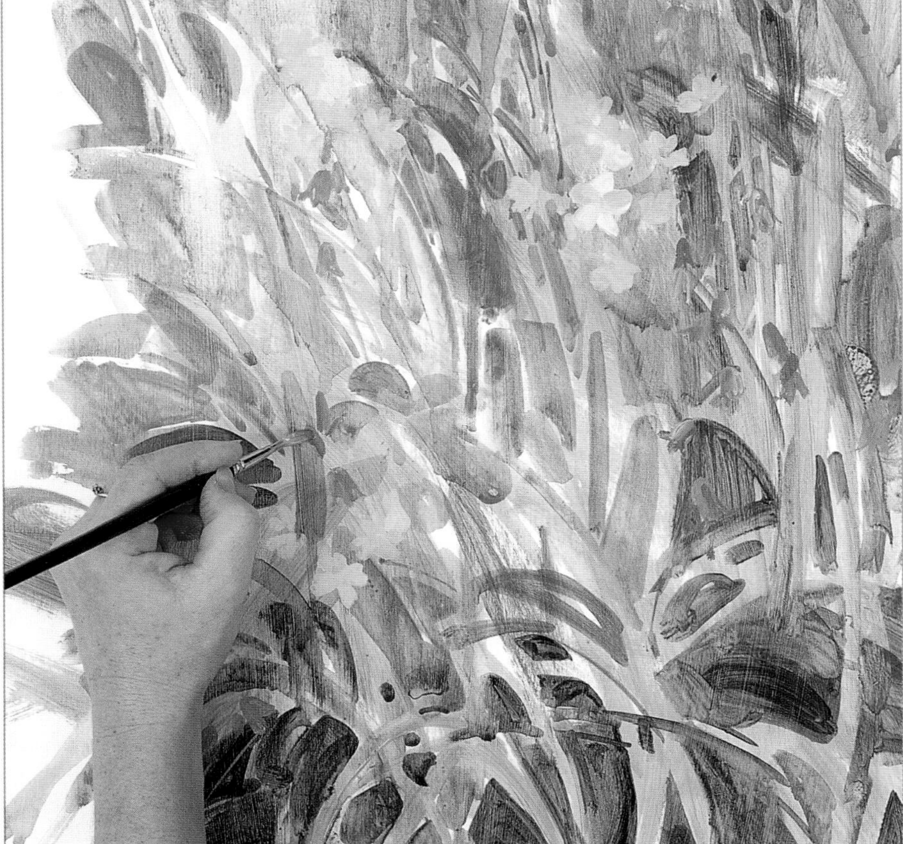

4 Start the petals of the flowers, working from the lightest colors in the undiluted paints. The white and yellows stand out against the darker greens automatically, but for now concentrate on finding the positions and shapes, rather than aiming for more contrast. Move on to the pink and purple petals.

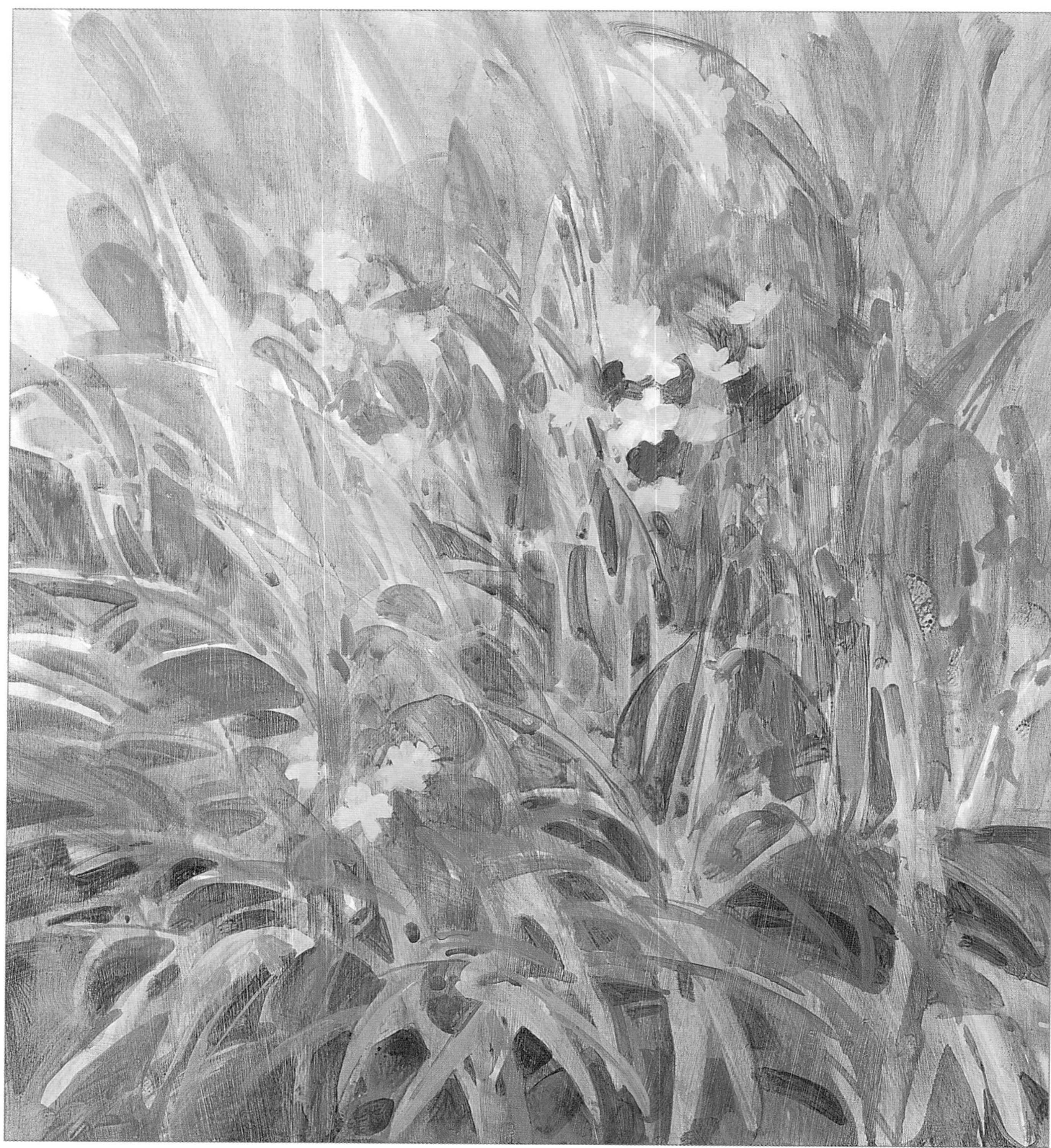

5 With everything in place, apply very light glazes across the back with the large brush to simplify the directions and mute the colors. Draw into the nearer flowers and grasses with the smaller brush, working both light and dark. Introduce verticals to provide movement and structure.

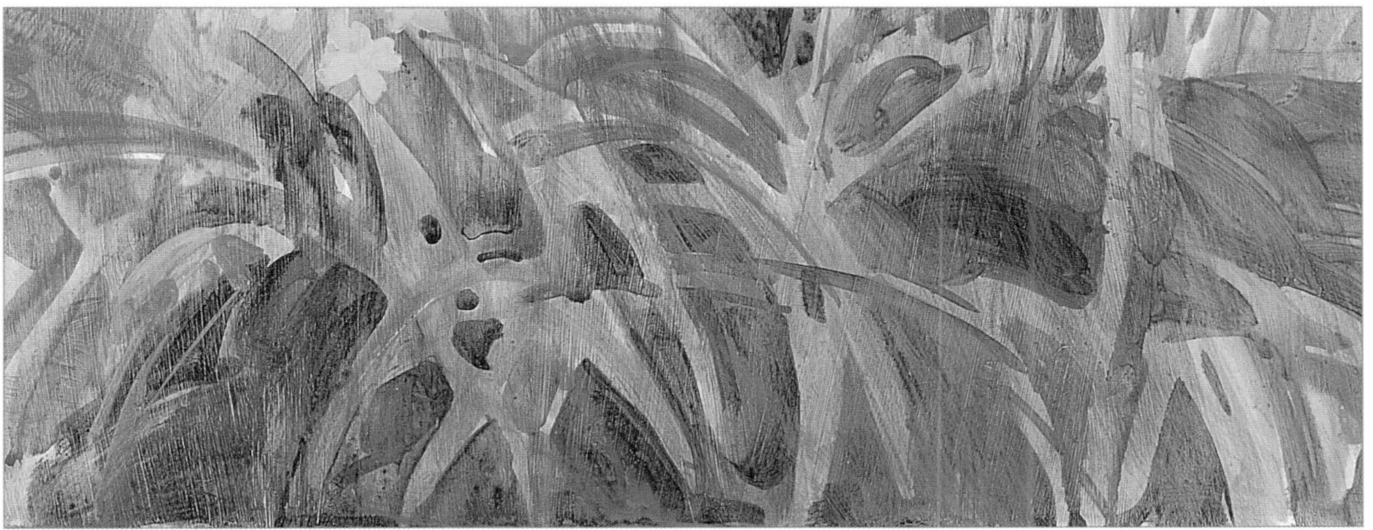

6 For the foreground details, lay in light opaque lines, and then develop the shaded areas beneath the foreground leaves—this both gives a three-dimensional effect and makes the background areas more patterned and recessive. Move across the whole picture to keep a sense of unity.

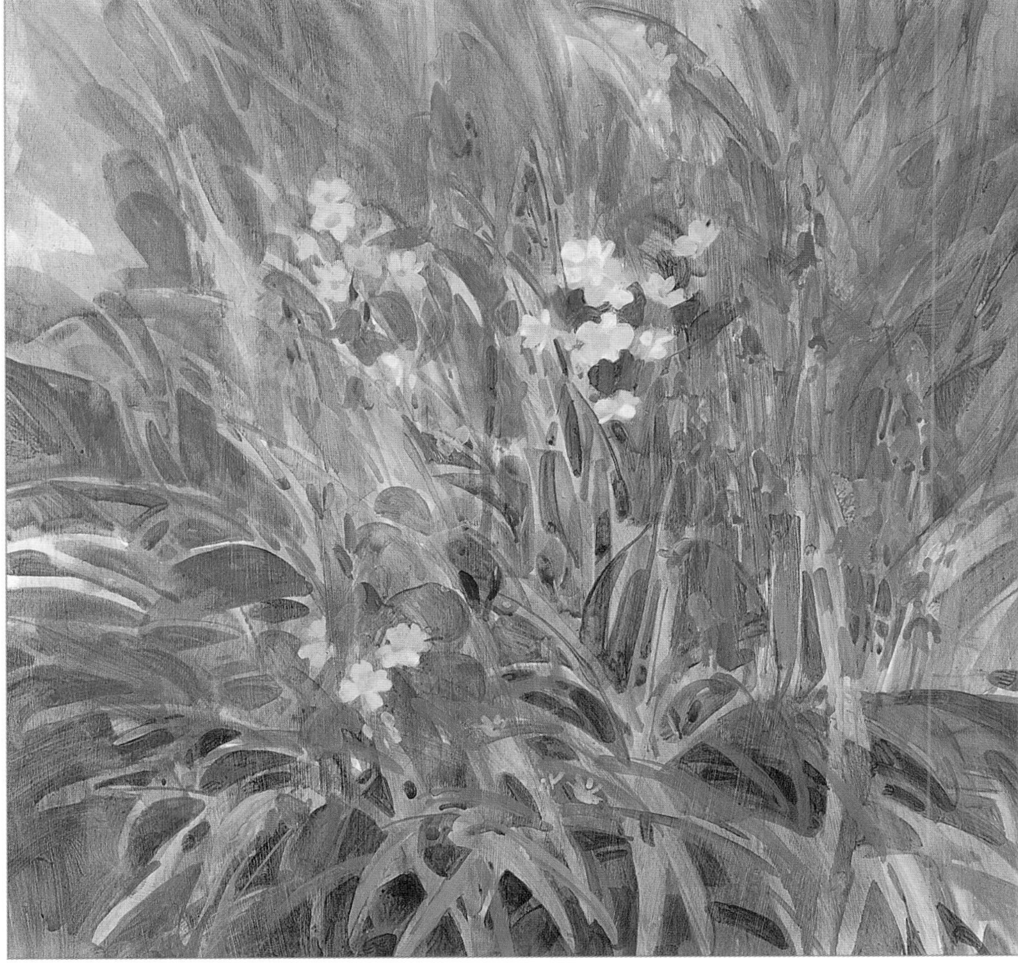

7 Stand back and look objectively before deciding how you want the painting to develop from here. Use the large brush and diluted washes to flatten the background, but keep the movement so as not to lose the chaotic nature of the scene. Add a cedar green around the yellow petals to make them stand out.

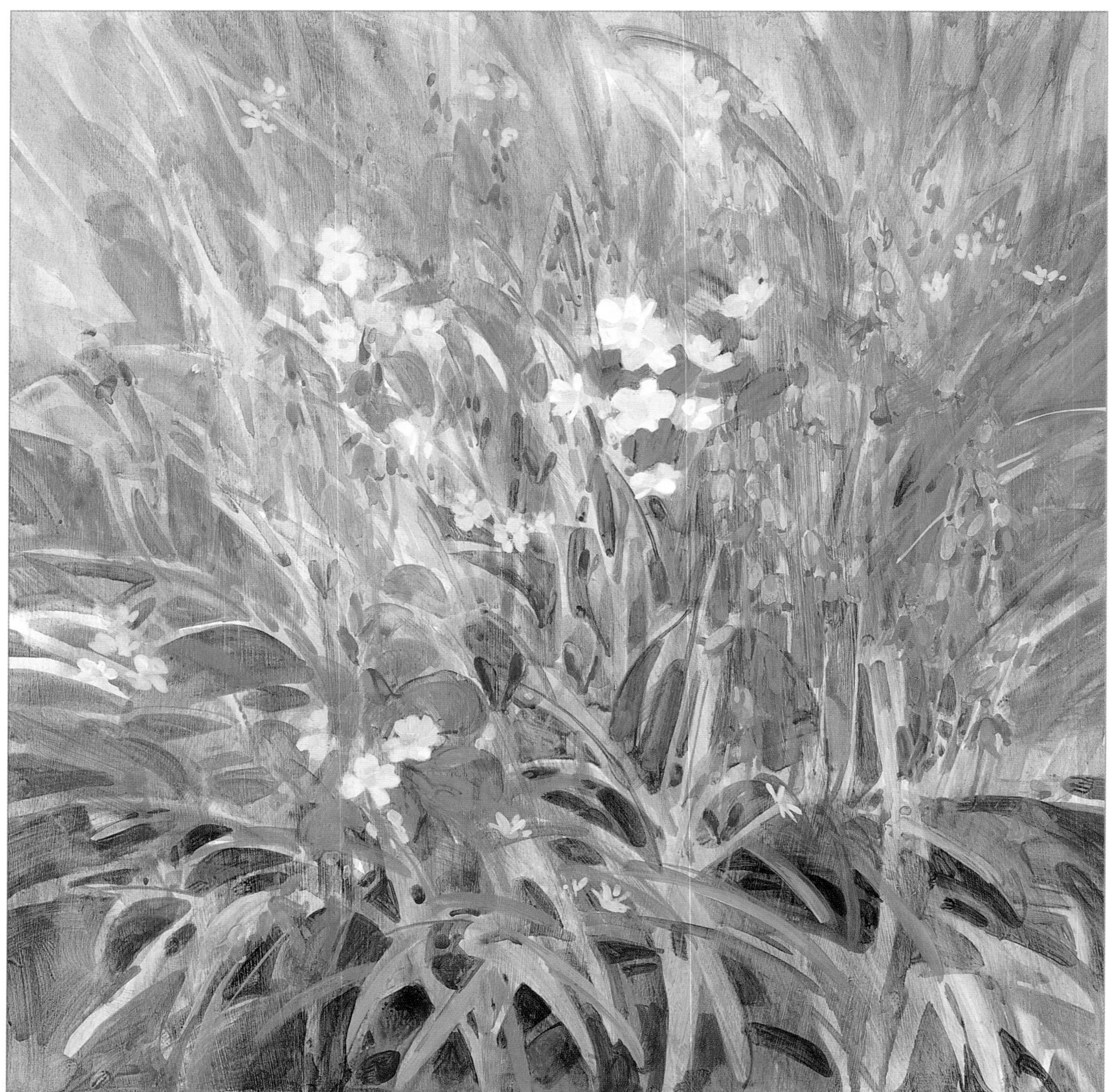

8 Find the position and shape of the reddest flowers, working with full-strength white into magenta. Reinforce the pinks and purples, and look to find the vertical lines of the stalks. Use a rag to knock back overly dominant colors. Finish by strengthening the paler petal colors.

Daisies: Conté crayons and watercolors on semi-rough watercolor paper

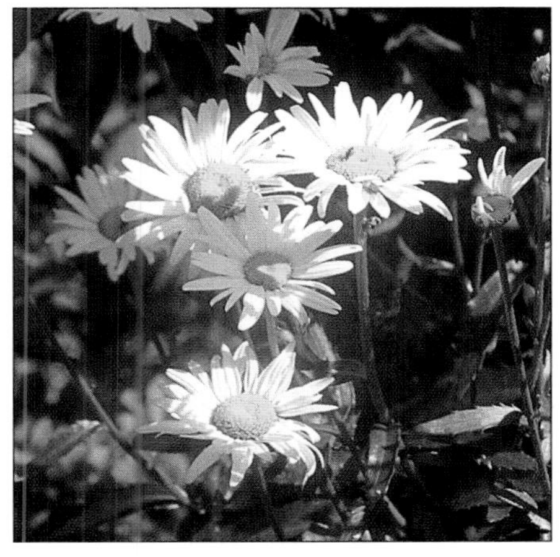

Instead of using colored paper as a basis for pastel drawing, an interesting effect can be achieved by painting a watercolor wash with semi-abstract, wet-in-wet brushwork onto white paper. This gives a rich base for interesting effects very quickly—the dense, opaque qualities of Conté crayons make them ideal for drawing over watercolor.

Materials

- Semi-rough watercolor paper
- Large oriental brush
- Watercolor paints
- Clean water
- Conté crayons

1 With the brush and very fluid washes of various greens, vigorously apply a broken background onto pre-stretched watercolor paper. Work wet-in-wet, adding blues to the darker shadow areas and yellows for the flower centers. Cover most of the paper, giving a range of colors, textures, and tones.

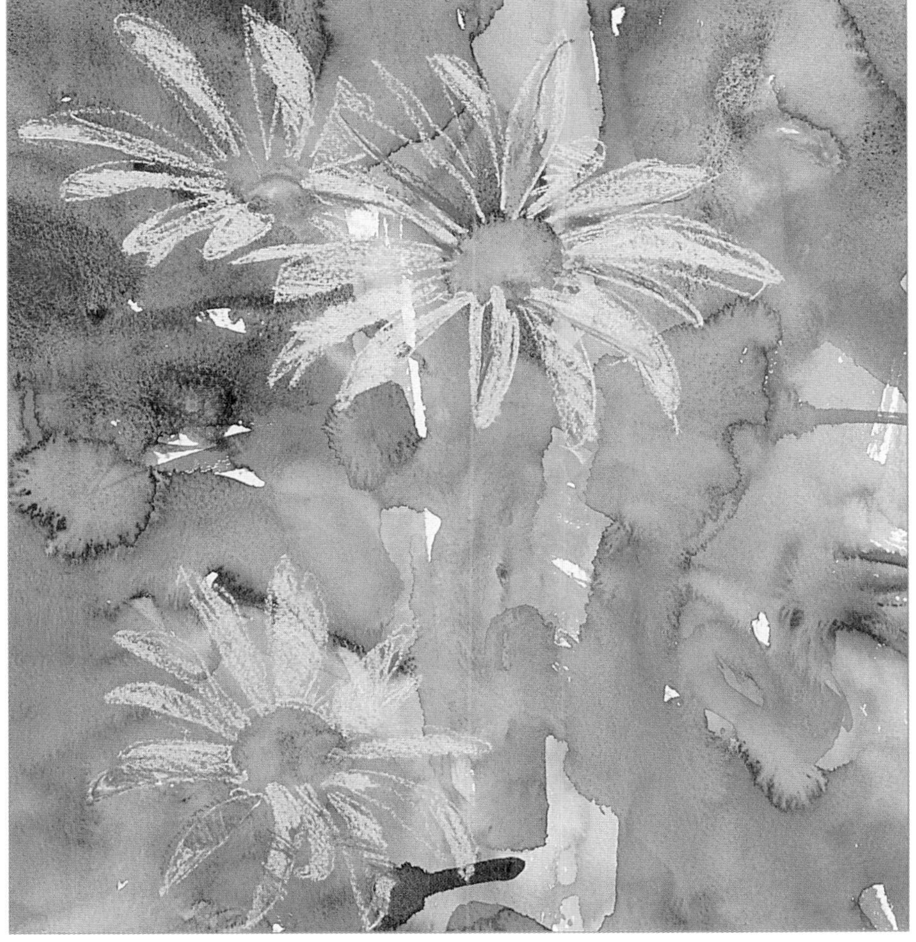

2 When the washes are thoroughly dry, work around the loose areas of the flower centers, drawing in the shapes of the main petals with a white Conté crayon. Draw freely, capturing the irregular shapes of the flowers. Using mid- and pale-blue Conté crayons, add the shadow areas to the petals.

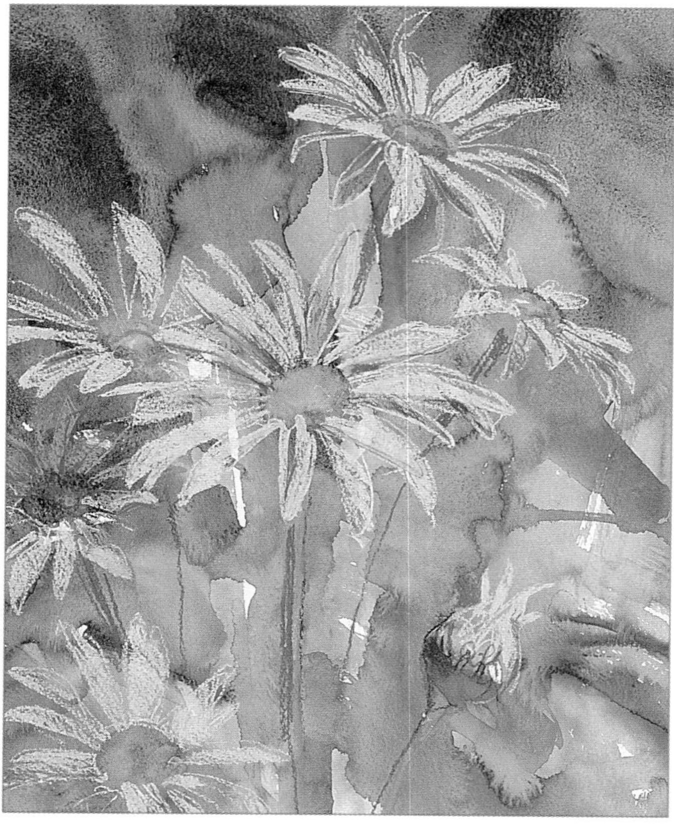

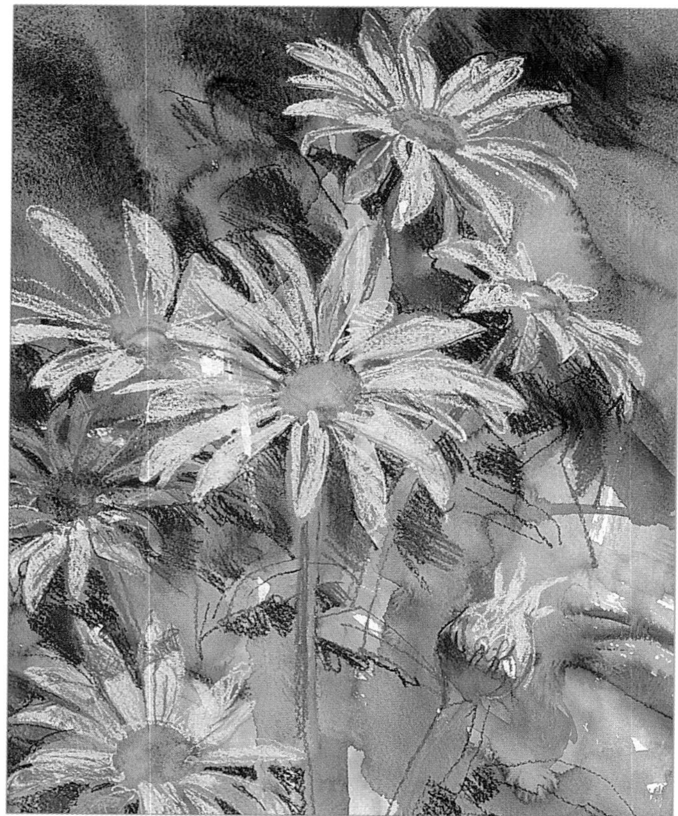

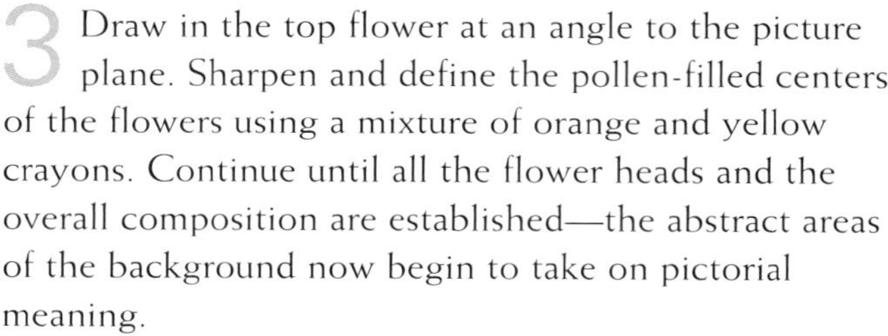

3 Draw in the top flower at an angle to the picture plane. Sharpen and define the pollen-filled centers of the flowers using a mixture of orange and yellow crayons. Continue until all the flower heads and the overall composition are established—the abstract areas of the background now begin to take on pictorial meaning.

4 Using slightly darker tones of the background colors, draw around the flowers to give them greater definition and bring them forward out of the surrounding areas—in effect, treating them as negative shapes. The hardness of the Conté allows for finer lines and more control than softer, chalk pastels.

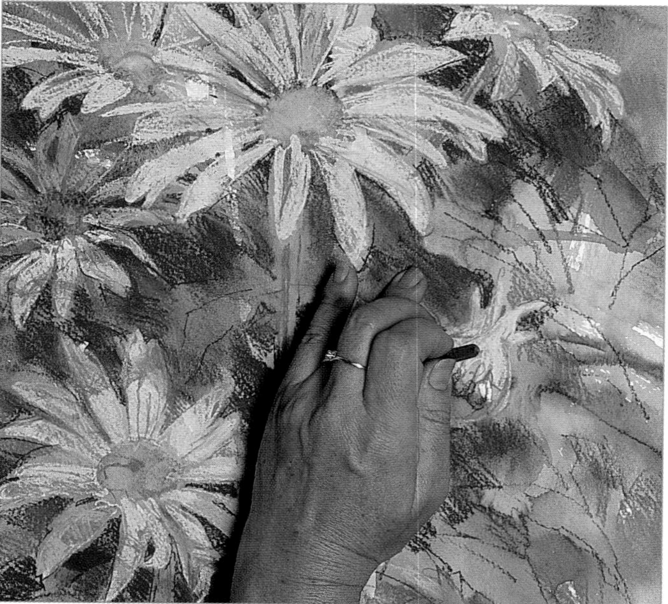

5 Continue drawing the background, defining the leaf and stalk shapes as you go. The dappled light sharply defines brightly lit areas, whereas other shadow areas melt into the background. Soften areas of shading using the edge of a finger—this allows the pastel drawing to blend in with the watercolor background.

6 Finally, assess the whole picture and finish any unresolved areas, defining and melting the shapes. Be very careful not to overwork the Conté colors—the end result should be a fresh and spontaneous rendition of simple flowers in dappled light.

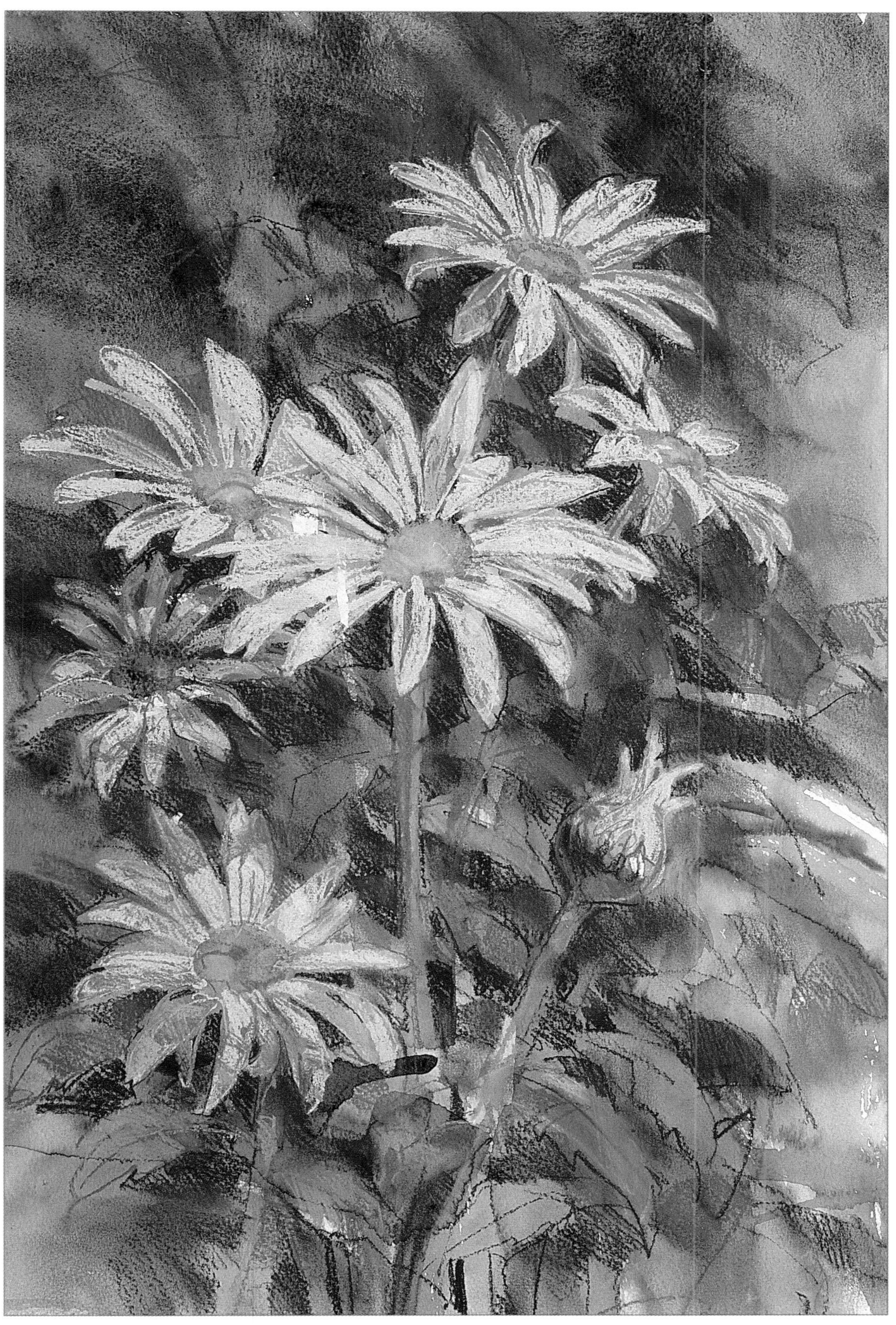

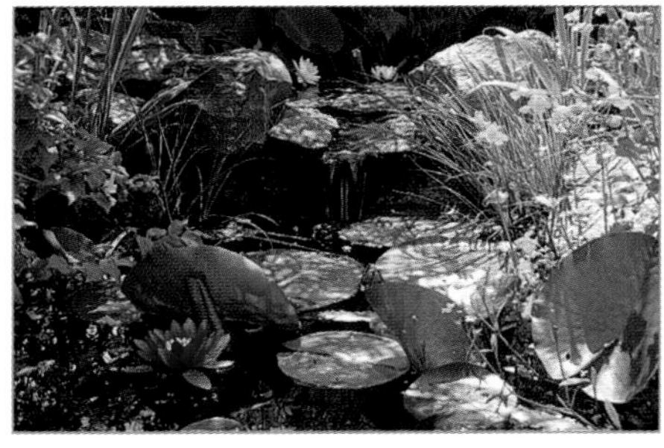

Ponds and water:

watercolors on semi-rough watercolor paper

Plants and water are always an appealing combination, and it's worth spending time to find just the right view for you. In this scene, the sunlight and dappled shade, water lilies, and one pink-red flower make an interesting challenge to capture in watercolor paints.

Materials

- Semi-rough Bockingford watercolor paper
- 3B pencil
- Sable brushes
- oriental brushes
- Watercolor paints
- Clean water

1 Draw out a guide preliminary drawing. There are a lot of different elements in this composition, so spend some time on the accuracy of the proportions, dimensions, and relationship of each part of the picture to the others.

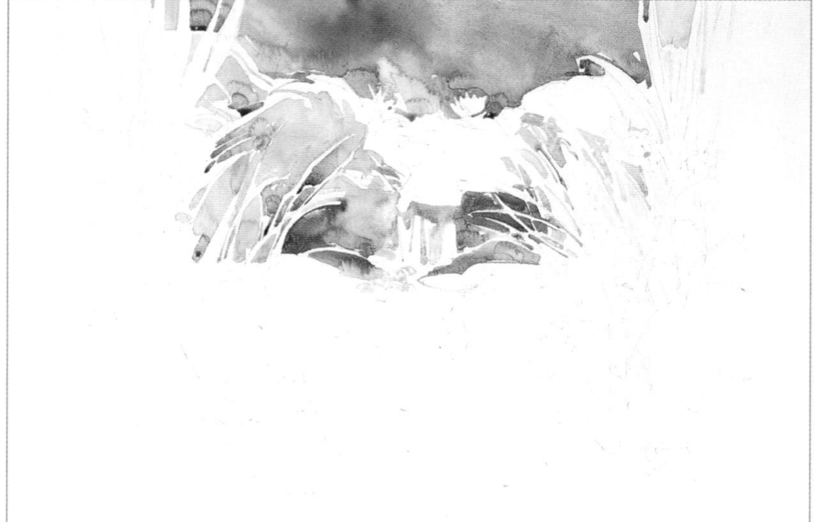

2 Lay in diluted blue, shadow areas that go to the far edge of the lilies and have the effect of knocking back everything behind the small waterfall. Add a little purple to the blue, dilute again, and use this with the oriental brush to lightly define the farthest area. On the next layer of rocks, look for the patterns of light, and aim to capture them.

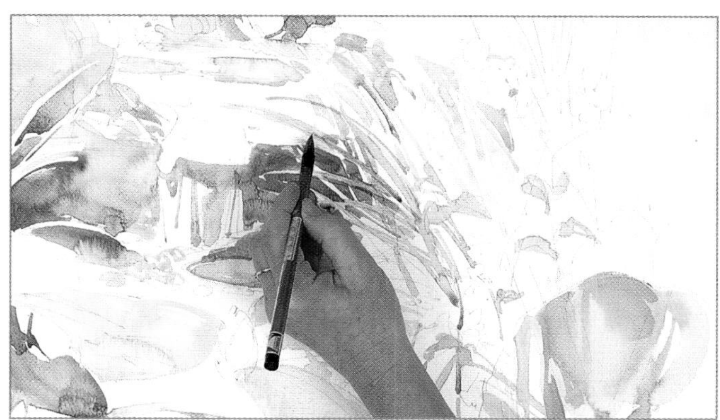

3 Introduce a variety of green washes, from light to dark, for the lily pads, being careful to leave white paper for the highlights. Using similar greens, paint in the long strands of grass through the shaded areas on the right.

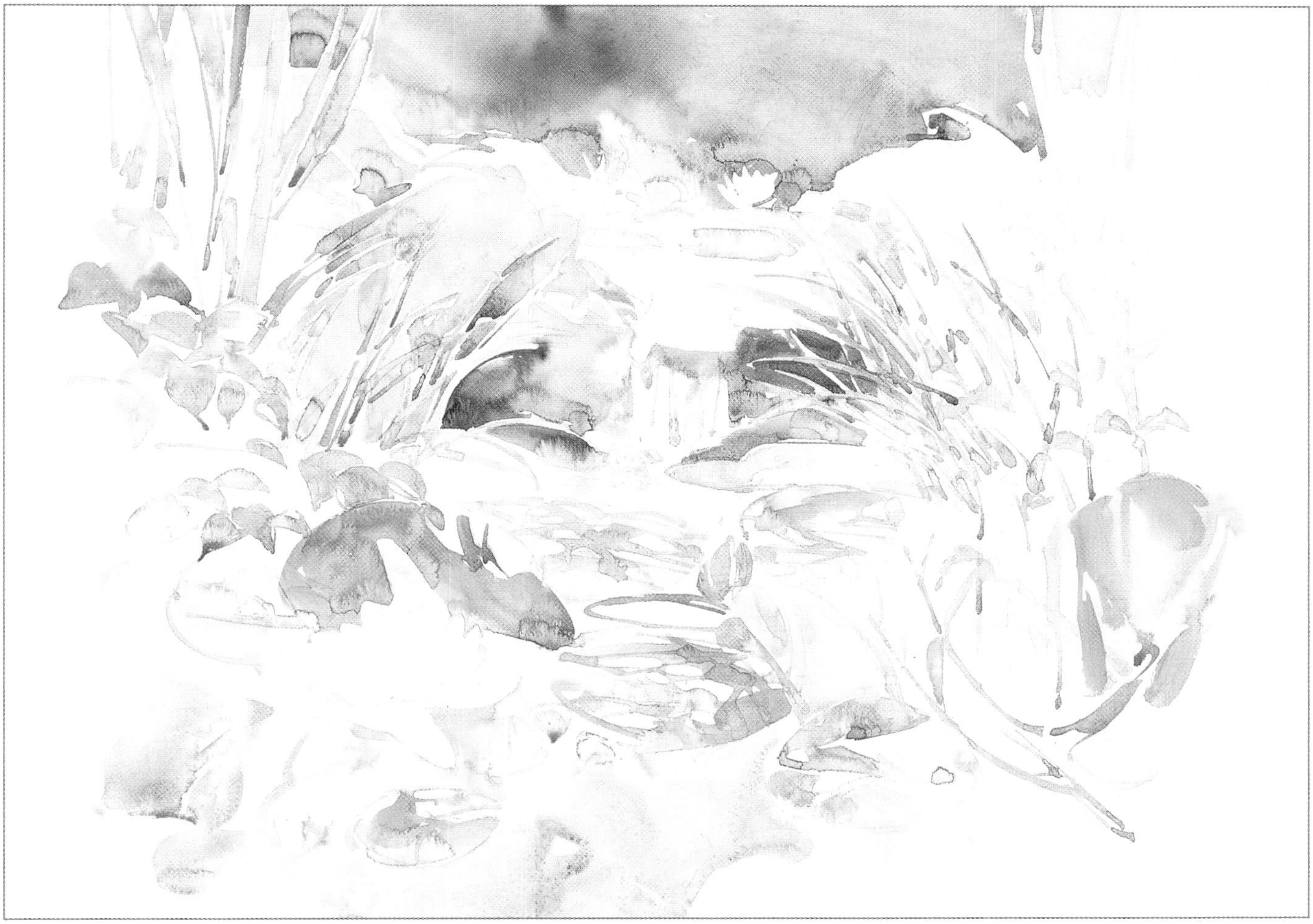

4 Move to the left-hand side and paint in the leaves and stalks, again leaving white paper for highlights—remember that you don't have to follow the lines of the preliminary drawing exactly, but use them merely as a guide. Use a very diluted blue wash for the area of foreground water.

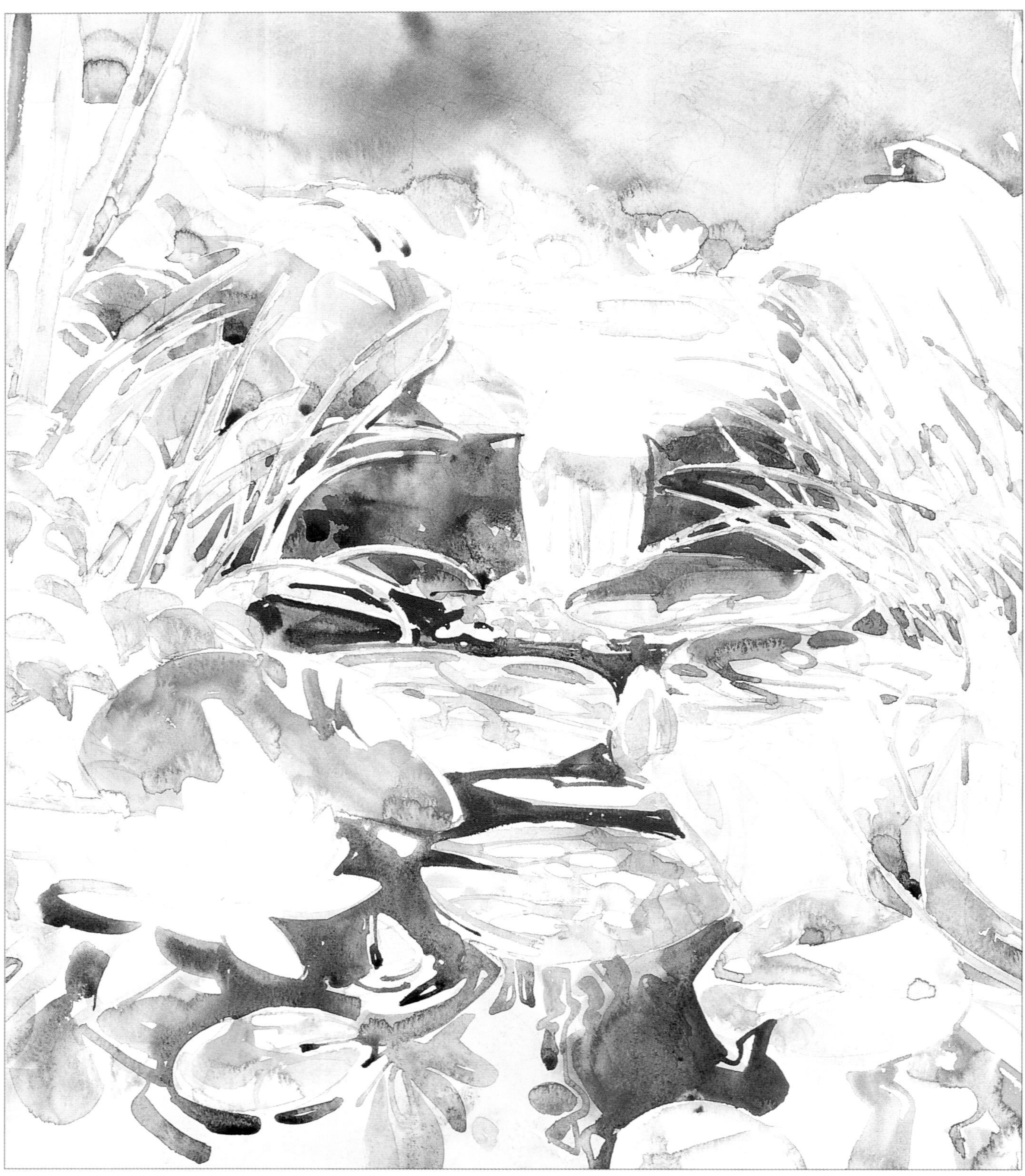

5 Make mixtures of purple, burnt umber, and blue, and use these to block in the darkest areas of water, keeping the flowers and leaves as negative shapes. As you bring these dark parts to the foreground, reinforce the swirl of the water, then work backwards to the waterfall.

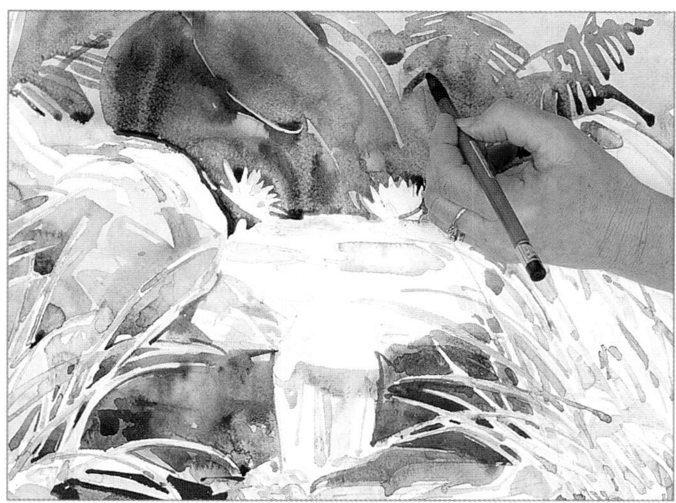

6 Add a few long, directional strokes to describe the fall of the water, and then concentrate on the plane beyond the waterfall. Start by picking out the outlines of the lilies, and next paint in the farthest leaves in the distance.

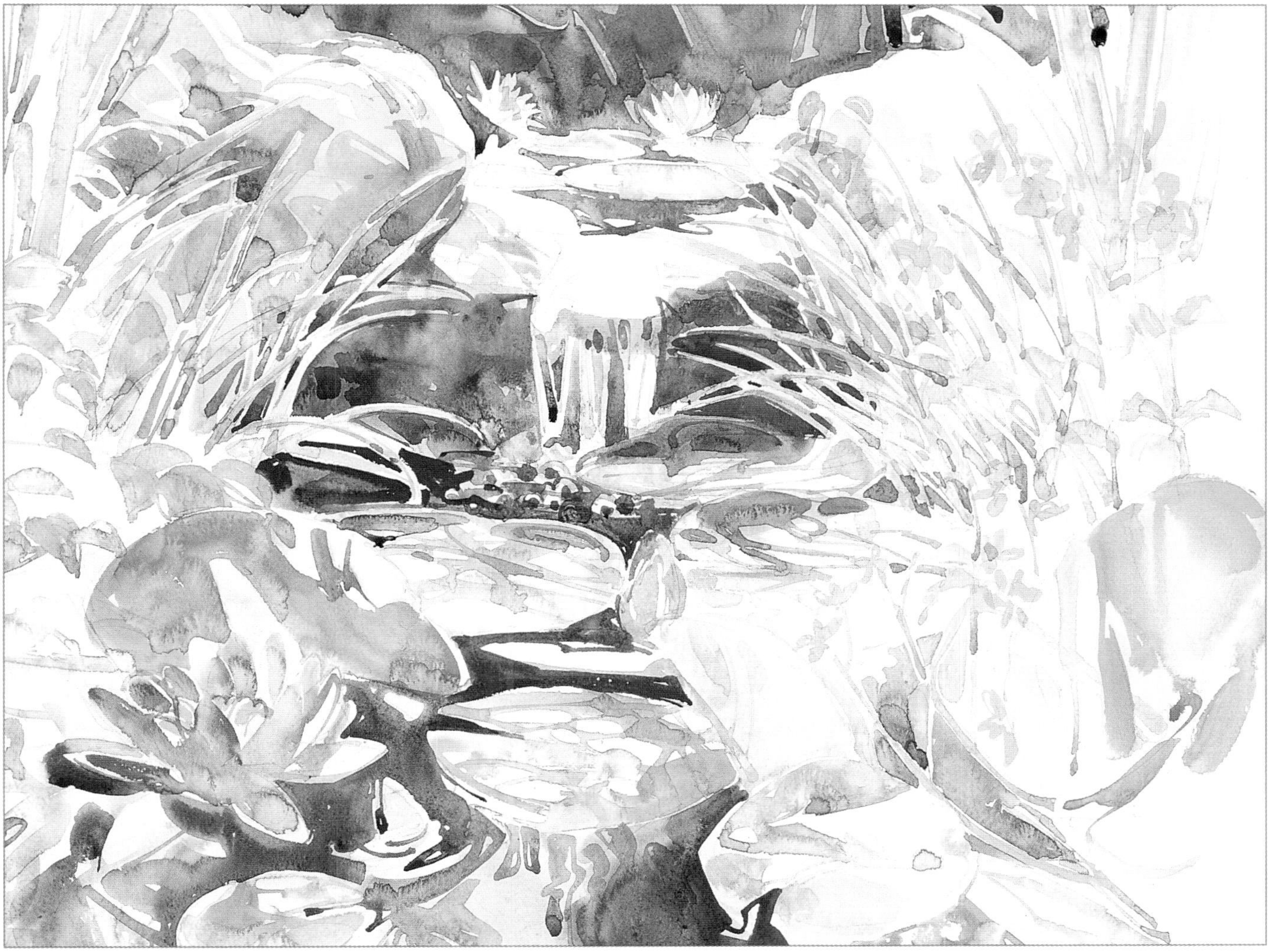

7 Make up a pale pink wash for the lily flower, and then use the oriental brush to fill in the white paper. Let the diluted wash make shadows and gradations of color. Allow to dry a little, use a very warm yellow for the flower centers, then move across to the right, and use the same color for the flowers on the tall stalks.

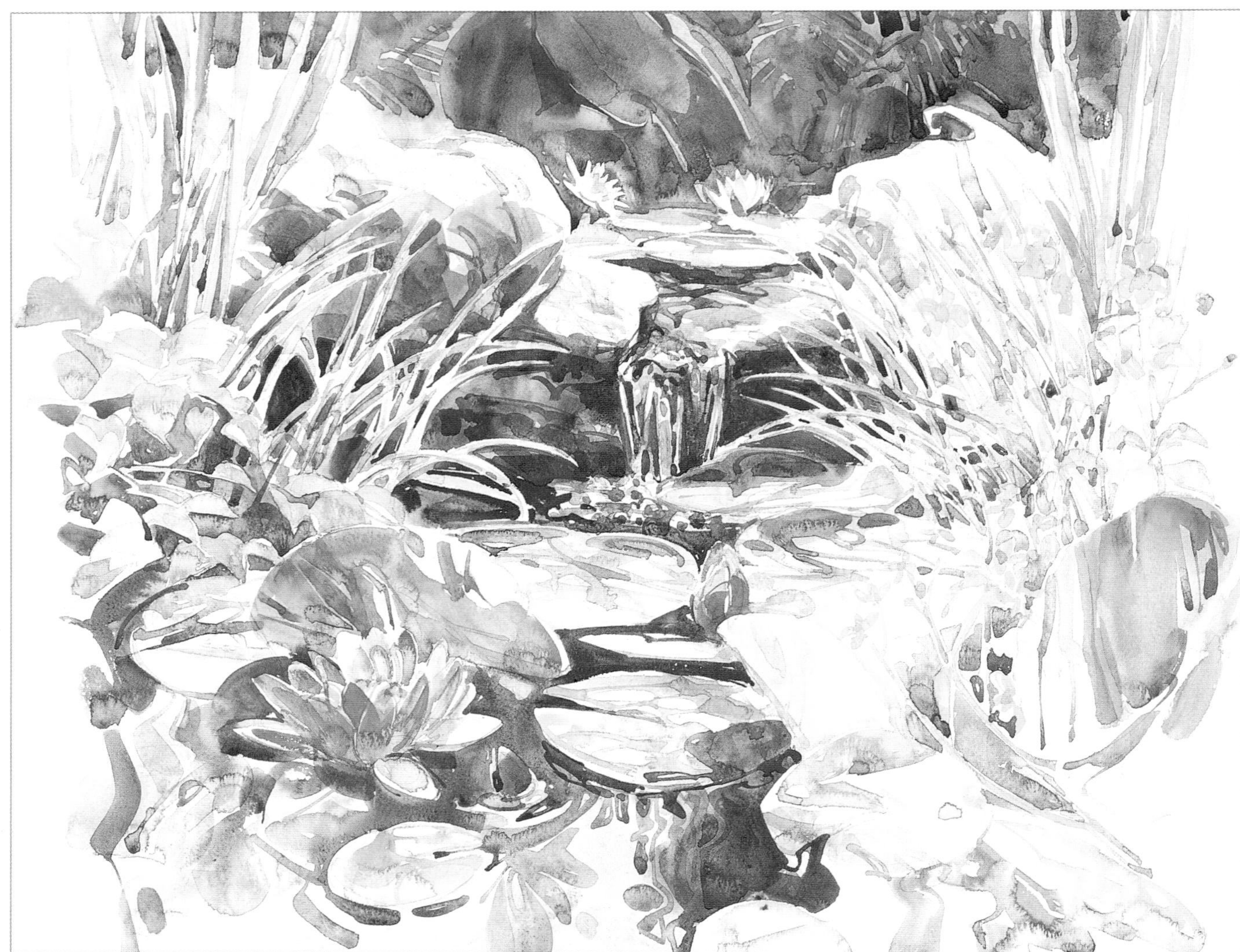

8 Strengthen the pebbles above the waterfall with yellows and ochers, then go around the whole painting, adding the long stalks and grass at each side, and the final lily pads. Mix up warm, dark shadow washes, and build up the shadows throughout the composition, then gradually reinforce the colors without losing the glow of the paints.

Exterior architectural setting:

watercolors, pastels, and Conté crayons on semi-rough watercolor paper

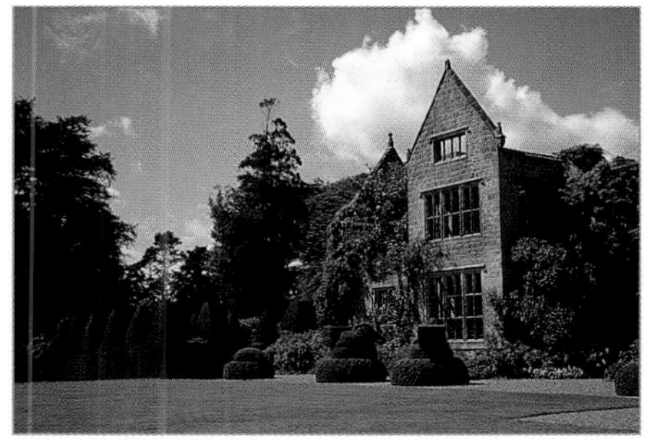

Working on such a large view means that you have to consider the trees, shrubs, and large hedges in the same "architectural" way as the building. The combination of using watercolor for blocking in, and pastels for shaping and highlighting, is an effective one.

Materials

- Semi-rough Bockingford watercolor paper
- 3B pencil
- Kneadable eraser
- oriental brush
- Large flat brush
- Watercolor paints
- Clean water
- Pastels
- Conté crayons

1 Sketch the composition lightly. Unlike some of the other preliminary drawings in these projects, this one can be quite tight, with much of the detail and shadowing mapped out as a guide. You can go over the pencil with pastel later.

2 Lay down some light washes with a large, flat brush, blocking in the sky and empty window spaces with light blue. Use quite a lot of water to spread the color. Apply light yellow for the path in front of the house.

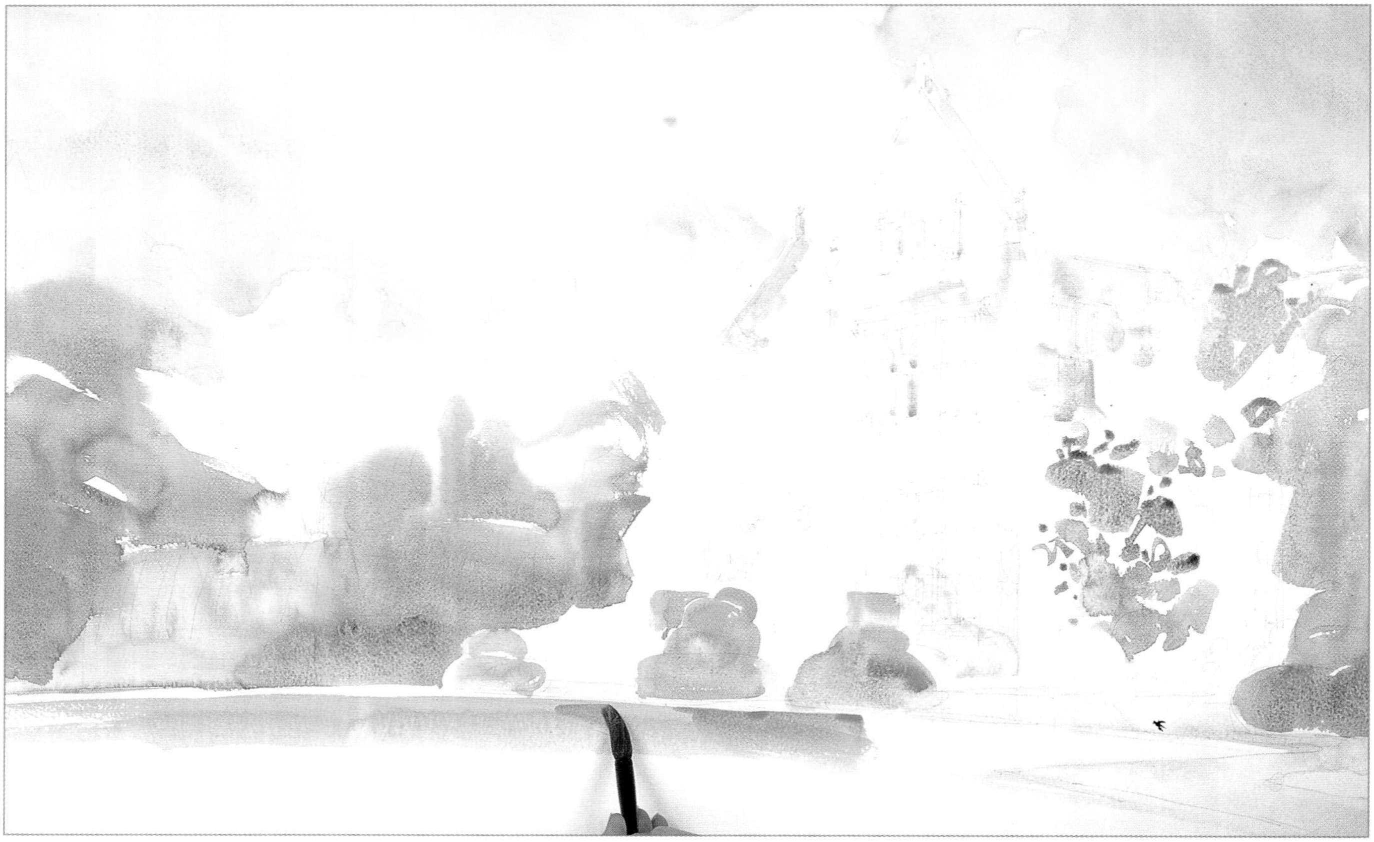

3 Put a wash over the face of the building, spread the blue sky with more clean water, then blend sienna and orange for the building side. Apply very diluted green washes for the tree areas, both sunlit and shadowed, and start to sweep on the foreground grass.

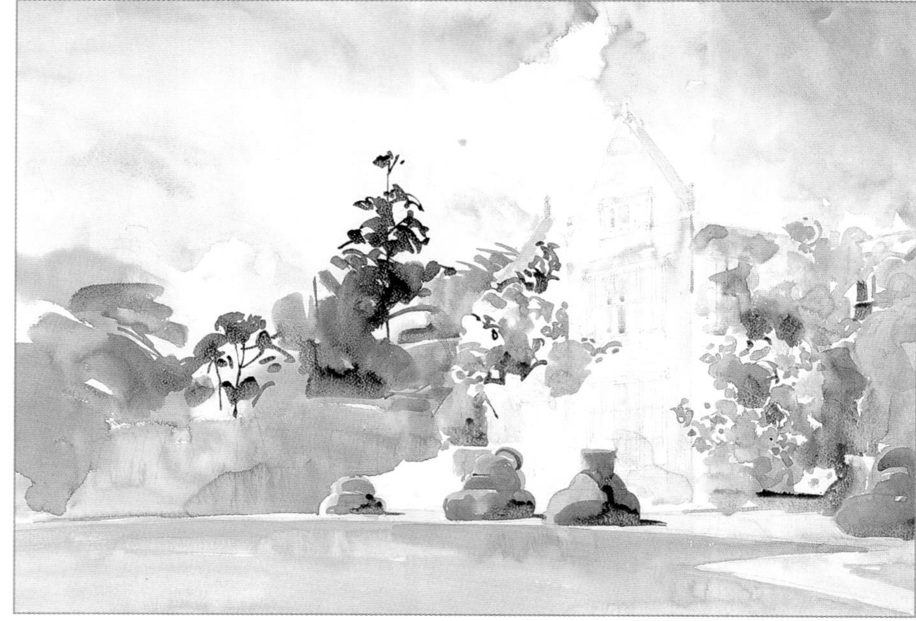

4 When washing in the greens for the foliage, leave some white paper for highlights. Add burnt umber to the trees on the building's left, and a dark purple for the cast shadows to the right. Use an oriental brush for the tallest trees.

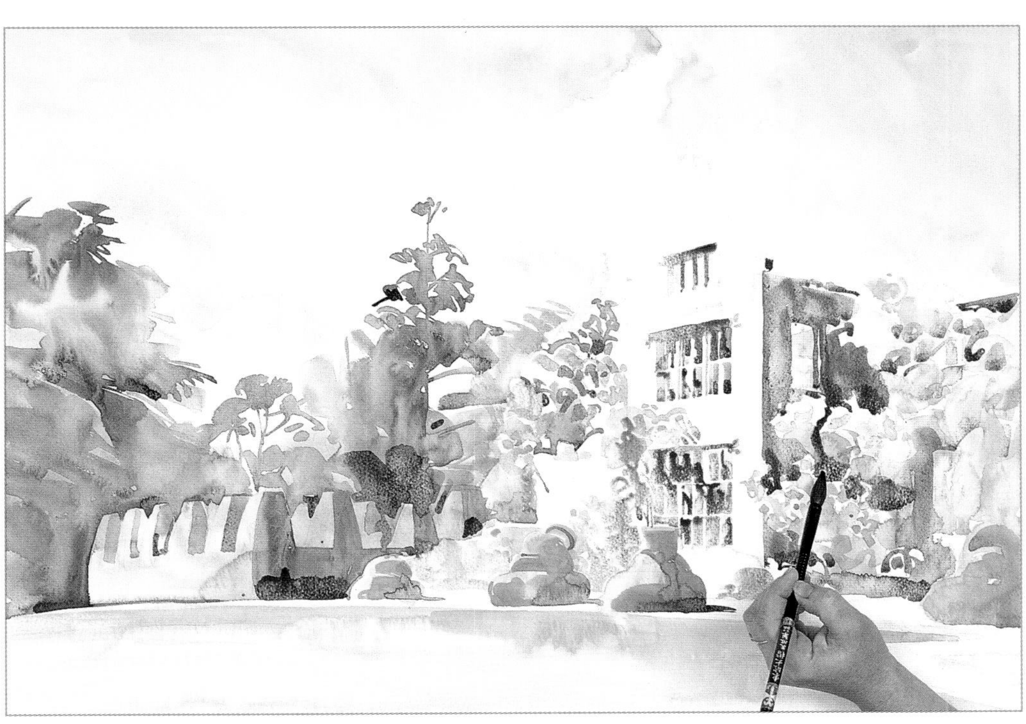

5 Paint loosely as you sweep in the greens, from dark to light, to suggest the angles and movement of the trees. Add blue to the purple shadows on the building, then block in the lower windows and the shadow areas on the castellated hedge on the left.

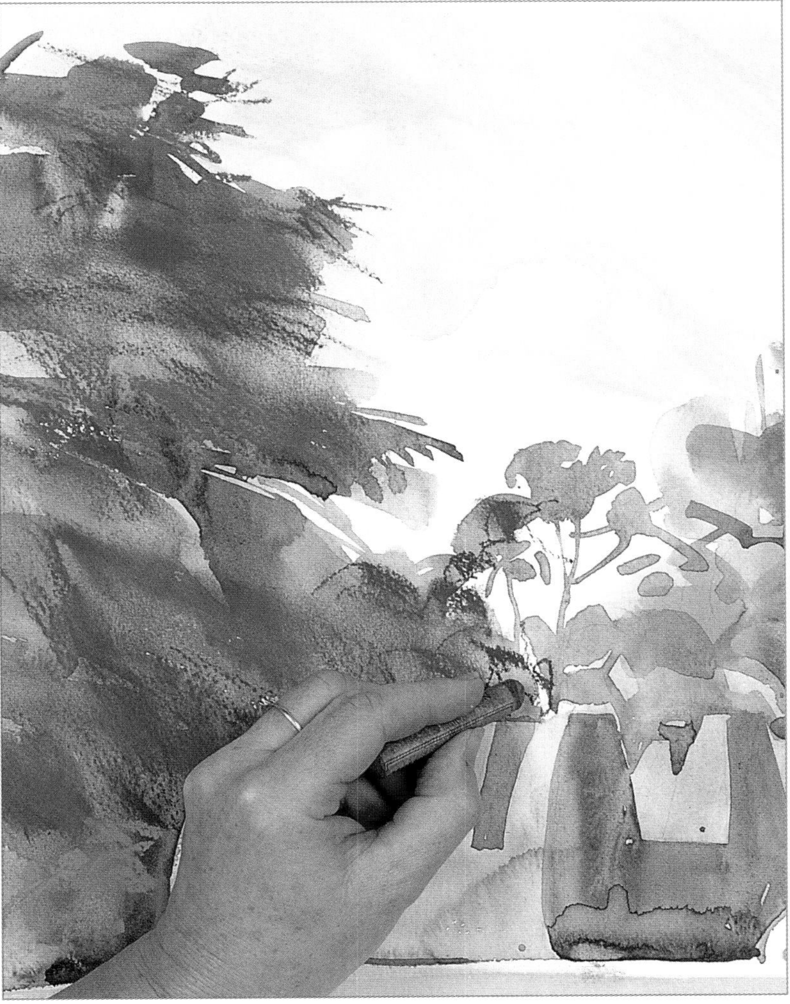

6 This is your last chance to erase some of the pencil lines before applying pastel. Let the painting dry completely, or use a hair dryer. Start with a pale blue pastel in the sky area, then make abstract marks on the left-hand trees, blending with your hand.

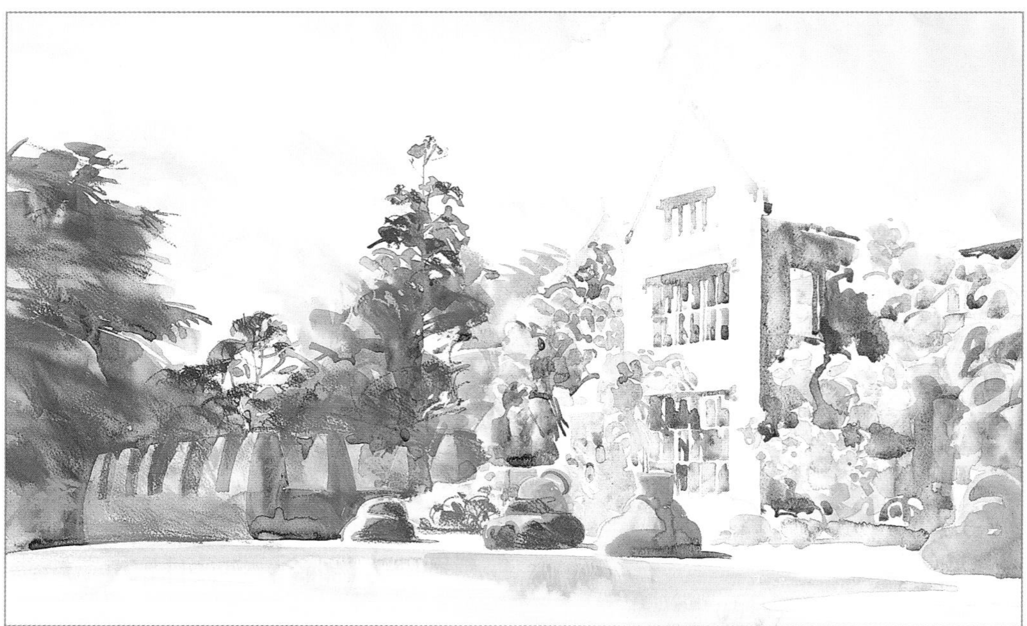

7 Use Conté crayons to refine the colors over the whole picture, refining and sharpening for variety and depth. Work between the crayons and pastels on the tallest trees and the topiary, and use white pastel for the highlights between the branches.

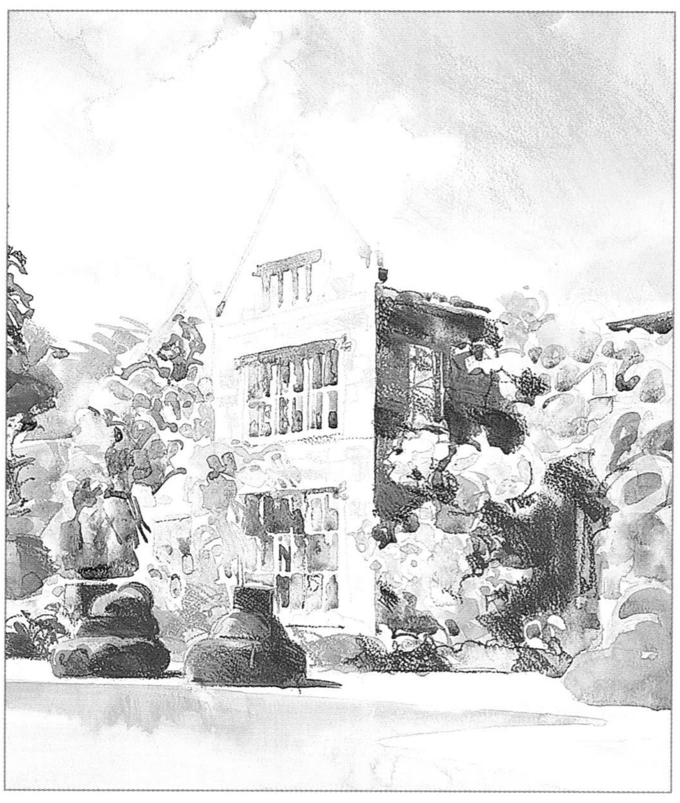

8 As you define and strengthen the pastel colors, use the watercolor washes as an underpainting for the shadows and highlights on the topiary, the side of the house, the warmer colors in the windows, and the stone on the front of the building.

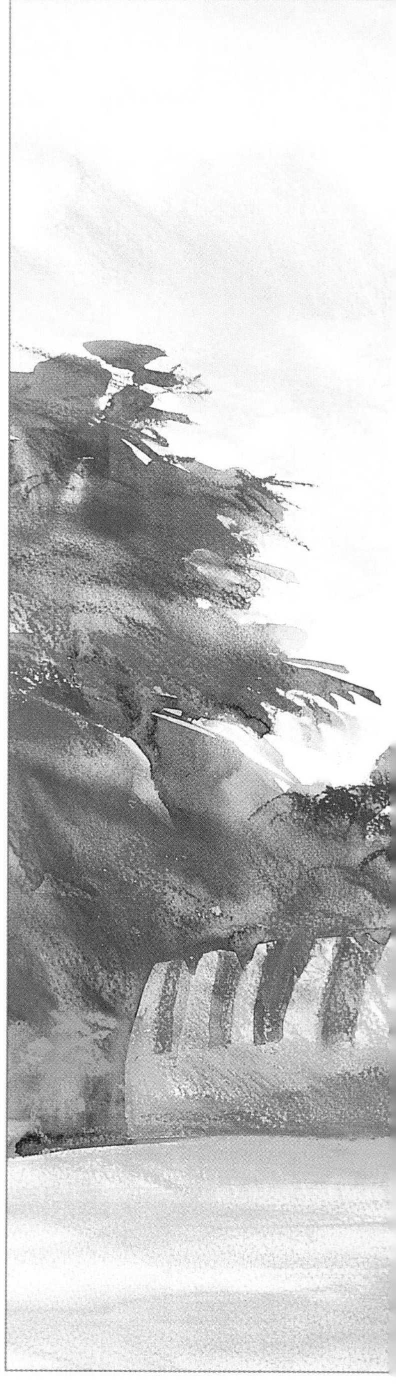

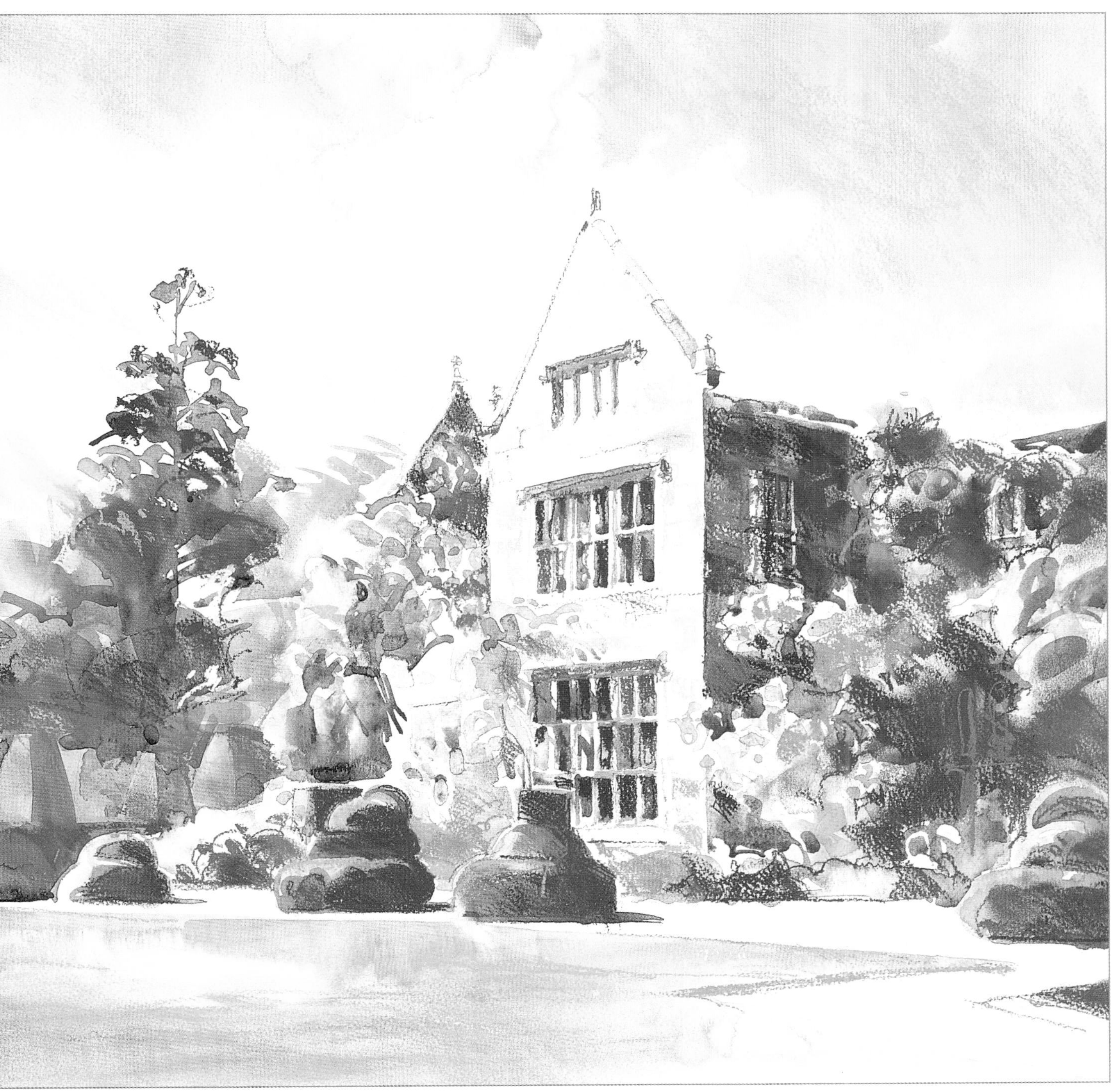

9 Use the tip and side of a green Conté crayon to introduce contours and shades on the foreground grass, before finishing the front and windows of the building. Knock back overly prominent areas, and cover the white paper with pastel highlights.

Winter scene: watercolors on semi-rough watercolor paper

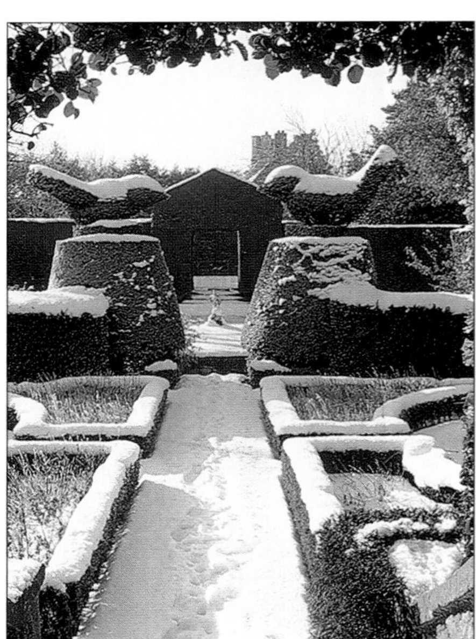

In a scene like this, where a large amount of the view is snow or ice, the amount of tonal and color contrast in a drawing or painting will be much more than during other seasons. Using masking fluid is unfeasible in this sort of situation, so you have to be brave in your approach and plan the composition carefully beforehand through sketches and studies.

Materials

- Semi-rough Bockingford watercolor paper
- 3B pencil
- Kneadable eraser
- Oriental brushes
- Watercolor paints
- Clean water

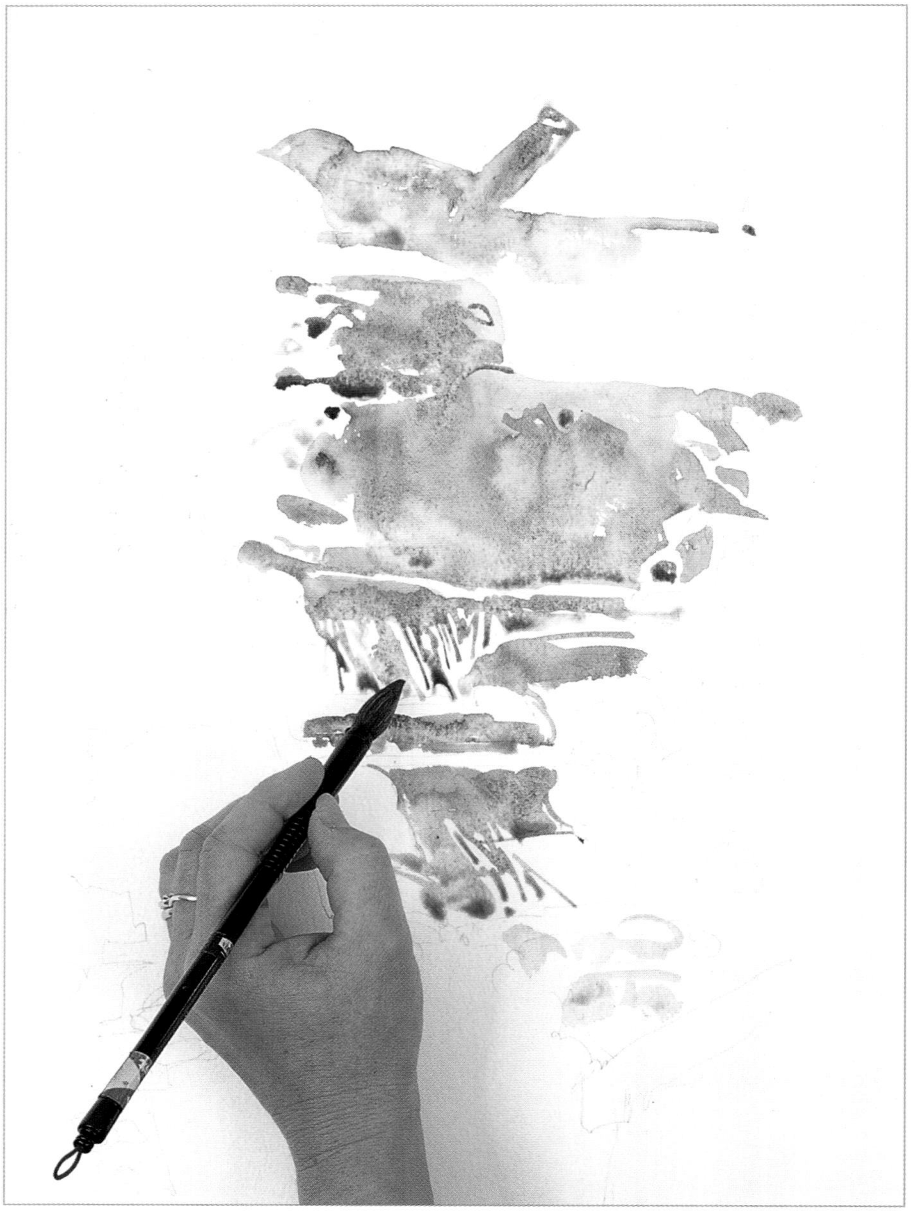

1 When making a preliminary guide drawing, include both the main positive and negative shapes, and the shadow areas that play a major part in defining the form and contours. Lay in a very diluted pale blue wash in the sky area, painting over the pencil marks. Make up a very weak mixture of purple and blue, and apply it over the shadow areas of the right-hand topiary bird and hedge below, working around the snow-white parts. Add more blue for the coldest shadows.

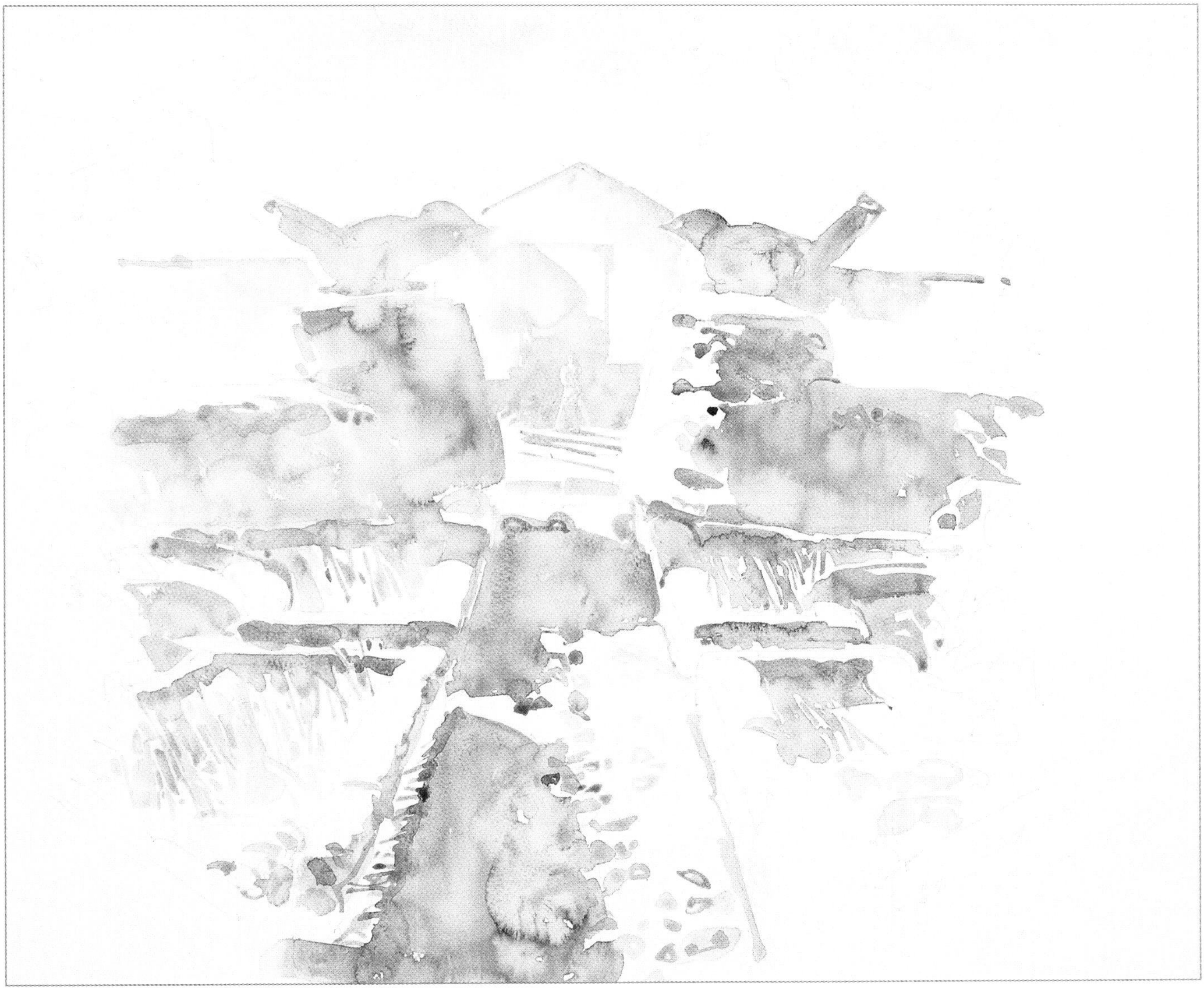

2 Move across the central path area with the shadow washes, then along the nearest left-hand edges. Because the shadows are not a uniform color, let the washes do much of the work of blending and moving the colors. Add the footprints on the path, and work up the more shadowed left-hand side, before catching the sheen on the distant frozen pond.

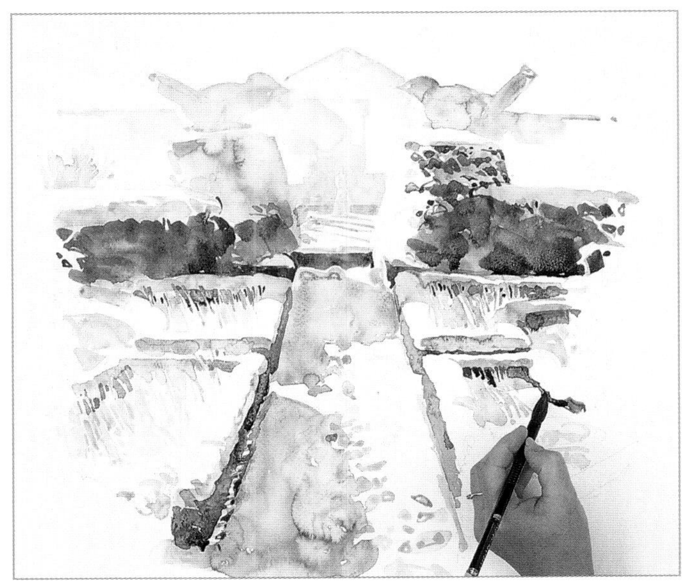

3 Put in the highlighted topiary on the right-hand side with short brushstrokes of light green, then move to a darker green for the parts not in direct sunlight, working alongside the shadow and snow areas of white paper. Use a fine oriental brush to form the darkest recesses of the topiary, and make a start on blocking in the left-hand hedges.

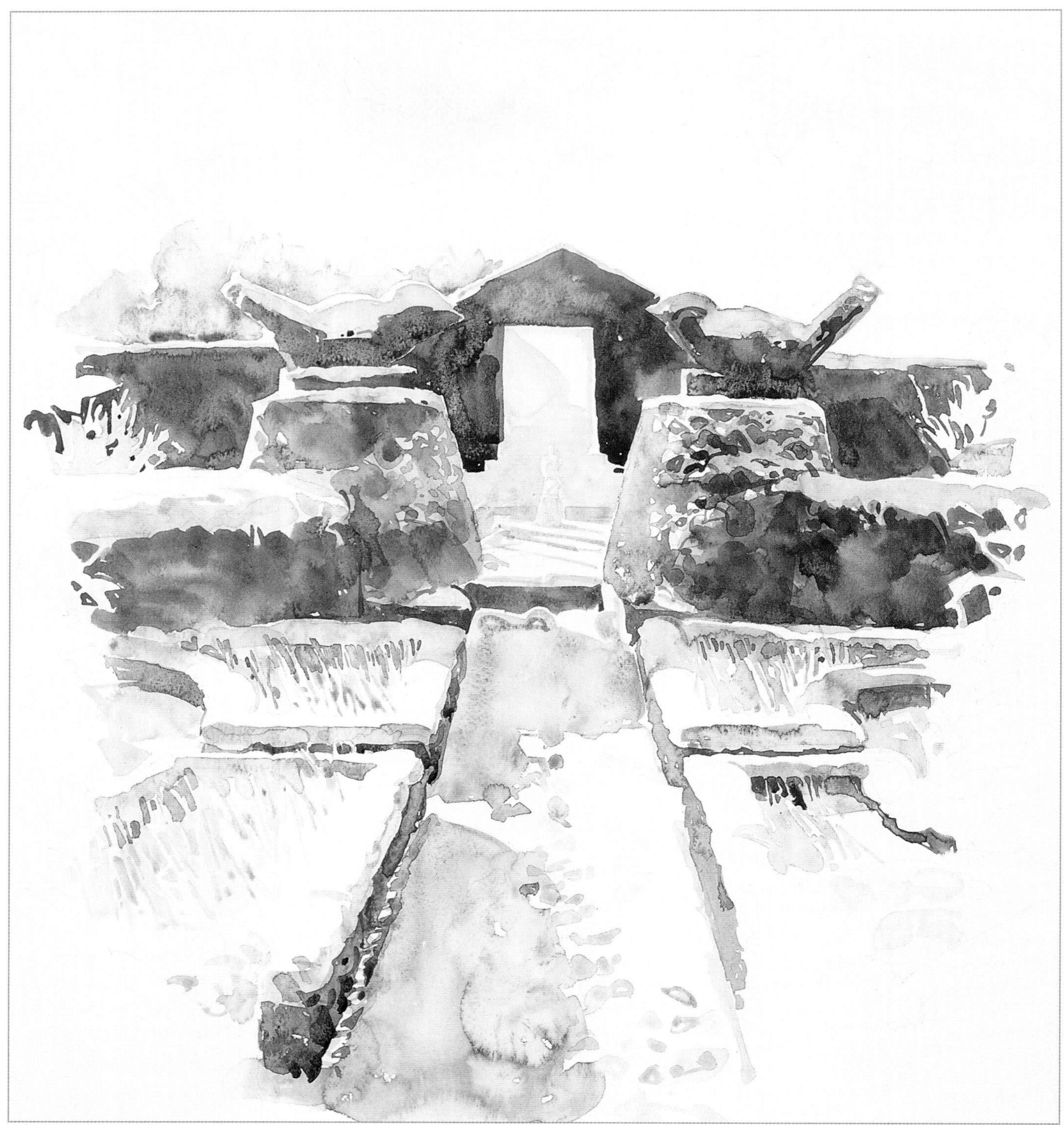

4 When blocking in the greens, go over the shaded wash on the hedges and birds. Leave the background washes in place, and paint around the blue of the right-hand bush. Use layers to build up texture on the large blocks of green. Loosely paint in the trees in the far right background, using very diluted washes of light green and emphasizing the distance.

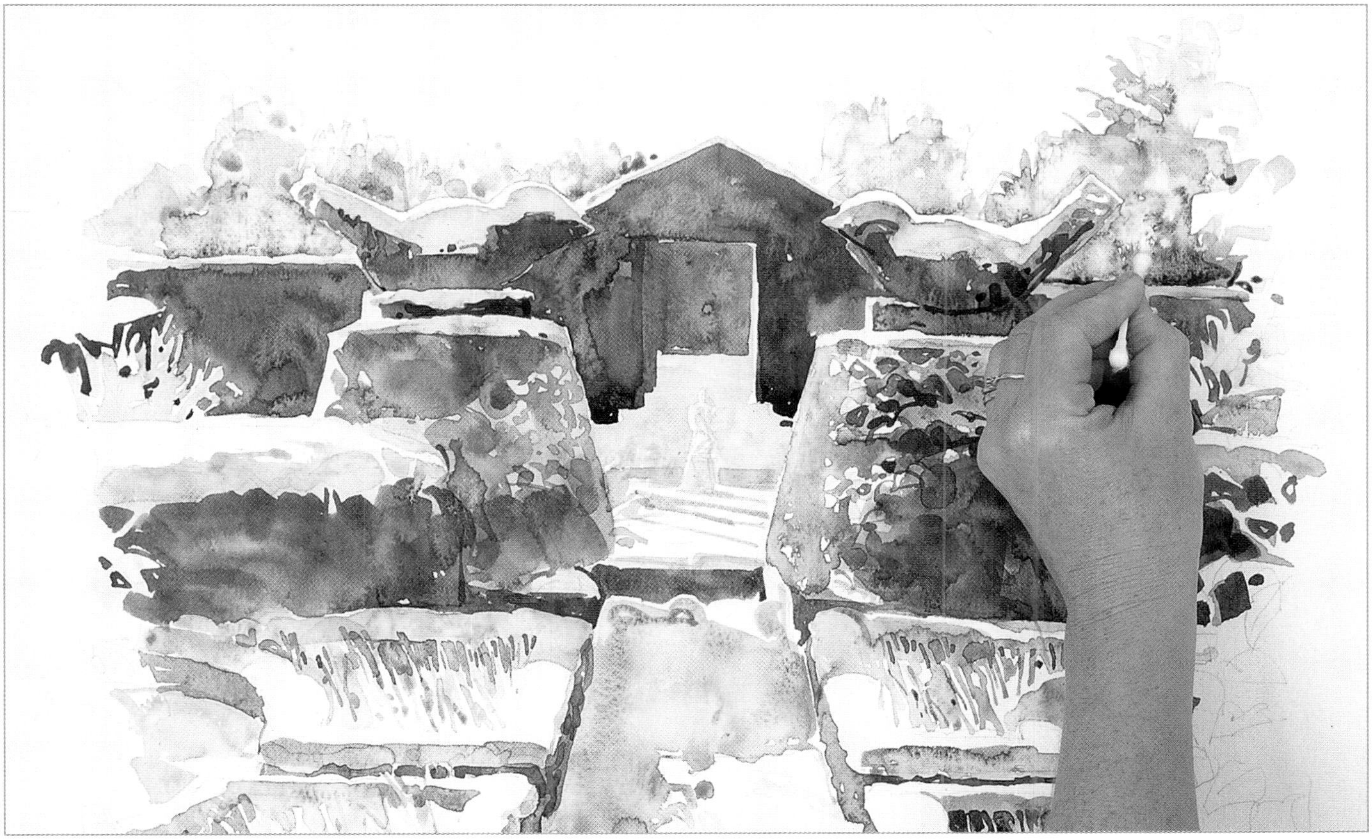

5 Apply the muted greens of the background trees on the right-hand side, then add a few tiny touches of warmish copper color to them and to the statue. As you paint the far right-hand trees, dilute the colors by pulling out the pigment with cotton balls or cotton swabs, then wet the area with clean water for a muted effect.

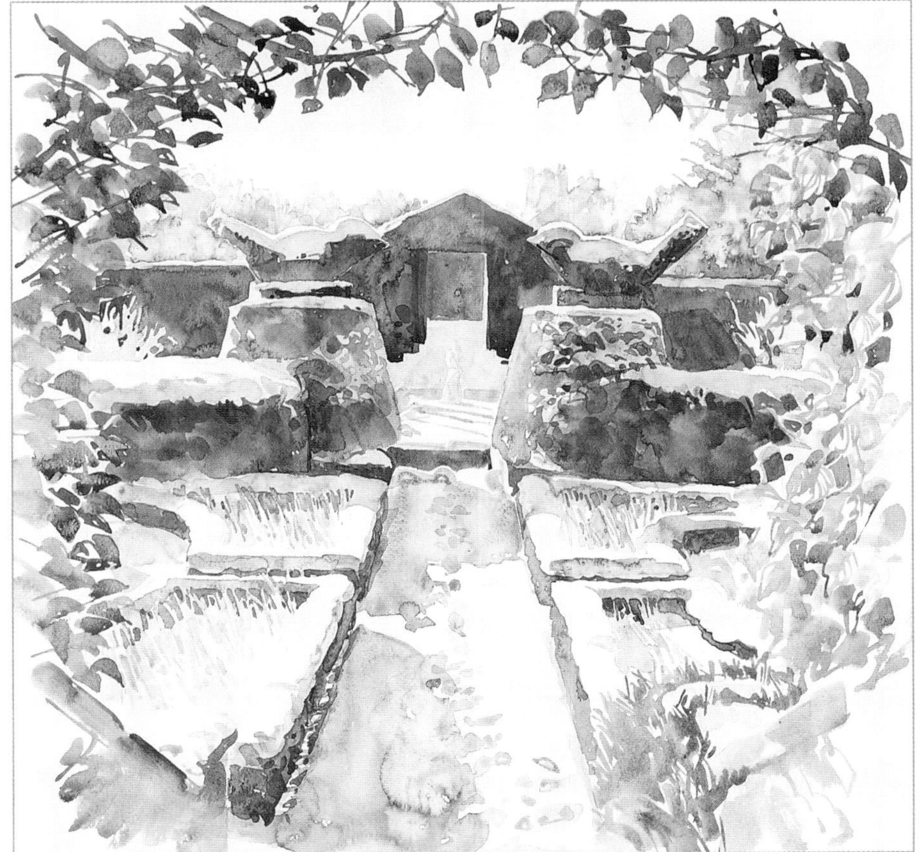

6 Add the warmer colors of the coppery leaves in the foreground, starting with the light yellows and deepening the washes as you go along. Work around this arched frame that leads you into the garden, loosely blocking in the leaf shapes and then moving on to the brown branches. Concentrate on the variety of colors as a contrast to the cold effect of the main scene.

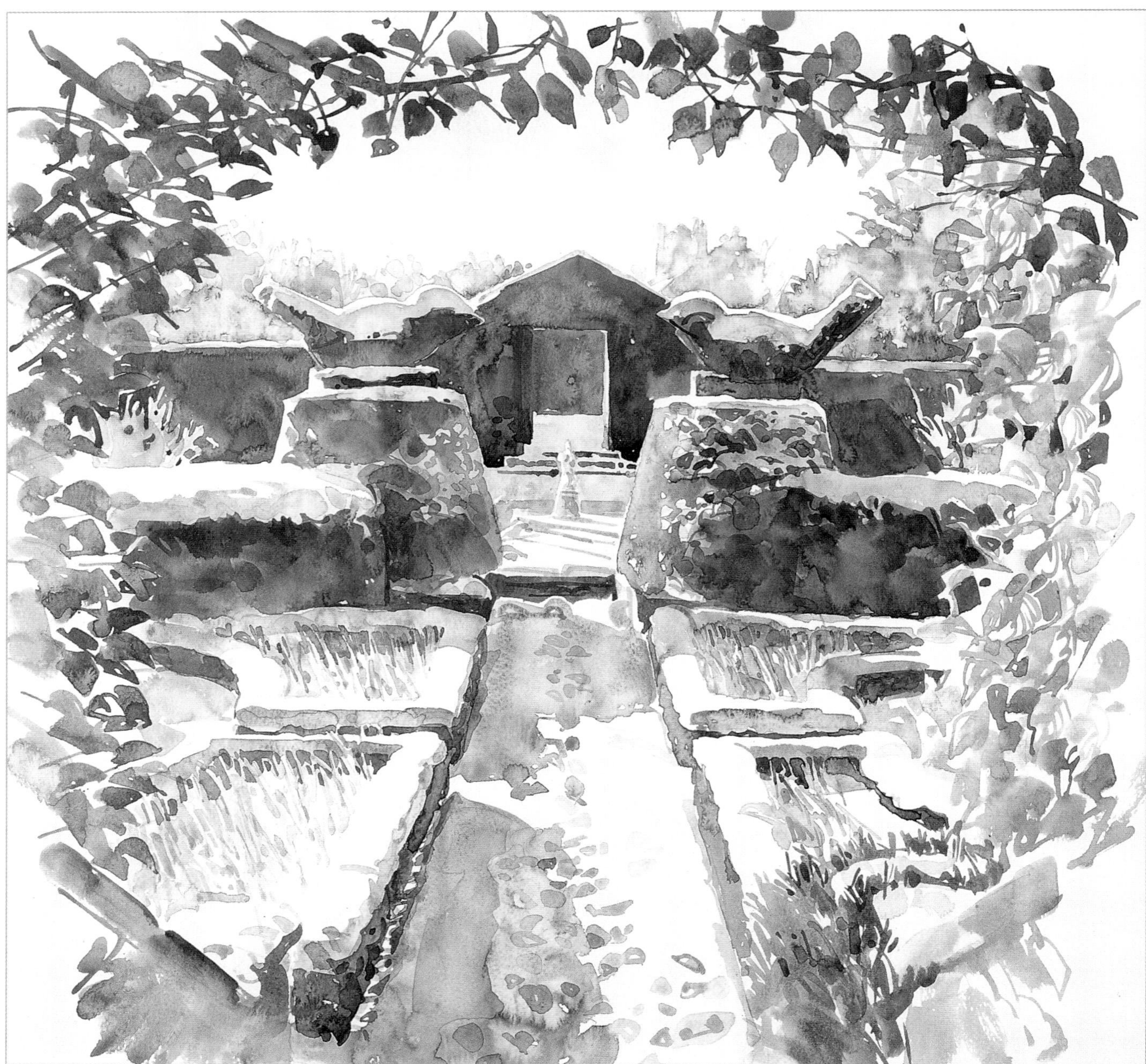

7 Use a small oriental brush to paint in the dark brown steps by the statue, and to warm it up a little. Mix red-brown to warm up the lavender stems inside the shaped hedges, linking up the warm colors from the foreground arch. In the right foreground, reinforce the cold blues. Take a look at the colors of the reflected shadows in the middle foreground, and amend them if necessary before erasing the last pencil marks.

Spring scene: watercolors and colored pencils on semi-rough watercolor paper

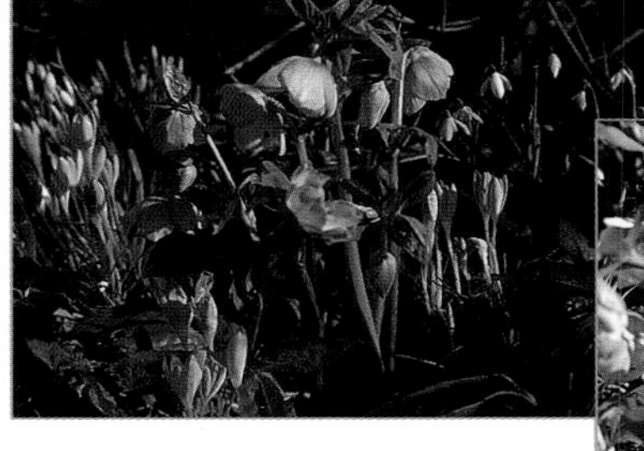

This painting is a composite of two views—the main one, from which most of the composition is taken, had a lot of areas that made the overall feel too dark. Some crocuses and hellebores were added from another viewpoint, and the small bird sculpture on the right was placed for extra visual effect.

Materials

- Semi-rough Bockingford watercolor paper
- Colored pencils
- Oriental brushes
- Watercolor paints
- Clean water

1 Use colored pencils to lightly sketch out the basic composition. With a medium oriental brush block in the sculpture and the nearby shadows with pale washes of reds and light browns. Paint in any shadows, and add the deep purples around the crocuses in the foreground.

2 Start to apply the lightest leaves with pale green washes, painting into the negative shapes, and creating new positive ones as you block in the colors. Move to stronger washes for the deeper green leaves, then work with the same color across the whole painting. Stand back regularly to check on your progress.

3 Freely wash in the trunk and branches of the tree in the background, starting with a dull crimson graded into the darker shadow areas. Again paint into the negative flower shapes, and blend in different colors to block in the main bulk and blank out the top half, creating more shadow areas.

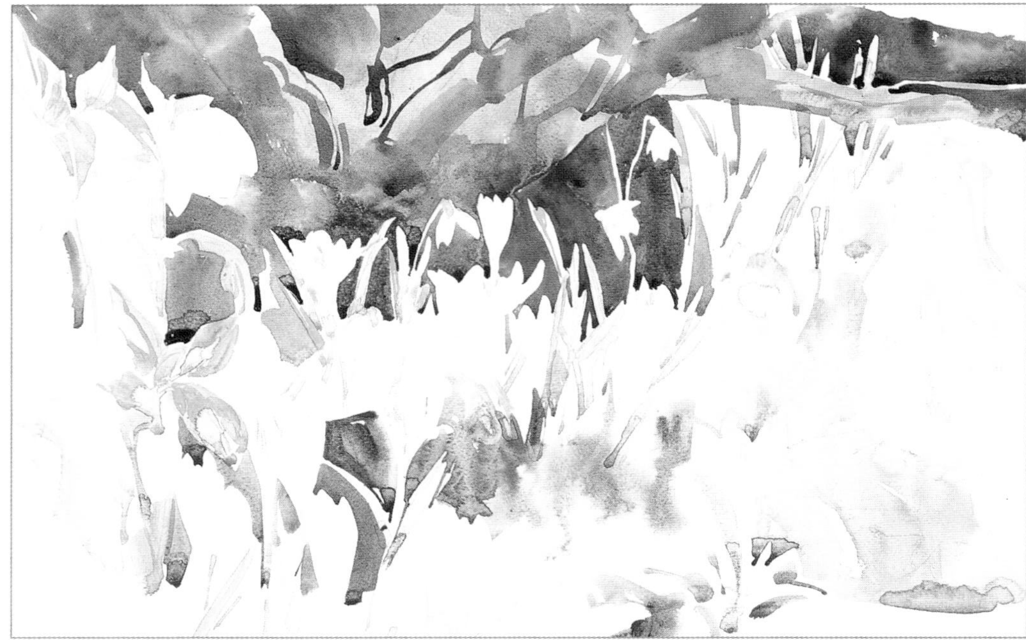

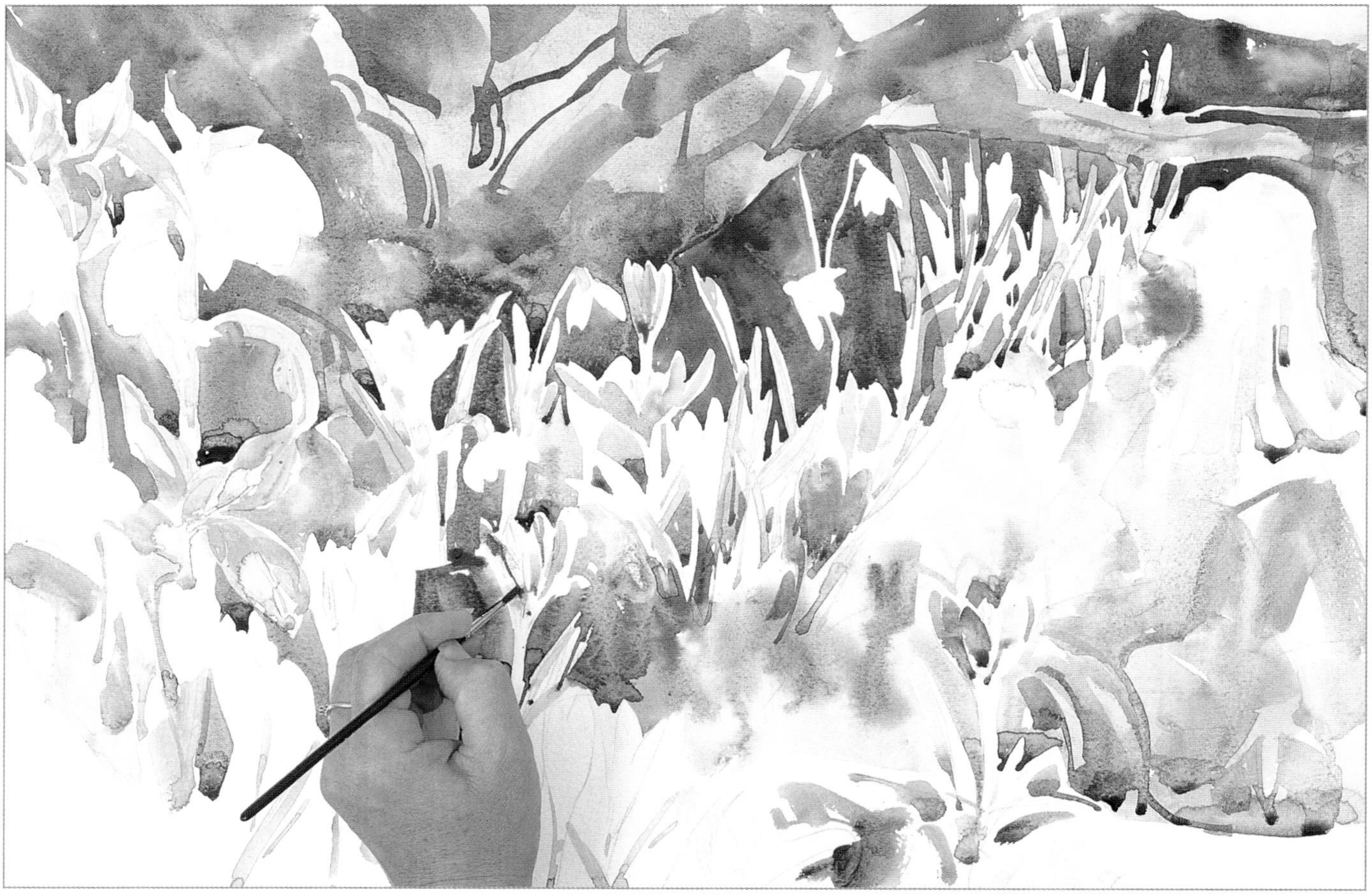

4 Paint down from the tree trunk into the leaves and around the sculpture, then add some washes to the latter to establish its tonal values. Fill in the left-hand tallest leaves with varied strengths of green, then switch to a small brush to add the first pink washes on the crocuses.

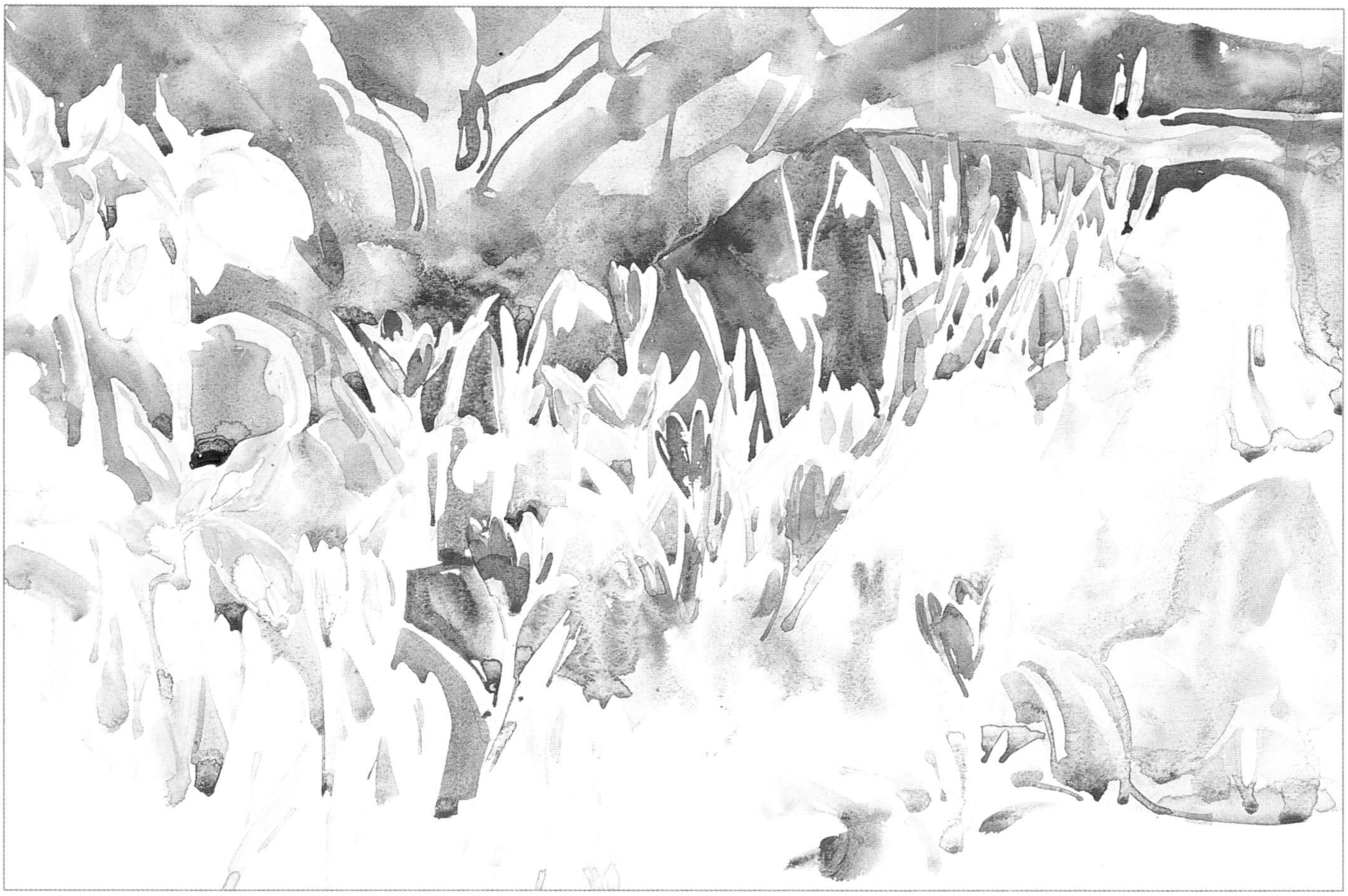

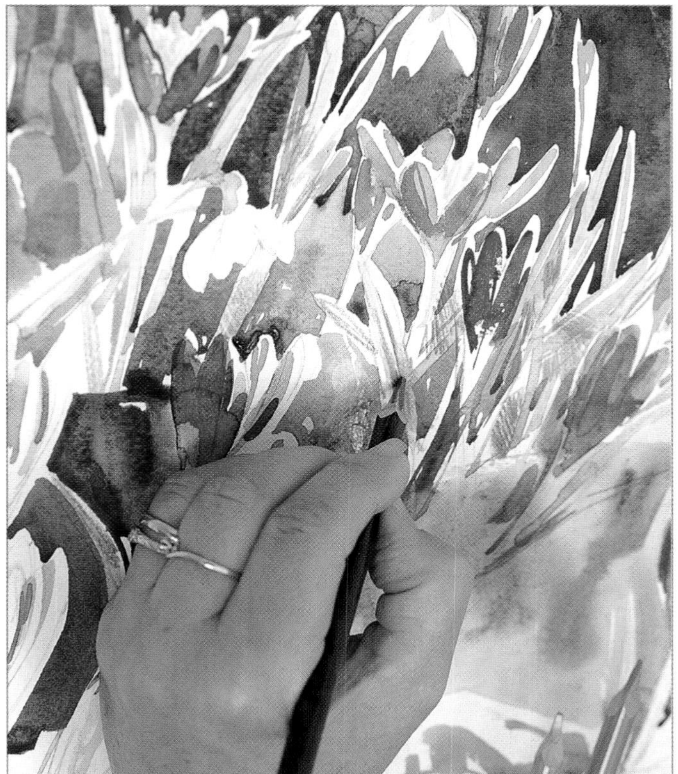

5 Continue to fill in the positive shapes of the leaves and flowers, leaving the paper white for the lightest parts—colored pencils don't work to their best over watercolor washes. Mix a very pale red for the petals of the hellebores on the far left. Let the washes dry completely, or use a hair dryer to speed up the process.

6 Use colored pencils to define the shapes of the crocuses, and add green to the leaves to tighten up and deepen the pale washes. As you work across the colors, remember that building up the strength of the tones and textures is the aim—the details aren't that important, but the feel and light are.

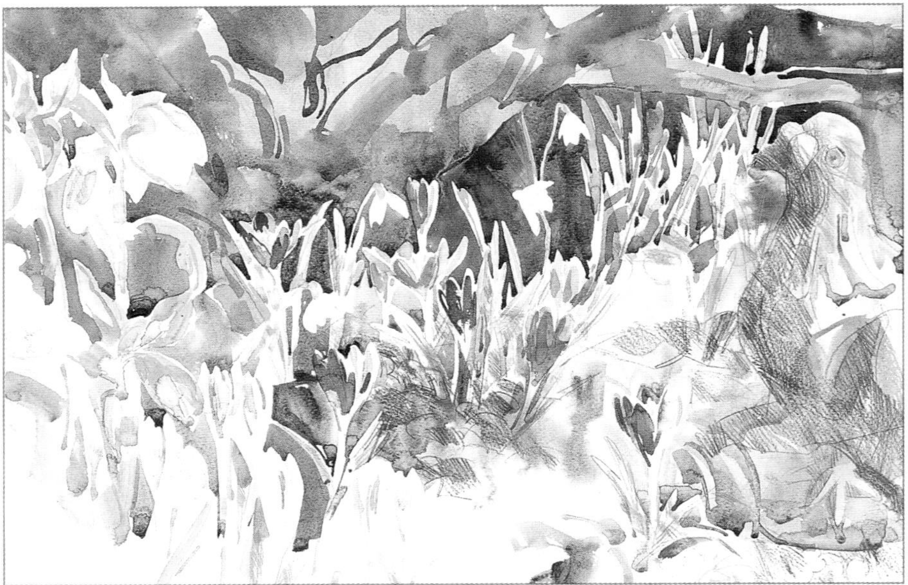

7 Use brown colored pencil to put in texture on the areas of ground—here you can work quite speculatively, because you can go over the area with washes. Add some features and shading on the bird sculpture, hatching and crosshatching to show the contours and tone, then apply green for the verdigris on the head.

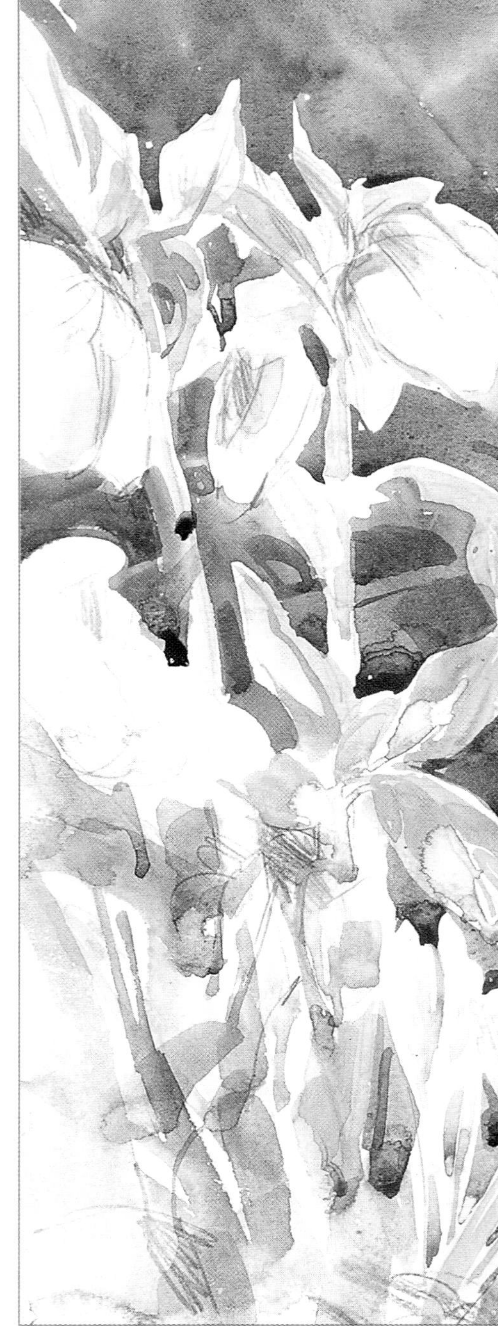

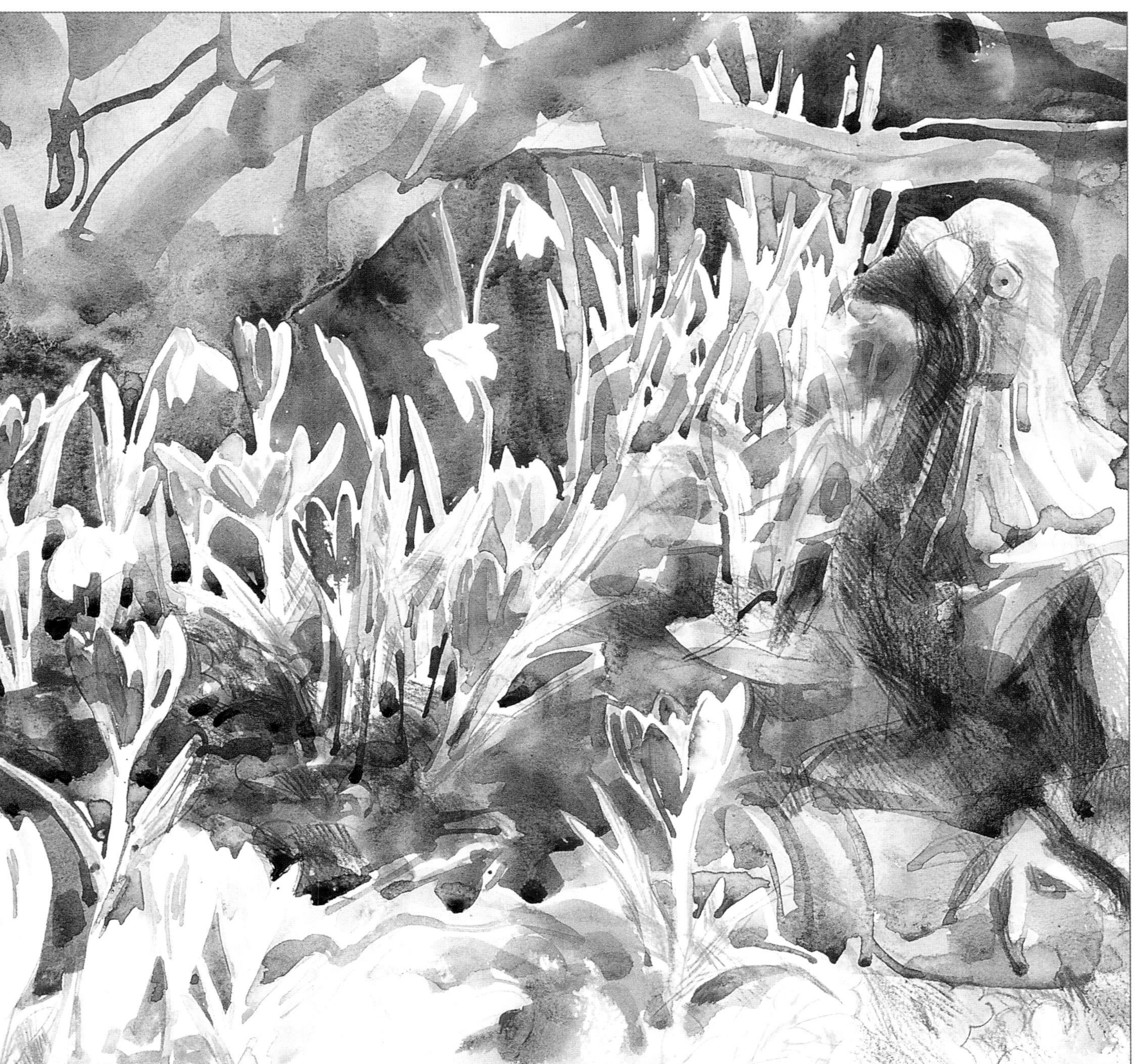

8 Use large brushstrokes to build up layers of shadows, going over the pencil marks where necessary, and use the lines to emphasize the outlines of the flowers. Working across the whole picture, move back to colored pencils to create texture on the hellebores. Finish by building up the tones that hold the highlights, and add a little blue pencil to the shaded parts of the white snowdrops.

Summer scene: watercolors on semi-rough watercolor paper

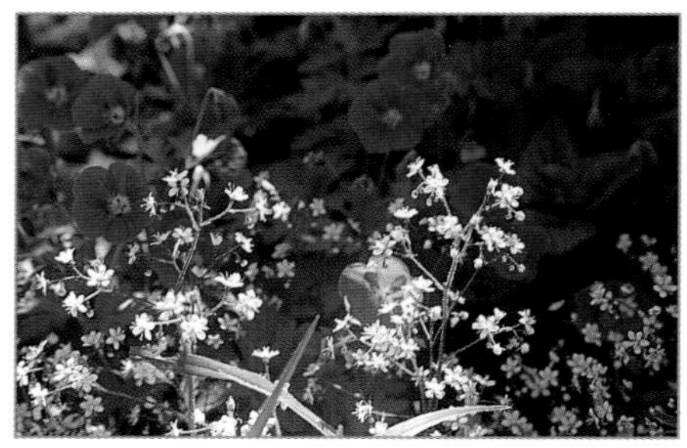

The highlights of this scene of summer blooms in sunlight are a profusion of little, white "Pride of London" flowers. It would be very time-consuming and laborious to leave the paper white while laying washes, so use masking fluid to cover it. Gum arabic gives a slight sheen to the paint and restricts spreading of water washes.

Materials

- Semi-rough Bockingford watercolor paper
- 3B pencil
- Kneadable eraser
- Masking fluid
- Rubber-tipped color shaper
- Watercolor paints
- Gum arabic
- Oriental brushes
- Small, round brush
- Clean water

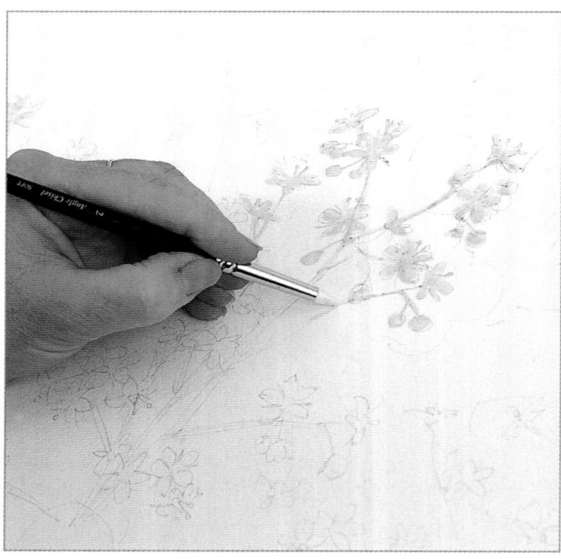

1 After drawing a guide, use a rubber-tipped color shaper to fill in the whitest petals with masking fluid. These shapers are better than brushes—they are more precise and they don't lose their shape, and they allow more control.

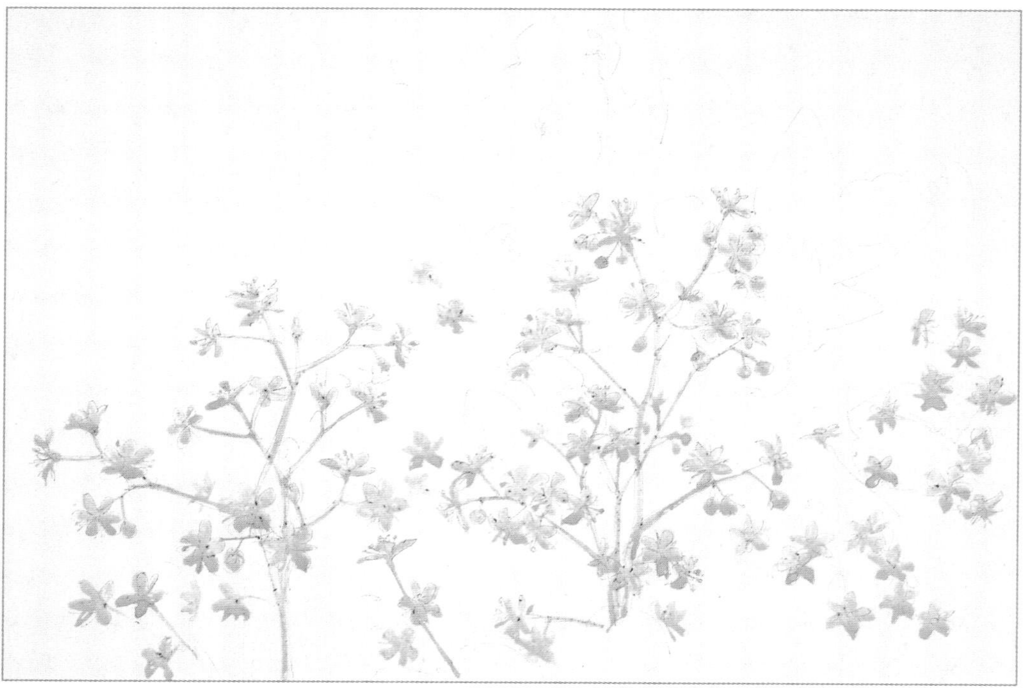

2 Work carefully and accurately, and clean the tip of the shaper regularly when the masking fluid dries on it. Pencil marks under the fluid can be erased later. Go over the flowers that are not to be in the bright sunlight. Use a hair dryer to dry the fluid.

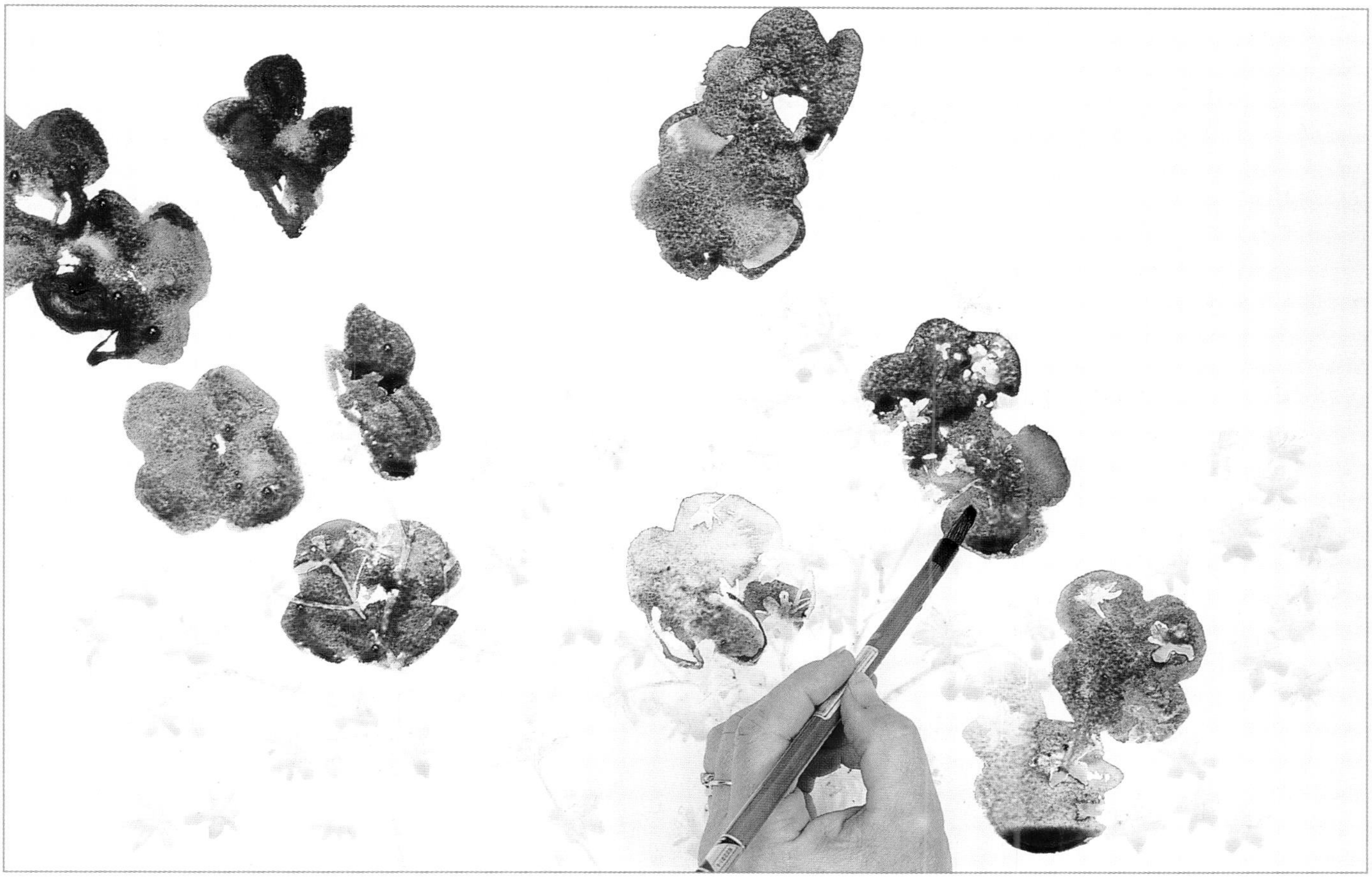

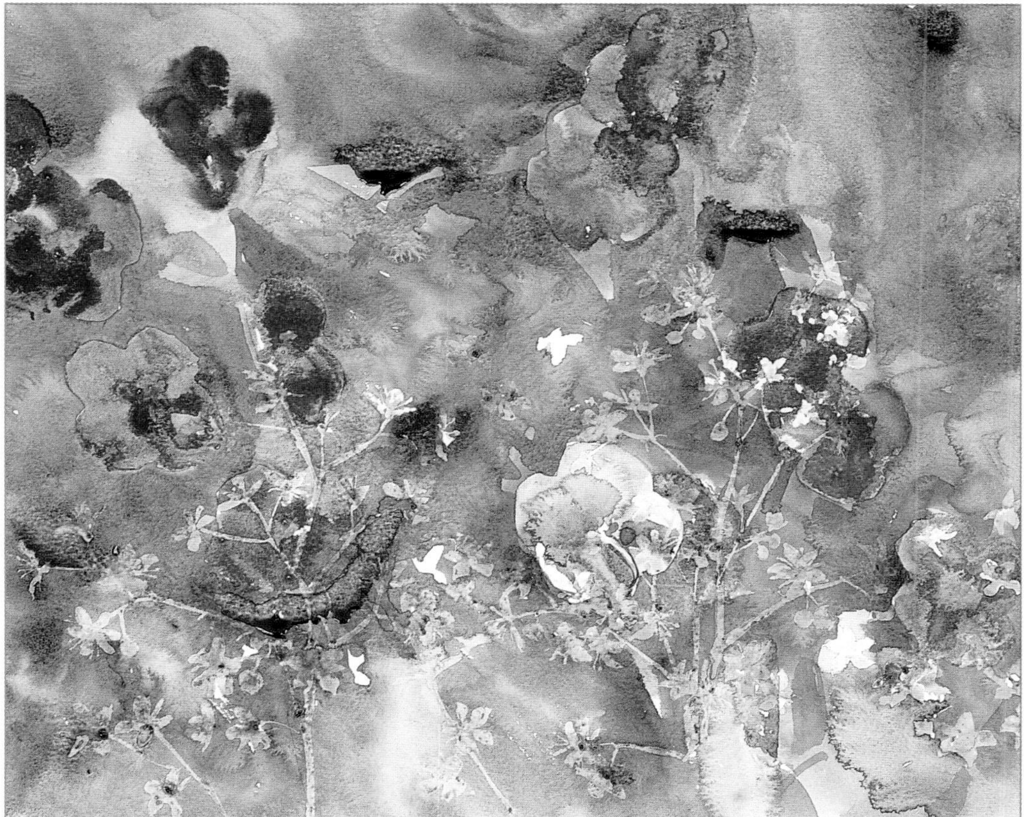

3 With the fluid completely dry, lay the board flat and make the first pink wash with an oriental brush, capturing the movement of the petals. Add a little gum arabic to the wash with purple, and paint the edges of the petals.

4 Use yellow and gum arabic for the flower centers, and red to go around and on the yellow. Before the paint dries completely, freely apply shades of dark green up to the flower edges—they will only bleed a little. Cool down the background with blue washes, emphasizing the light.

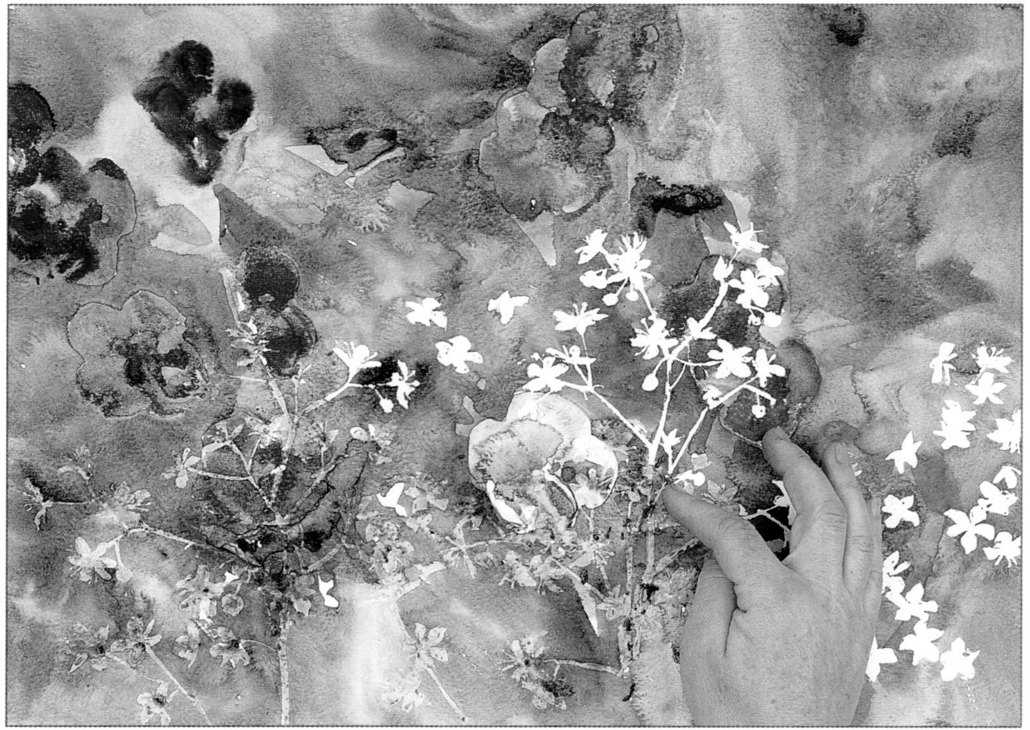

5 Allow the paint to dry thoroughly, then rub off the masking fluid with a finger, exposing the white paper beneath the washes. Use an eraser or the flat edge of a craft knife for the areas covered by gum arabic and paint.

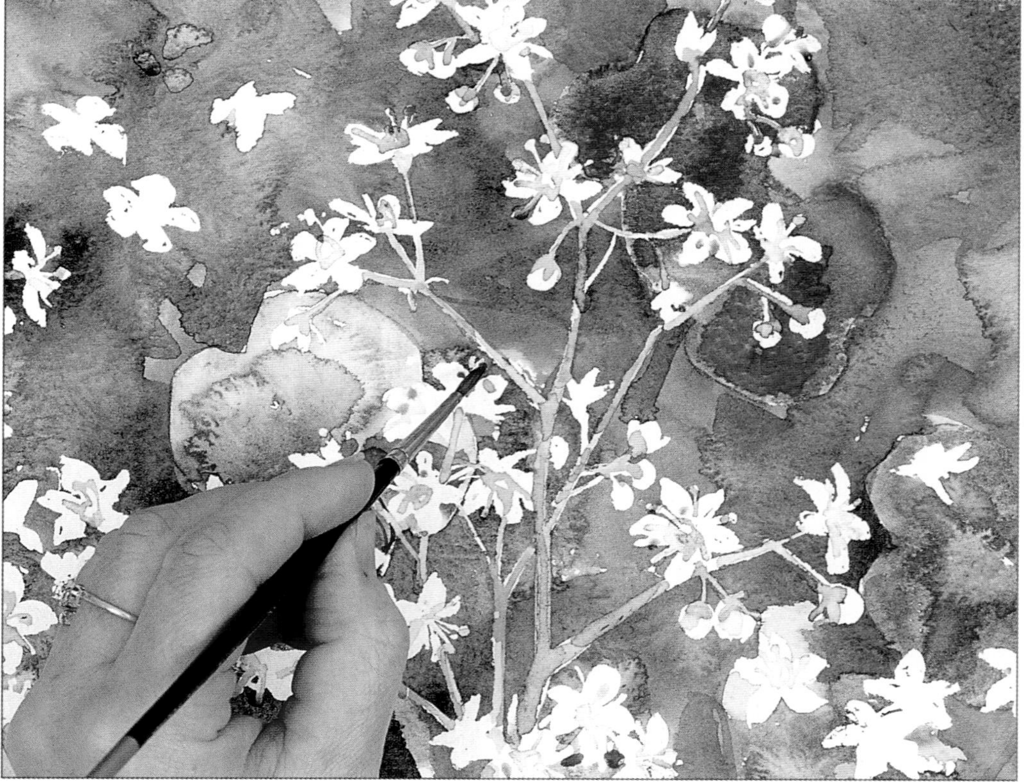

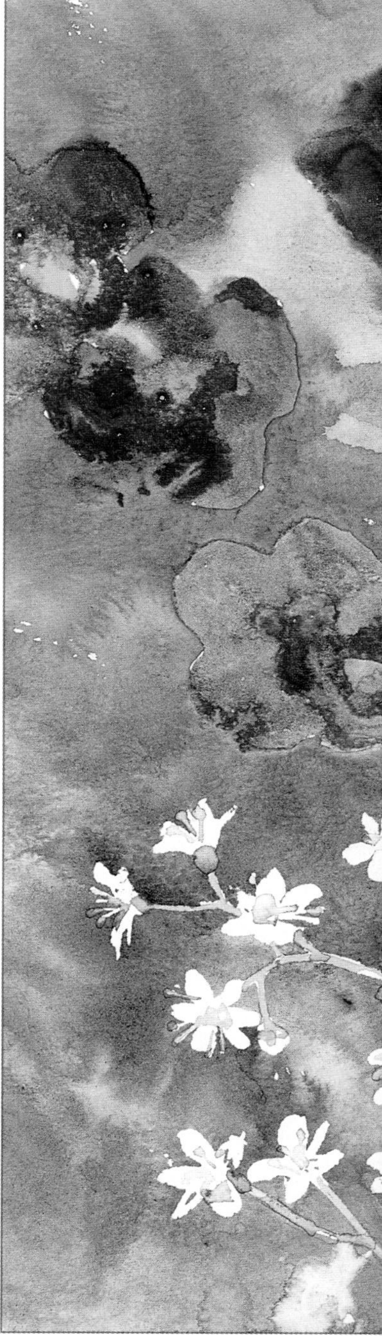

6 Use an eraser to clean up the pencil marks before adding the stalks with a small, round brush and a mixture of yellow and pink. Use the same brush to paint in the red/pink centers of the "Pride of London" flowers.

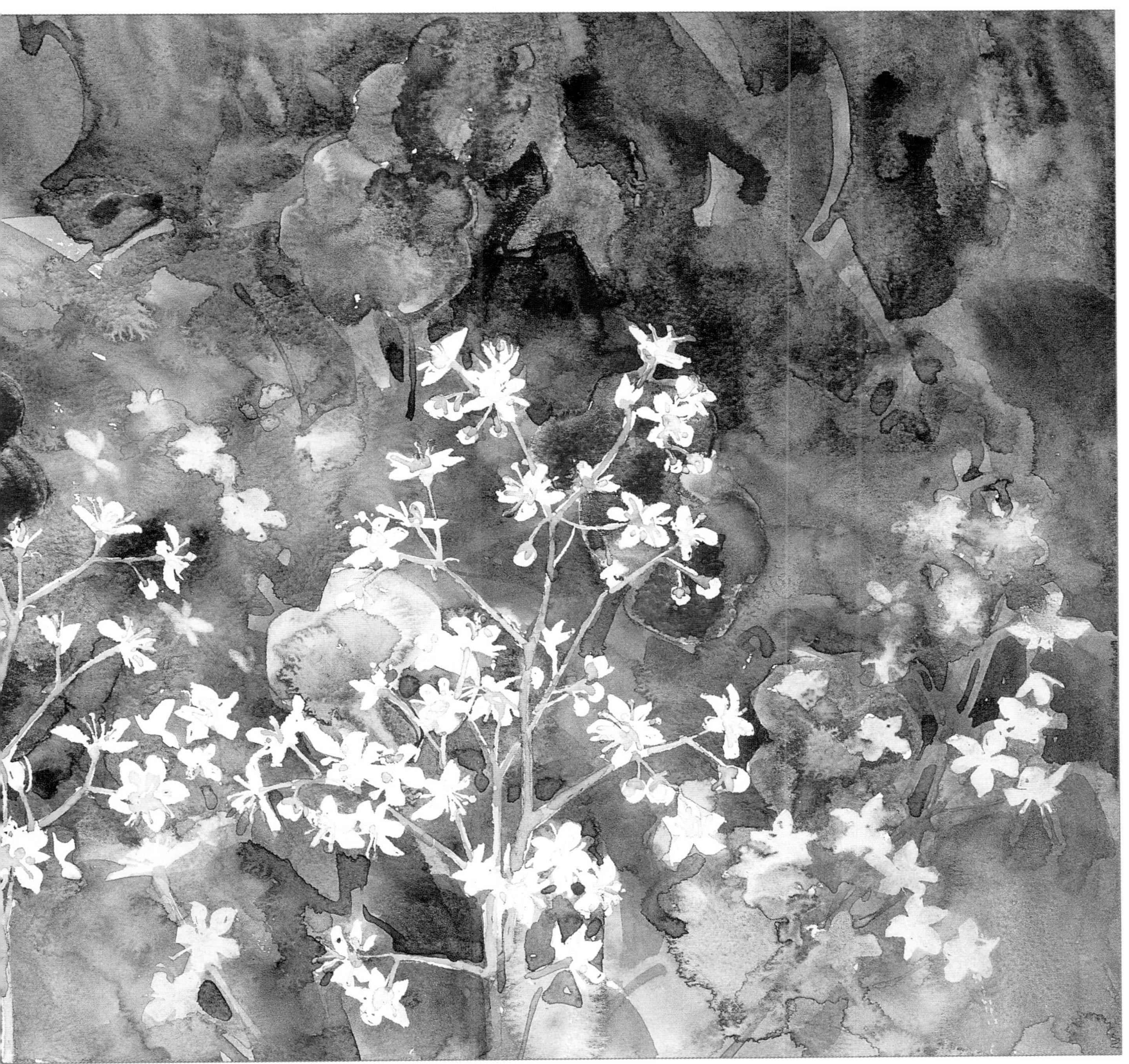

7 Using a large oriental brush and a very diluted, pink wash, knock back some of the white flowers in the shade. A diluted, blue wash gives a cool color to the shadow areas, or you can dab water onto a dark wash and move it. Darken the background to bring the stalks and flowers forward.

Fall colors: watercolor inks on semi-rough watercolor paper

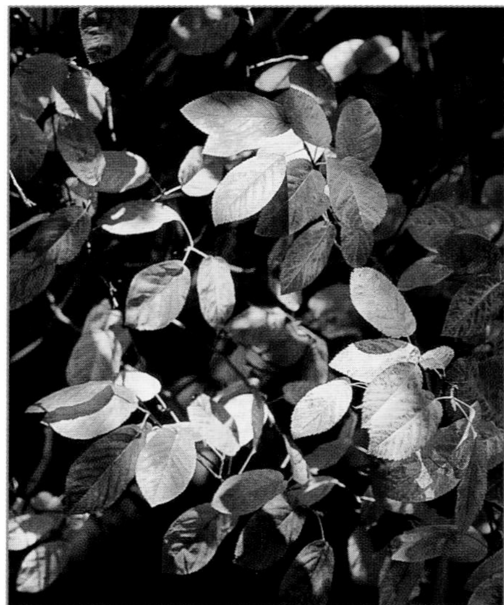

The glorious reds, yellows, and browns of fall leaves are a delight to capture, and there are many mediums that are suited to the task. Watercolor inks have a particular brightness, but at a cost—they are quite impermanent, and some colors fade quickly when exposed to daylight for any length of time.

Materials

- Semi-rough Bockingford watercolor paper
- 3B pencil
- Steel-nib dip pen
- Watercolor inks
- Oriental brush
- Clean water

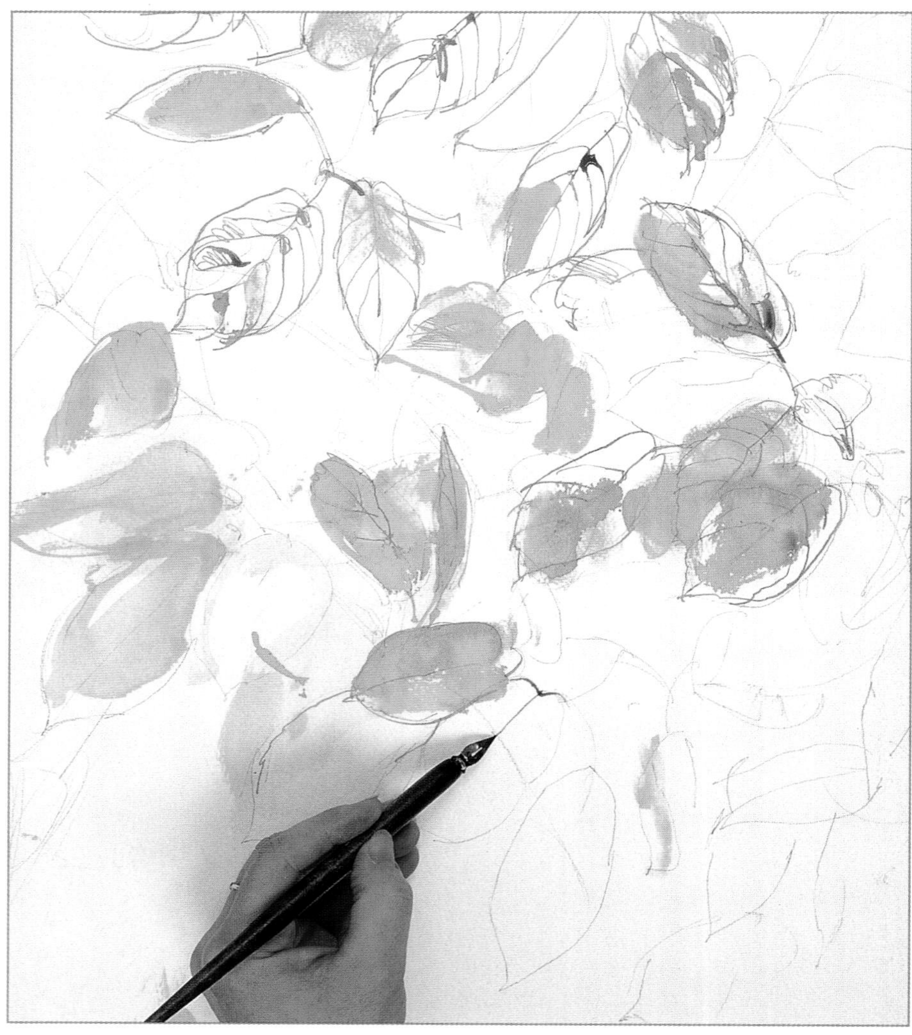

1 You can either make a preliminary drawing, as shown here, to find the basic composition and shapes, or go straight into working with the brush and nib. If the former, keep the lines loose so you don't feel bound to follow them rigidly.

2 Use a nib and yellow ink to draw the first oval-based leaf shapes and veins. For interesting color mixtures, don't rinse the nib before using new inks. For soft lines, draw into wet washes, and use a wetted brush to spread the inks.

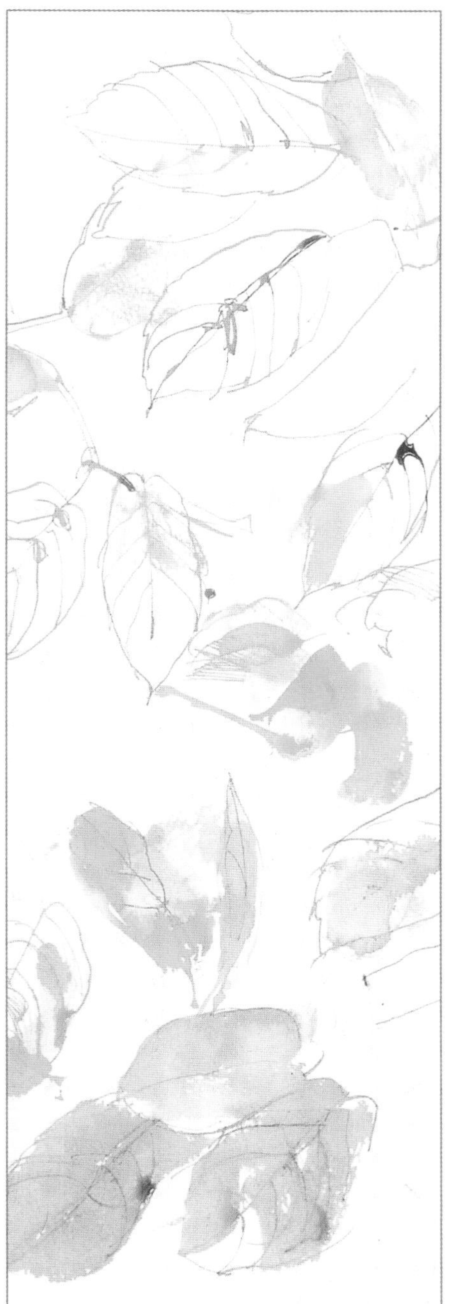

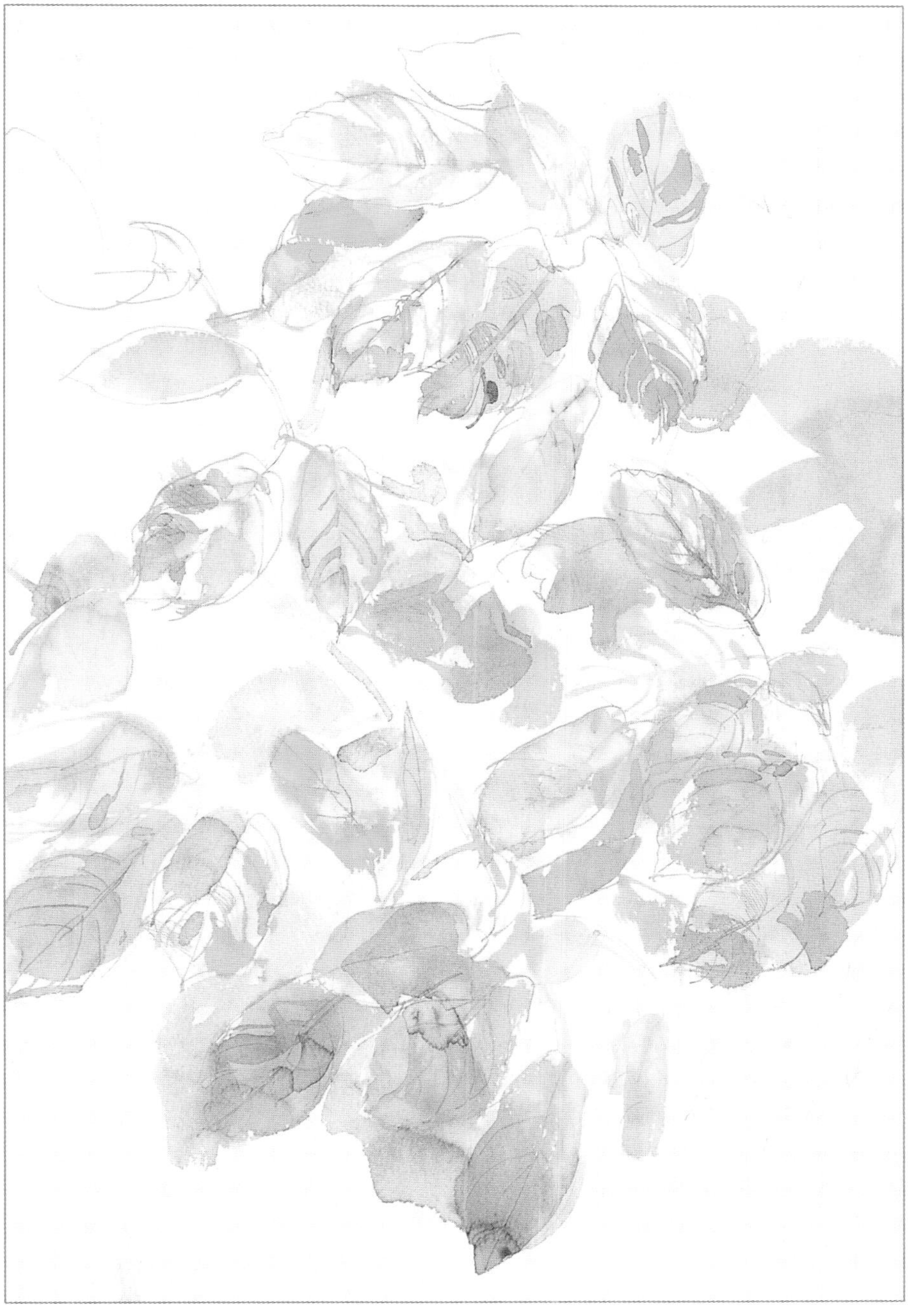

3 Move through the colors as you establish the shapes and first sets of tones. Block in some of the brightest leaves with the brush, trying not to make the wash too solid or opaque. Draw the veins in wet, then use a hair dryer to stop the spread before it goes too far.

4 Even when the inks have dried, putting a wet brush or finger across will move them. Add diluted green washes with the brush, then blue and purple to suggest the dark shadow areas, this time with brush, pen, and finger.

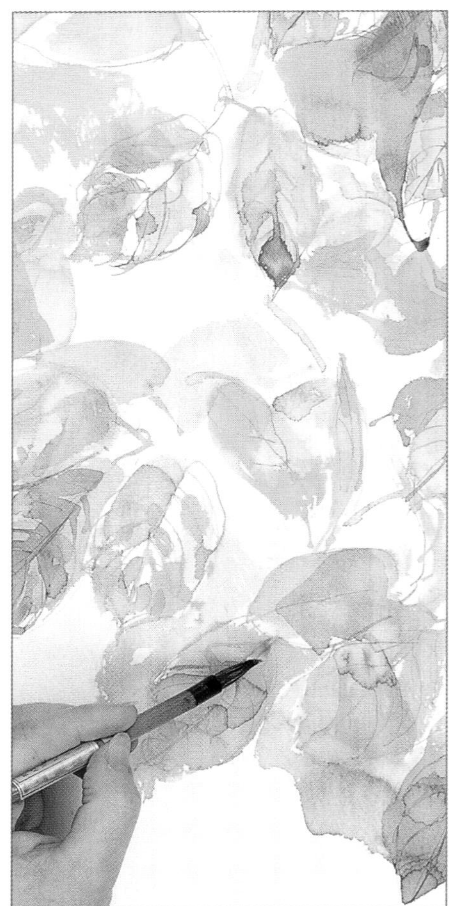

5 When the shapes are established, introduce some stronger colors across all the leaves—the richer, fall shades of reds, magentas, and greens—using the brush to block in some of the larger leaf areas.

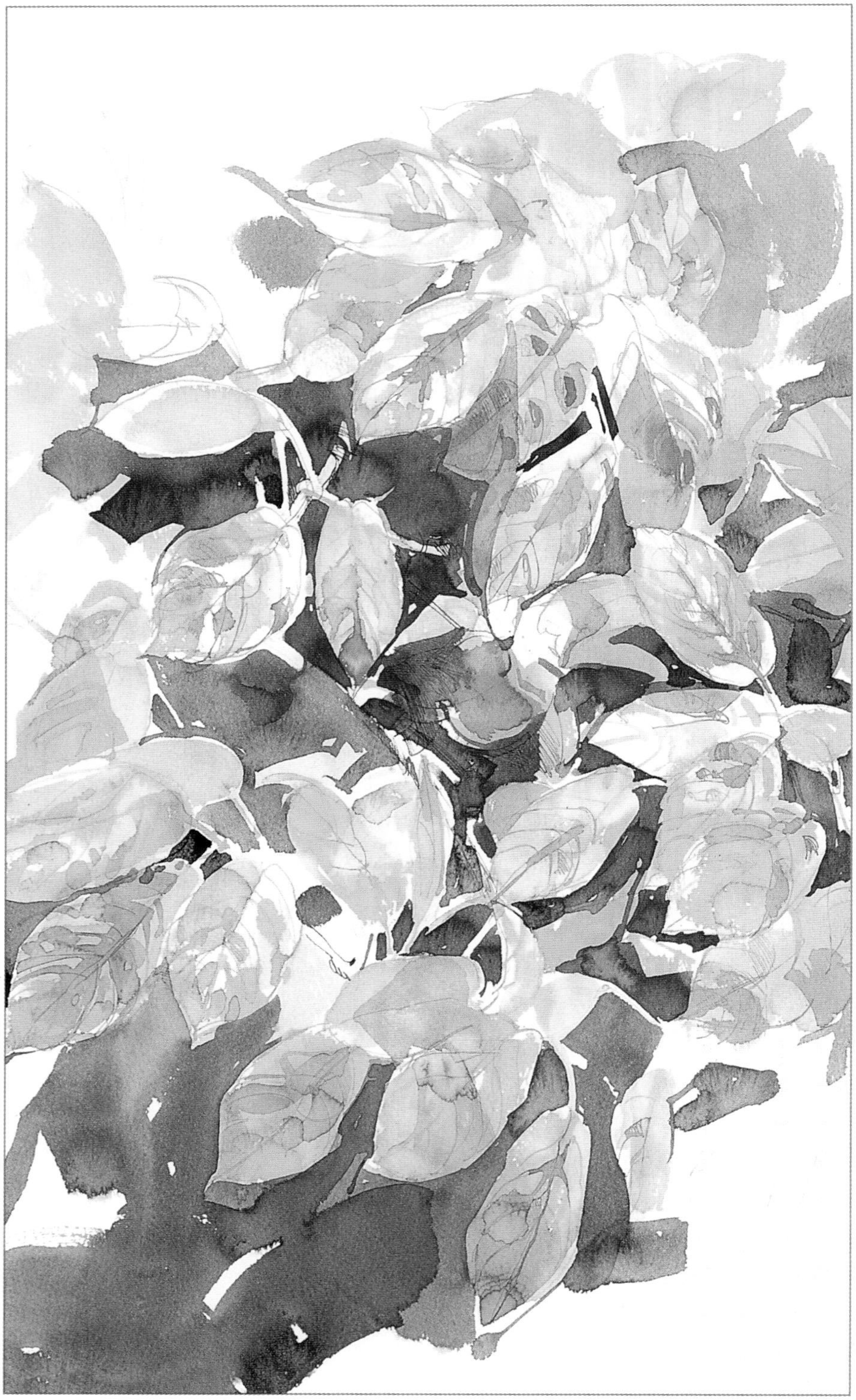

6 Make up darker mixtures using purple, sepia, and ultramarine blue, then block in the negative shapes with the brush, working broadly and freely. Vary the strengths and mixtures to suit, and only use the nib for texture and the finest shadow details.

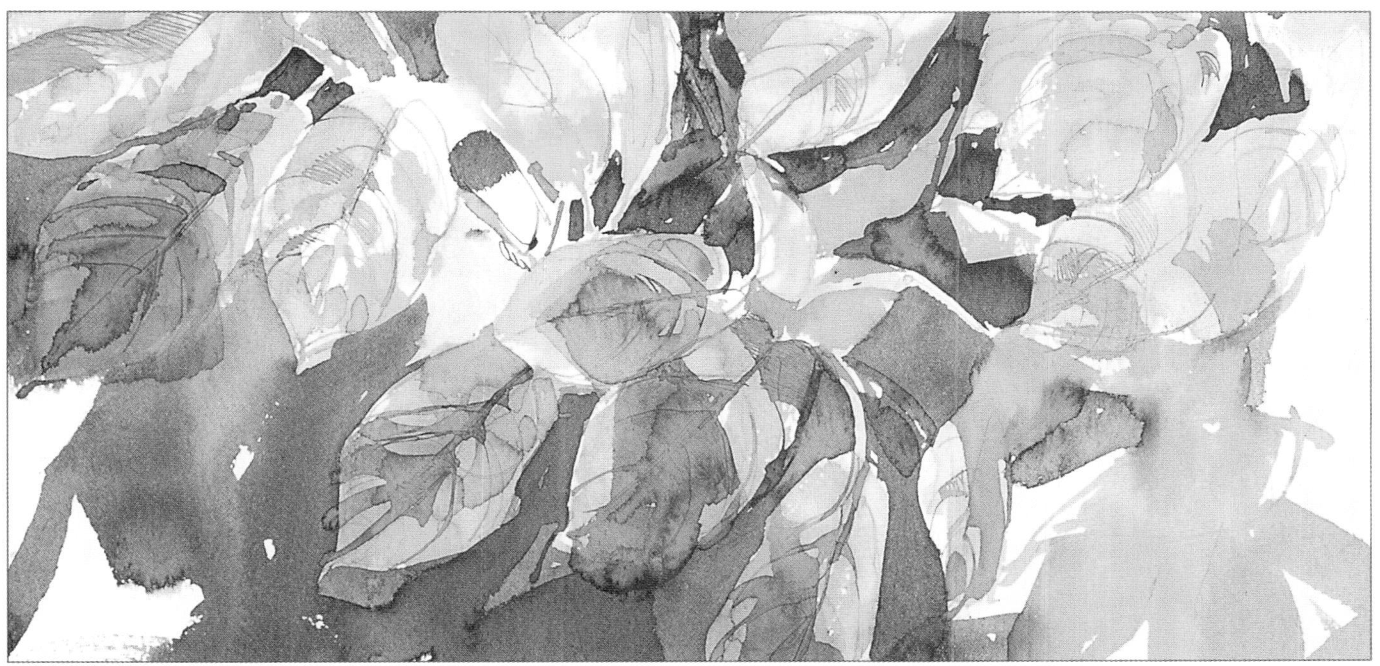

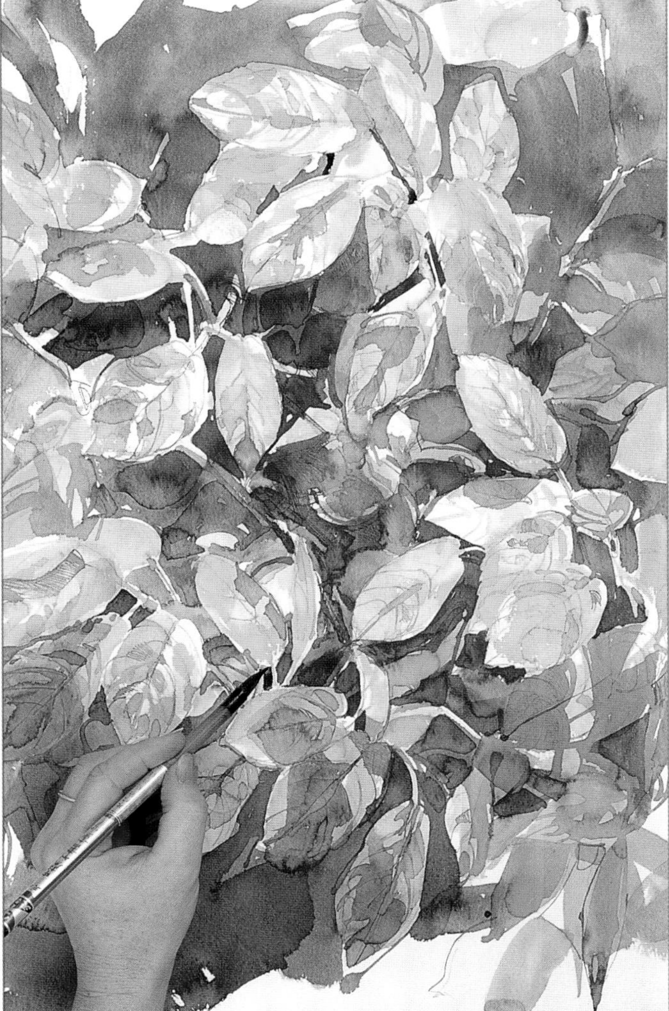

7 While you draw in more fine details on the leaves, using the nib and brush, look to link up all the various elements—leaves and shadows, positive and negative areas, tone and color—and amend and adjust the relative values as required.

8 When you are satisfied with the composition and colors of the central area, move outward to the edges of the composition. Build up the shadow areas around the outer leaves, adjusting the tones throughout as these dark parts increase. Most of the dark tones and the strongest contrasts are more central, to draw the eye into the composition.

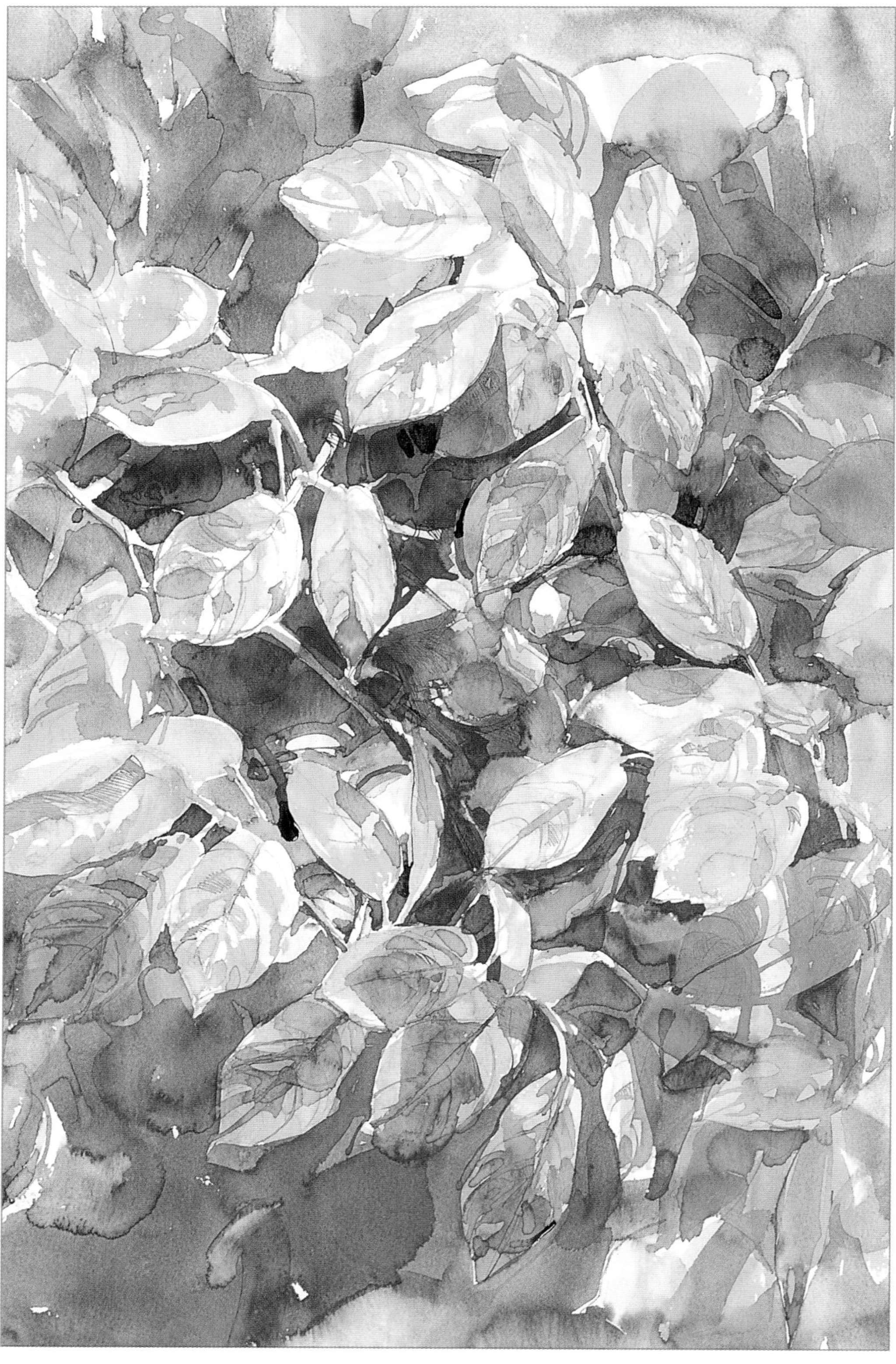

9 The shadow areas should be made up of color mixtures, not black, which gives you no room to add layers or make changes because it can deaden the shadows. Use the inks' layering qualities, but be careful not to overwork the picture, or to lose the freshness and appeal of the colors by adding too much detail.

Botanical gardens: watercolor pastels on semi-rough watercolor paper

For most of us, going to paint or draw in a rainforest or jungle is not a realistic option, but most people are within reach of botanical gardens, and a day or two spent sketching there is a pleasant break. Faced with such lush, chaotic and large plants, two different lights and views were combined for the picture, one concentrating on the left-hand leaves, the other on the right-hand flowers.

Materials

- Semi-rough Bockingford watercolor paper
- Neocolor watercolor pastels
- Oriental brushes
- Clean water

1 Use red and green watercolor pastels to clarify and simplify the foreground on the right-hand side, then add general, directional lines to give a rough basis for the tonal values.

2 Apply red into the flowers very lightly, then dip a small oriental brush into clean water, and make washes from the pastel lines and marks. Again, work lightly with the brush, and keep everything as clean as possible while delineating both the lighter and darker shadowed areas in the flowers.

3 Continue with the red washes only until the leaves are clearly shaped—too much work can look muddled, and loses the structure. Block in the green leaves with pastels and washes in the same way, with tiny touches of yellow on the left-hand tips. Add blue in the middle foreground for the shadowed areas between the leaves.

4 Use more pressure when drawing the lower left-hand leaves, as they are not very fanned out, and have deeper colors than those on the right. Form and gauge the negative shapes between the leaves to clarify the positive shapes, adding purple-blues for a cool effect. Blend, layer, and make textures using dry pastels at this stage.

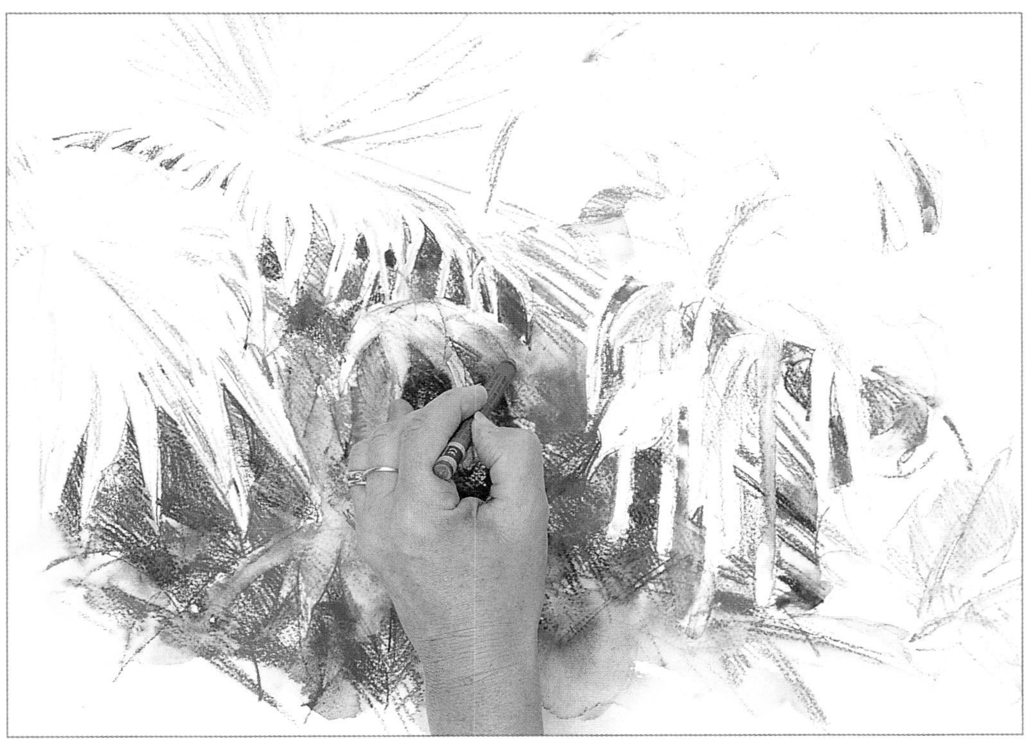

5 Load the brush with clean water, and start to make the washes. Don't worry about form or structure for now, but let the water do the work. Drag the colors around with the water for drawing, and only recharge the brush when it is dry. Working more pastel colors into the water gives very strong, definite colors. Let the washes dry.

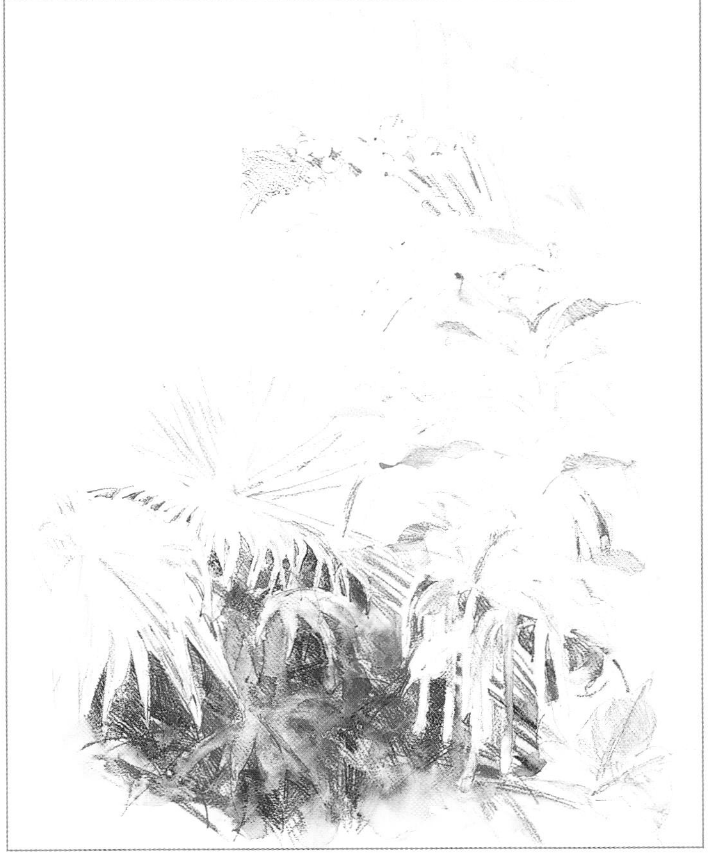

6 Use pale blue pastel to find the lightest top fan leaves and the ironwork of the roofing, which disappears into the foliage. Add water when the marks are set, and put in yellow strokes for the sunny highlights. Add the lightest green leaves on the right-hand side, and work across the picture to shape and block in the greens nearest the roof.

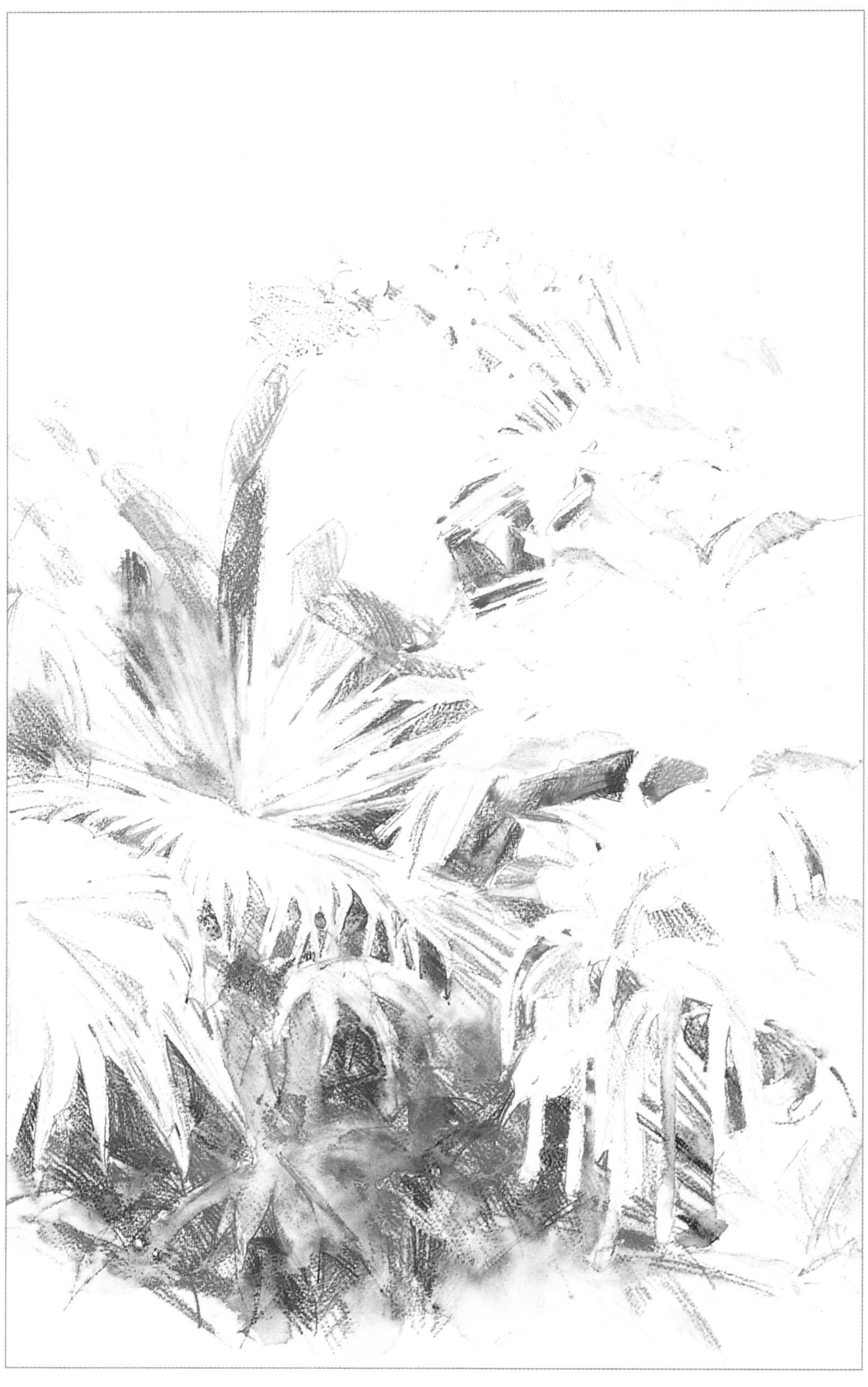

7 Move on to the more shadowed, large vertical leaf shapes, working a range of colors into the gaps between the fan leaves. Block in the shading on the middle ground area, concentrating on the darker shades, then go over with the watery washes. Spread the pigment as before, and draw with the brush.

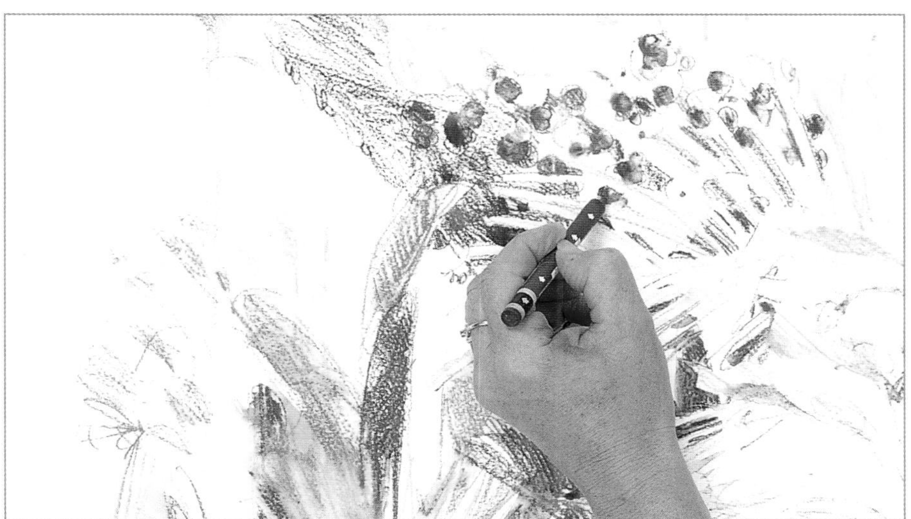

8 At the top of the picture, move onto the details of the architecture where it can be seen—the scrolls on the columns and the negative shapes—drawing in and blocking as you go. Include the yellow sunlight on the white ironwork. Add the rounded purple flowers, and adjust the surrounding blues and greens as required.

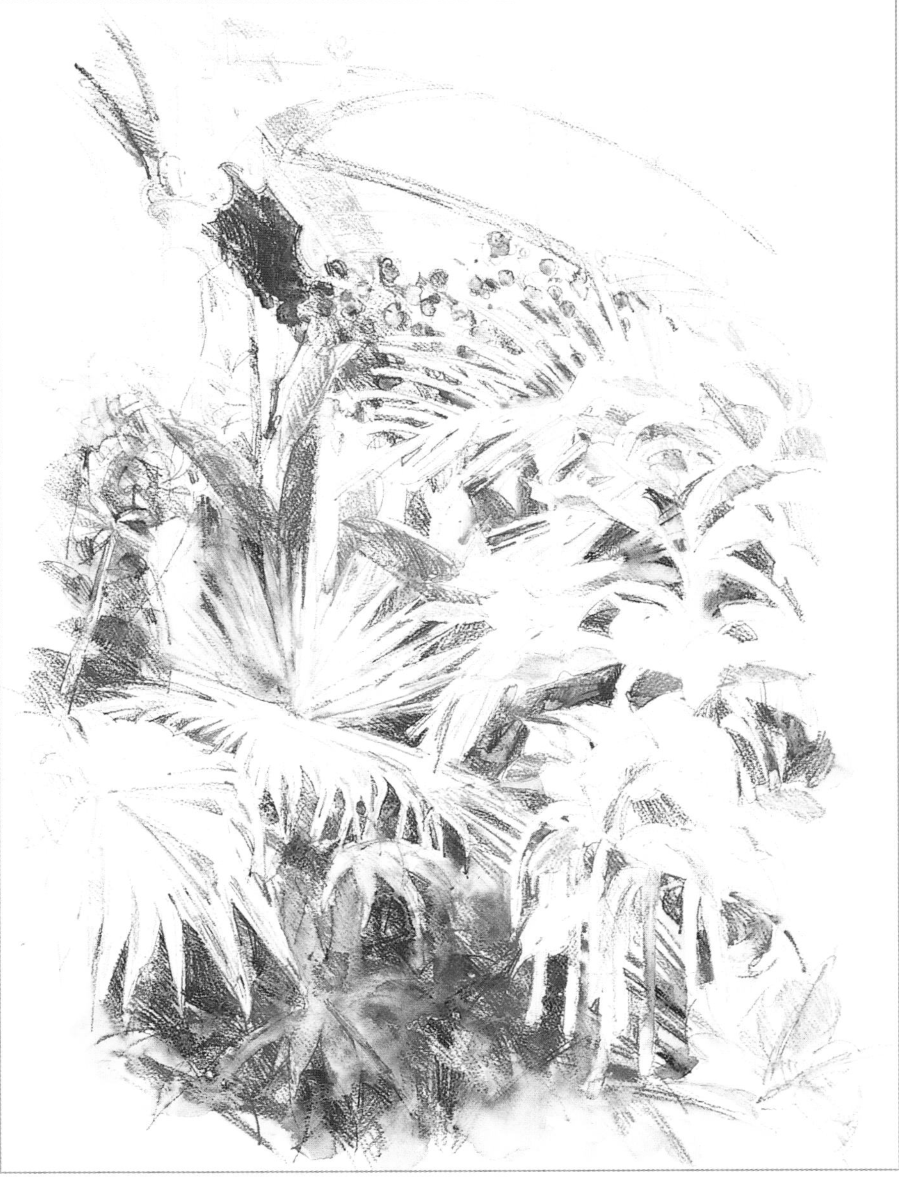

9 Continue to apply the background colors, and fill the spaces between the foreground reds and greens. This has the effect of bringing the right-hand flowers more into the foreground, which now appears to be paler in comparison to the built-up parts. Stand back and check over the whole picture, looking for patterns and tonal unity through the colors.

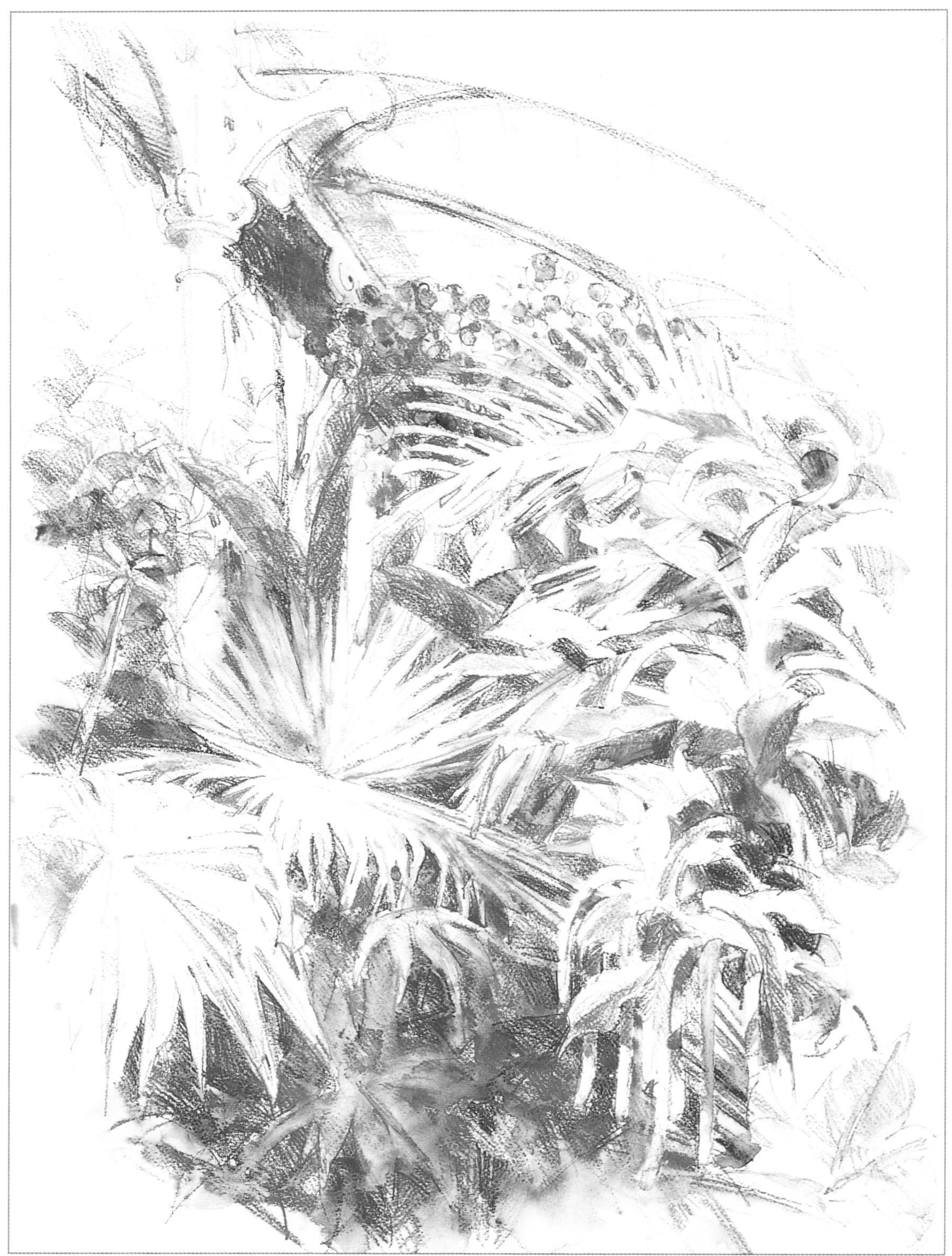

10 Add some warmer colors against the cool ones of the roof area, then reinforce the verticals of the ironwork columns and the leaves and stalks. Finish by adding the details, using strong colors for the shadows and darkest areas. Don't be tempted to make the most vivid shades too bold, or draw over too much white.

Informal set-up: watercolor pencils and colored pencils on semi-rough watercolor paper

Bright flowers draped across a tablecloth and combined with still-life elements can make an attractive, informal composition—although you may need to do a fair bit of adjusting to get it right before starting. Use the watercolor pencils for their dry and wet qualities, first drawing and then making washes out of the pencil marks to block in more solid areas of color.

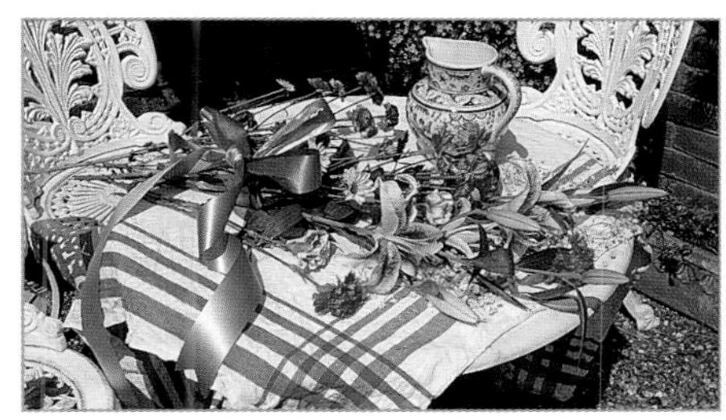

Materials

- Semi-rough Bockingford watercolor paper
- Watercolor pencils
- Colored pencils
- Small, round brush
- Clean water

1 Use colored pencils for the preliminary drawing—a light green to capture the direction and splay of the flowers, and a light blue for the curves of the jug. Touches of pink and mauve then set the basic colors and tones of the petals. At this stage, use very free strokes to find and establish the lines.

2 Switching to watercolor pencils, apply a variety of greens, from light to dark, to the stalks before setting the reddest carnation heads. Push the reds into the paper quite strongly. Use light blue for the stripes on the tablecloth, and mauve and purple for the ribbons, finding the darker tones by applying more pressure on the loose strokes.

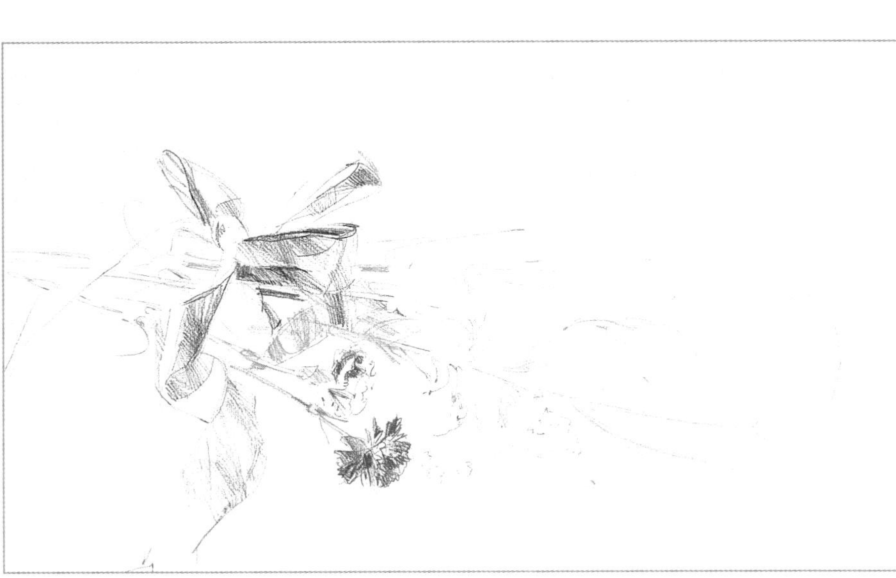

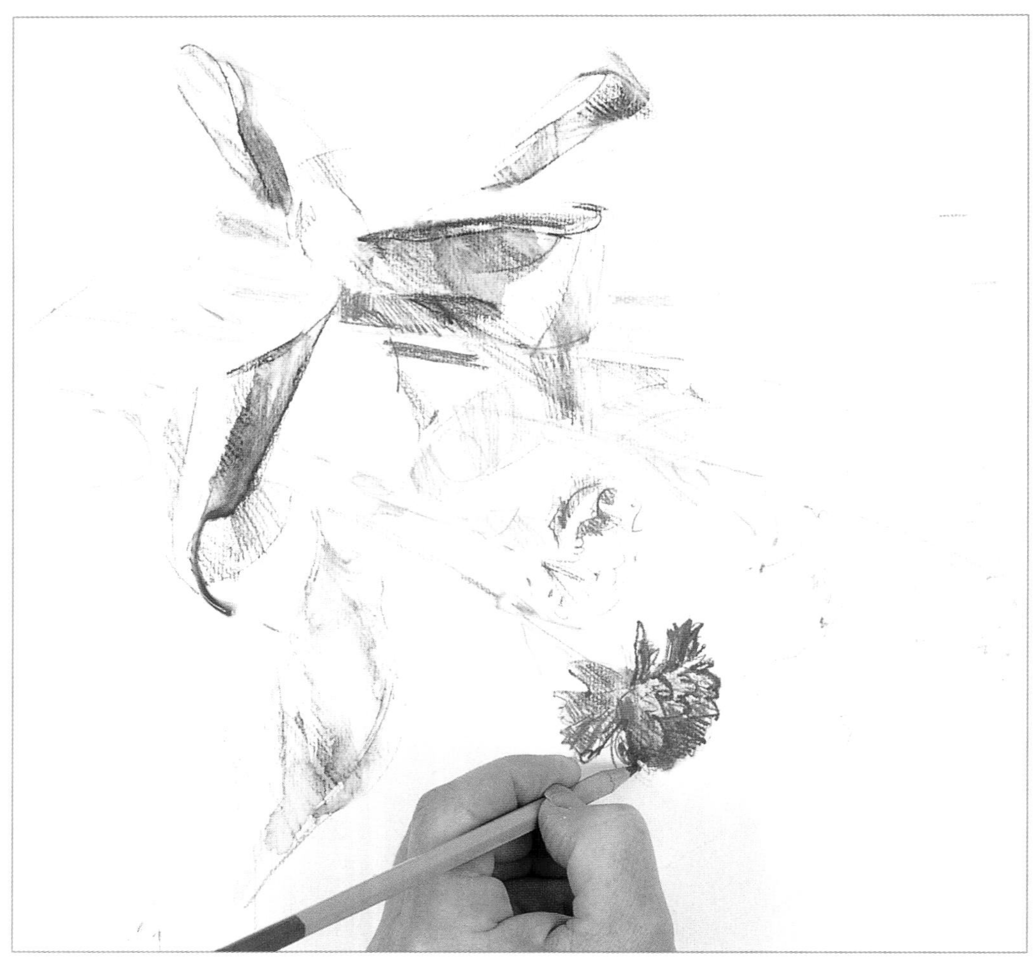

3 Using clean water and a small round brush, lay some water over the carnations. First solidify the blocks of color, then draw into the washes while they are still wet to build up the intensity. Rinse the brush, and repeat this process with the ribbon colors (or only semi-rinse, if you want to blend the red into the purples).

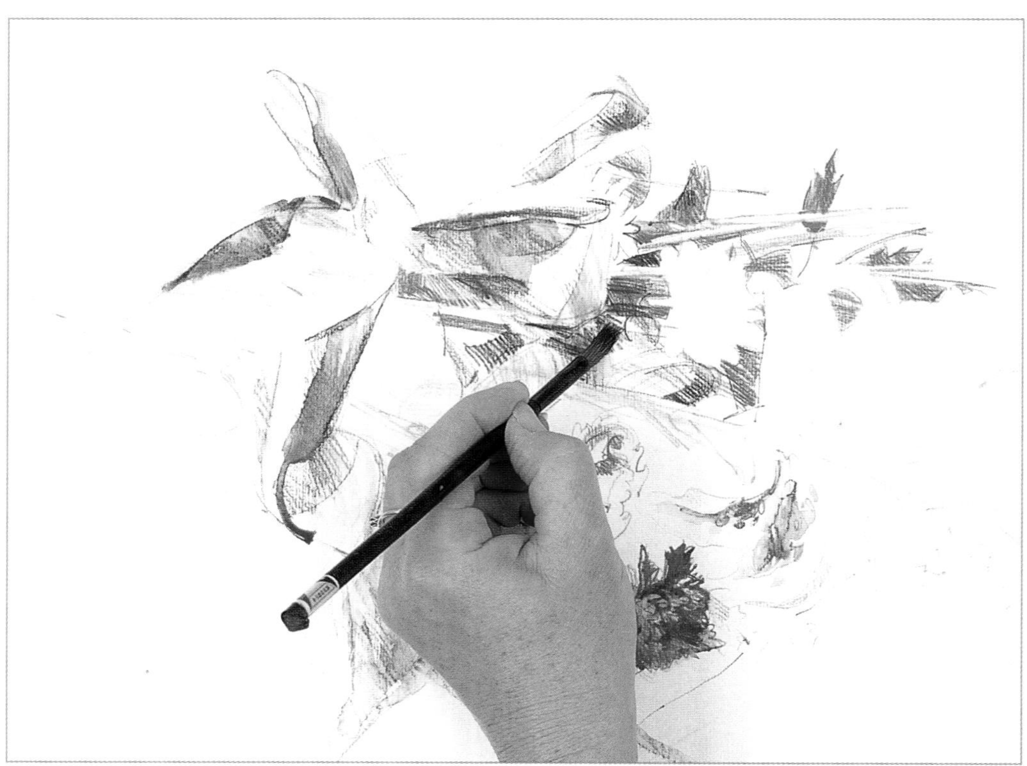

4 Draw in the petal details on the carnation, building layers of different hues and intensities. Next, work outward with blue to put in the longer tablecloth lines, solidifying these with brush and water. Build up the colors overall with watercolor pencils and brush, and block in the green leaves, stalks, and shadows, looking for the negative shapes.

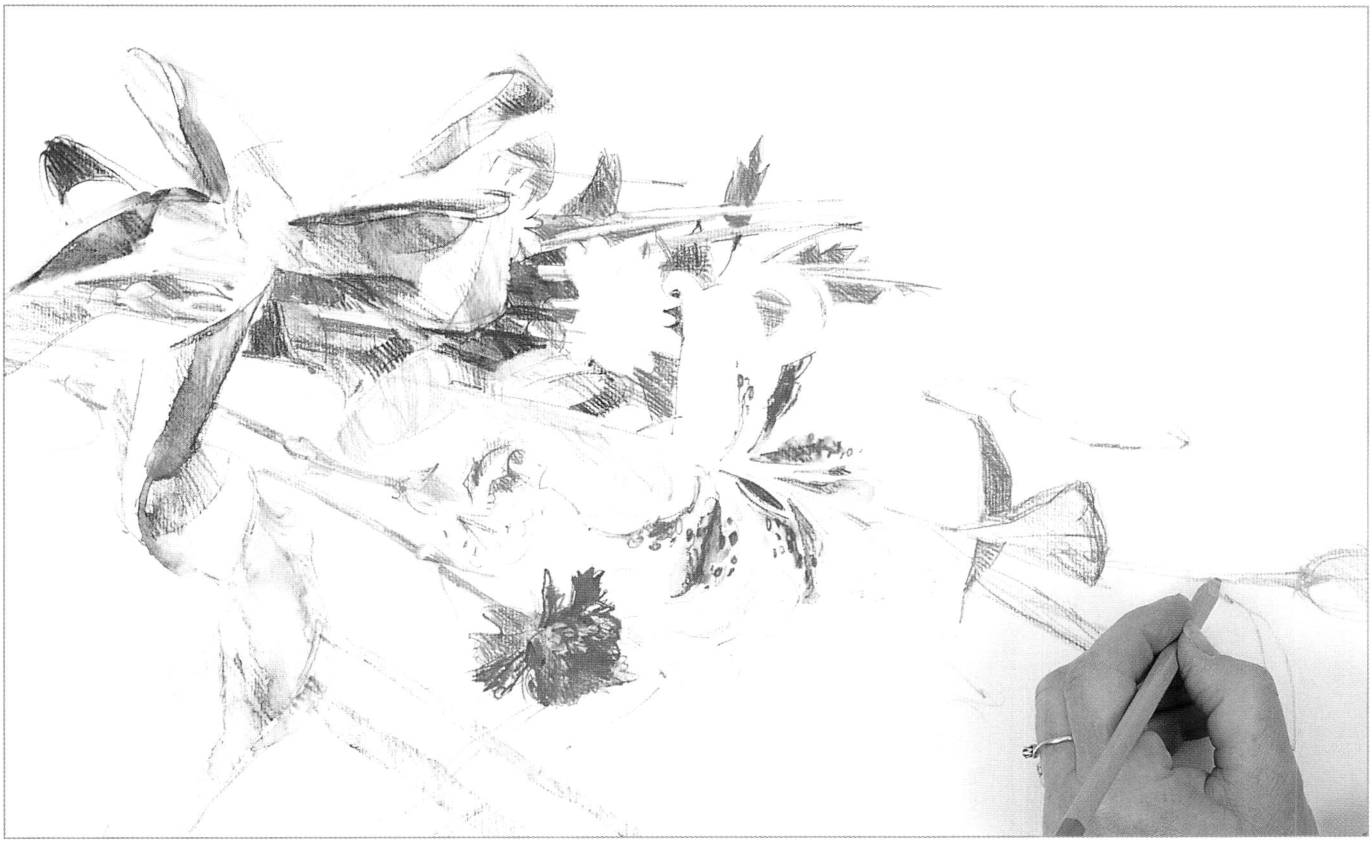

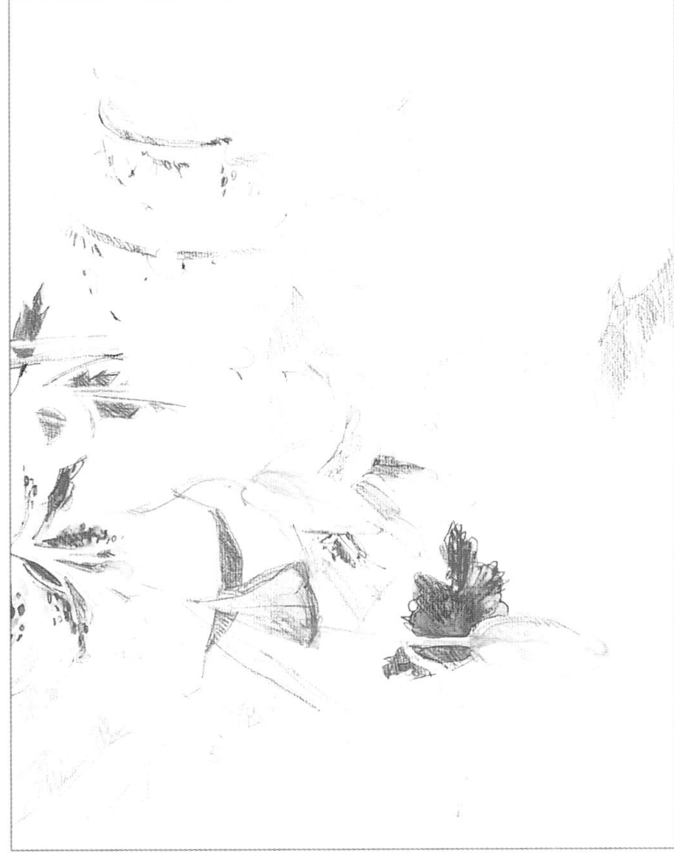

5 Apply the shadow areas and negative shapes around the stems using dark blues, again leaving the flower heads as negative shapes—alternate between free, loose, directional strokes and more detailed filling in. Work outward to the right-hand flowers, using the patterns to set the shapes and forms, then go on to the farthest leaves.

6 Block in the right-hand leaves and patterns with washes. Deepen the stripes on the tablecloth, adding yellow for the reflected sunlight, and include the patterns on the edges all around. Draw the outline of the jug, then darken the patterns on it to show the form and contours. Form the outline of the chair on the right, using the shadow areas to define it. These curves are useful compositional tools that help sweep the eye into the main grouping of the bouquet.

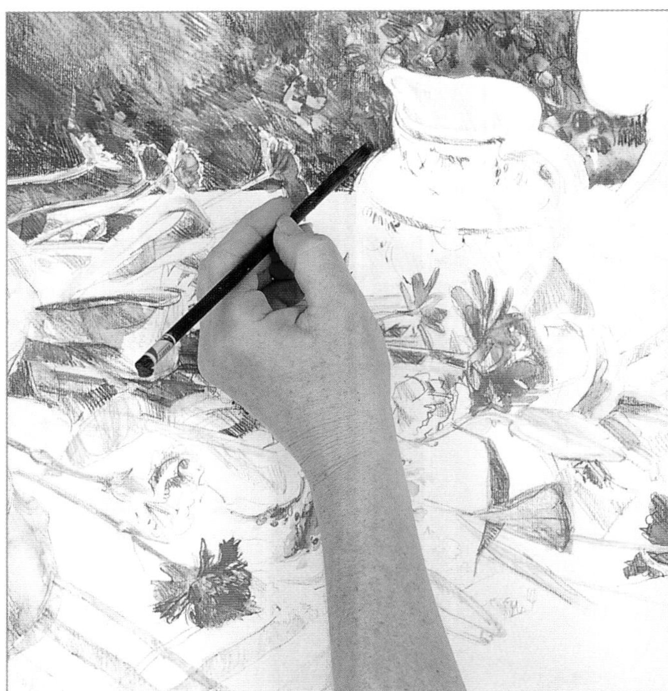

7 Fill in the petals in front of the jug, adding yellow and blue to shade the white flower head. Look across the whole picture, and add the flower heads at the top before starting to fill in the darkest background areas. Hatch and crosshatch loosely with brown, blue, and purple pencils, then make washes with plenty of clean water. Add the pink flowers around the chair. The background shading immediately brings the whites of the jug and chair forward, and solidifies their form. The grouping of flowers casades from the visual horizon formed by the back edge of the table.

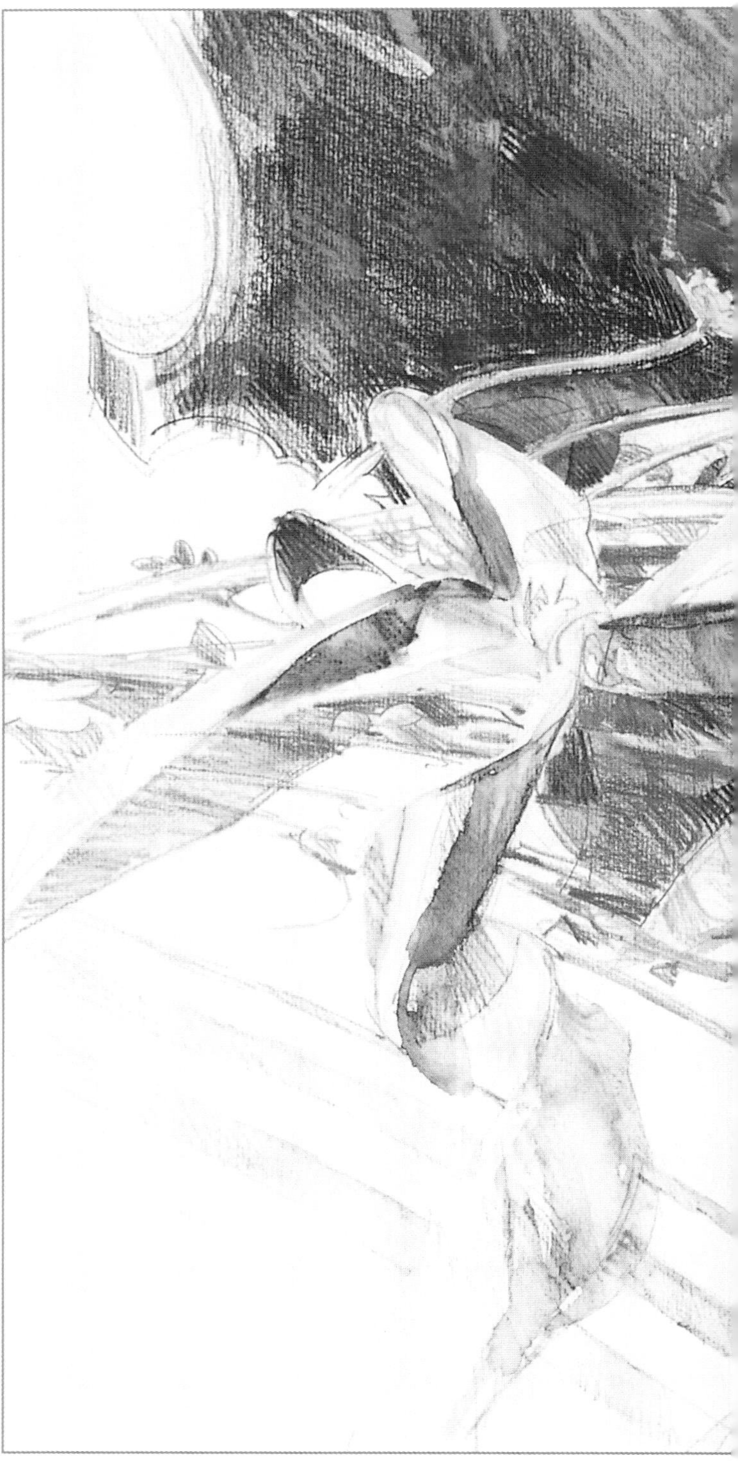

8 Add detail to the chair, following the lines and swirls of the ironwork, and filling the negative shapes with blue. Use the same color for the jug, then fill in the remaining negative shapes of the flowers and leaves, turning the pencil marks into washes and drawing with the brush. Keep the colors bright, and stop before losing freshness.

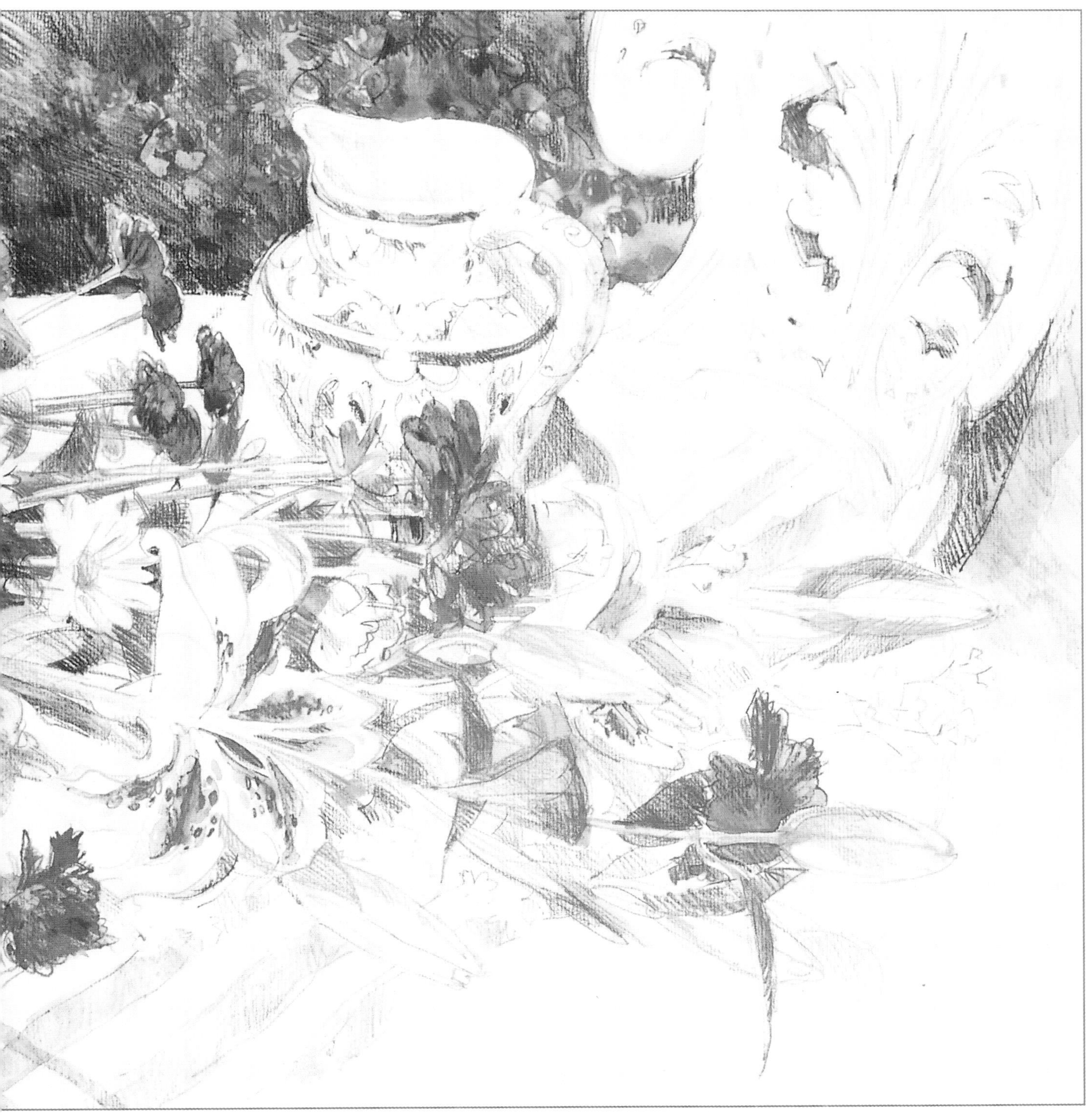

Formal interior with arum lilies:

watercolors on semi-rough watercolor paper

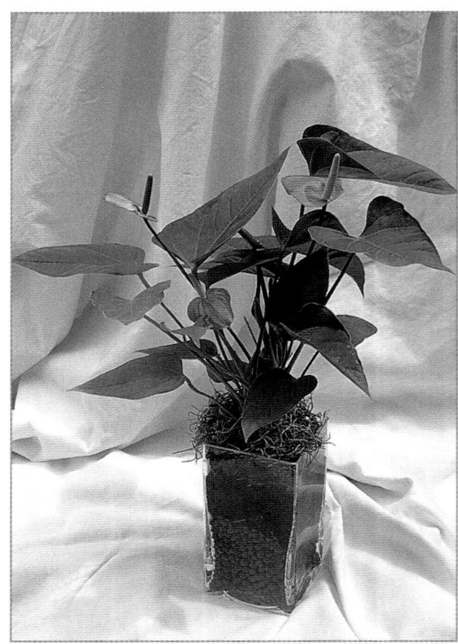

MATERIALS

- Smooth watercolor paper
- 3B pencil
- Oriental brushes
- Watercolor paints
- Gum arabic
- Clean water

The strong shapes of orchids, particularly the leaves, make them a compelling centerpiece for a drawing or painting. Choose your viewpoint and background carefully. Use a high viewpoint to be able to get as much of the leaves and petals in as possible, and keep the background simple and muted, which has the effect of throwing the vase and flowers into relief.

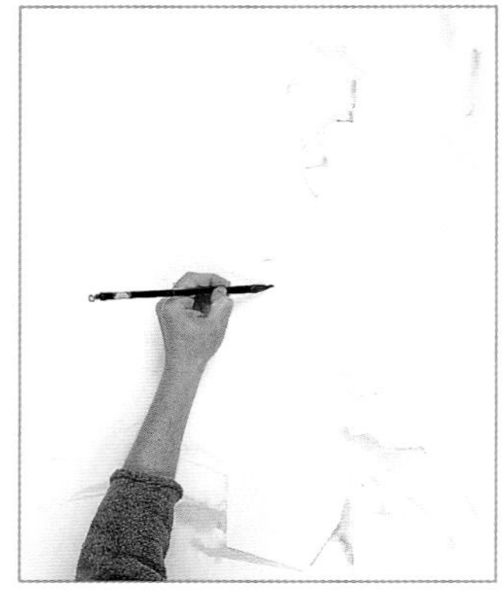

1 Make a preliminary drawing. Using smooth paper means that the pencil will not catch in the tooth, so work lightly and do not impress the drawing into the paper. Make up a mixture of blues, from cerulean to cobalt, with a little mauve, and use a medium oriental brush to apply washes loosely for the background fabric and folds. Work around the negative shapes of the flowers and vase, using extra washes of clean water to spread the pigment into the lightest areas.

2 With the negative shapes now beginning to show, continue loosely and fluidly with the background, letting the washes merge and blend to capture the recesses and folds. Introduce some yellow for the lighter area at the top, and then strengthen the blues.

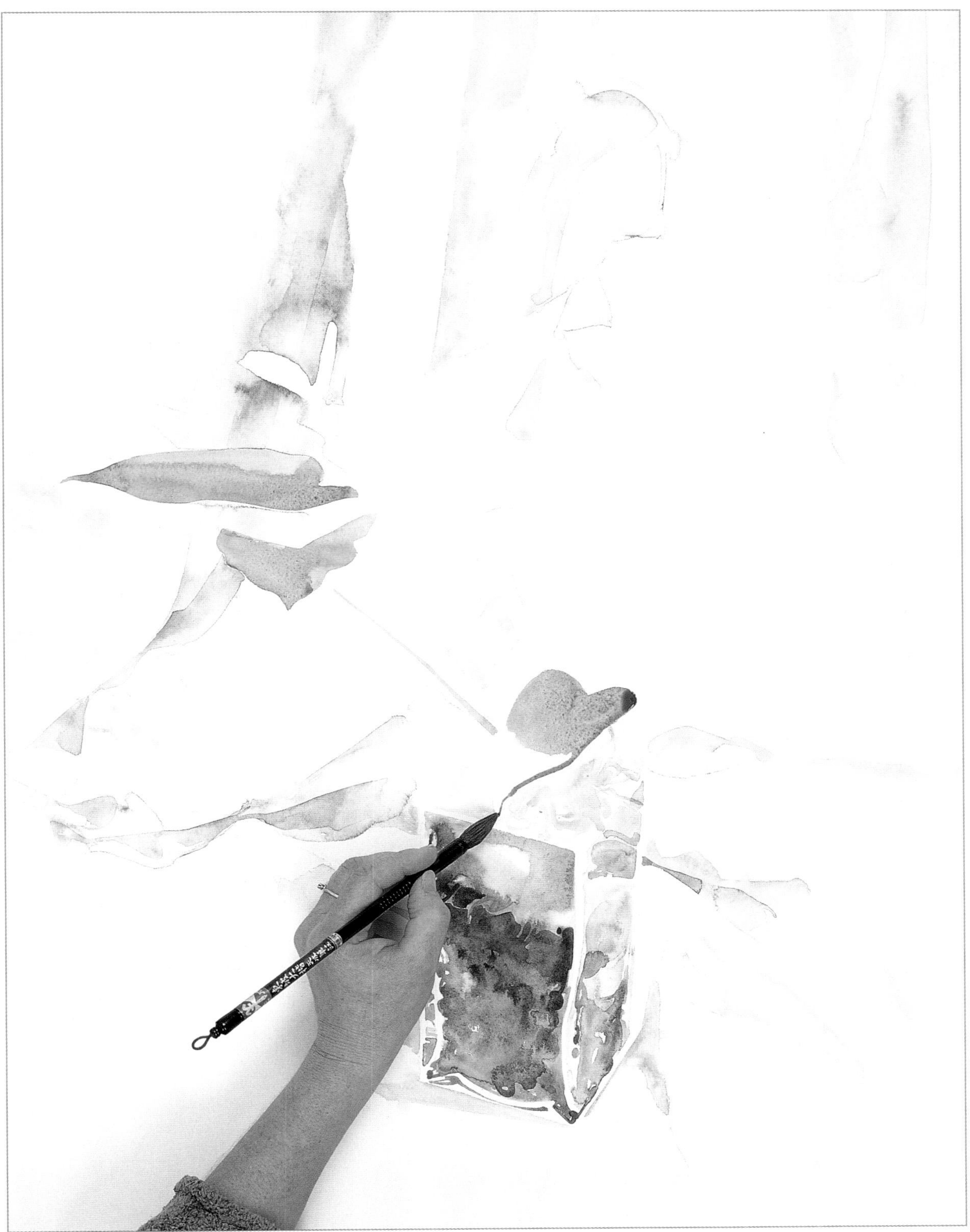

3 Apply the colors of the vase, using ochers, browns, and purples—take account of the reflections in the glass of objects outside the picture, as well as the fact that you are painting earth behind glass. Add the trailing moss covering with yellows and siennas, working around the negative shapes, and lay in the first pale leaves.

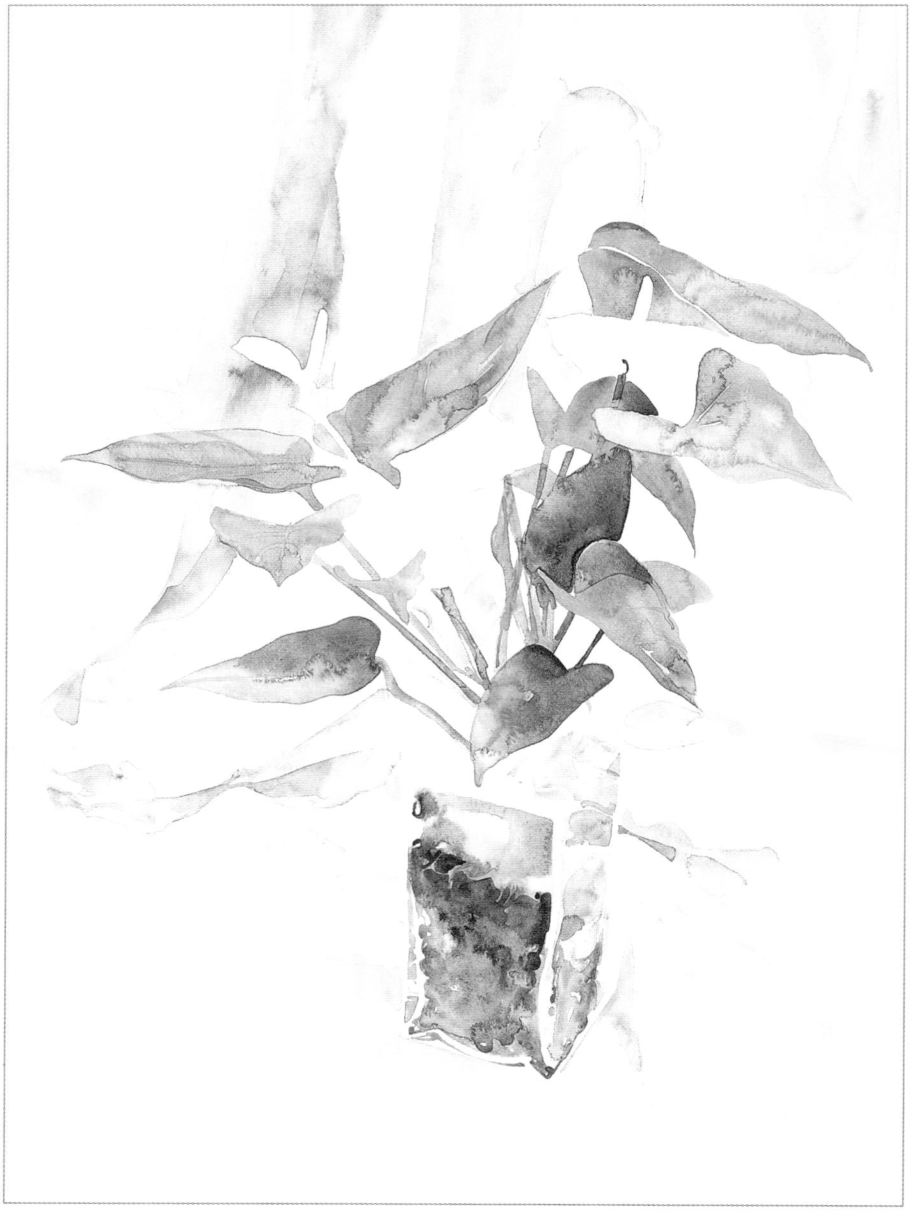

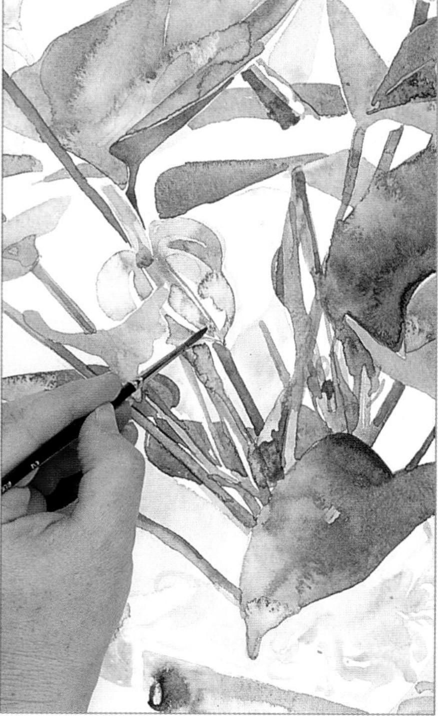

4 Keep the mixture pale at this stage for the leaves, and add yellow for the tips. When the first washes dry a little, draw in with darker and lighter greens for the veins and shadowed areas. Apply reds and browns for the stalks in the negative areas, looking to achieve an impression of the shadows here, rather than putting in each one tightly. To keep detail of the leaves to a minimum, look carefully at their shape and tone—you can still describe their form, curves, angles, and position against the rest of the leaves.

5 Mix up the petal colors with pinks, oranges, and reds, and use a small oriental brush to apply them—include darker washes for the shadows, and lighter ones for the highlighted areas. Allow to dry, then fill in the stamens lightly—the top left one has some yellow in it. Reinforce the greens around and across the flowers.

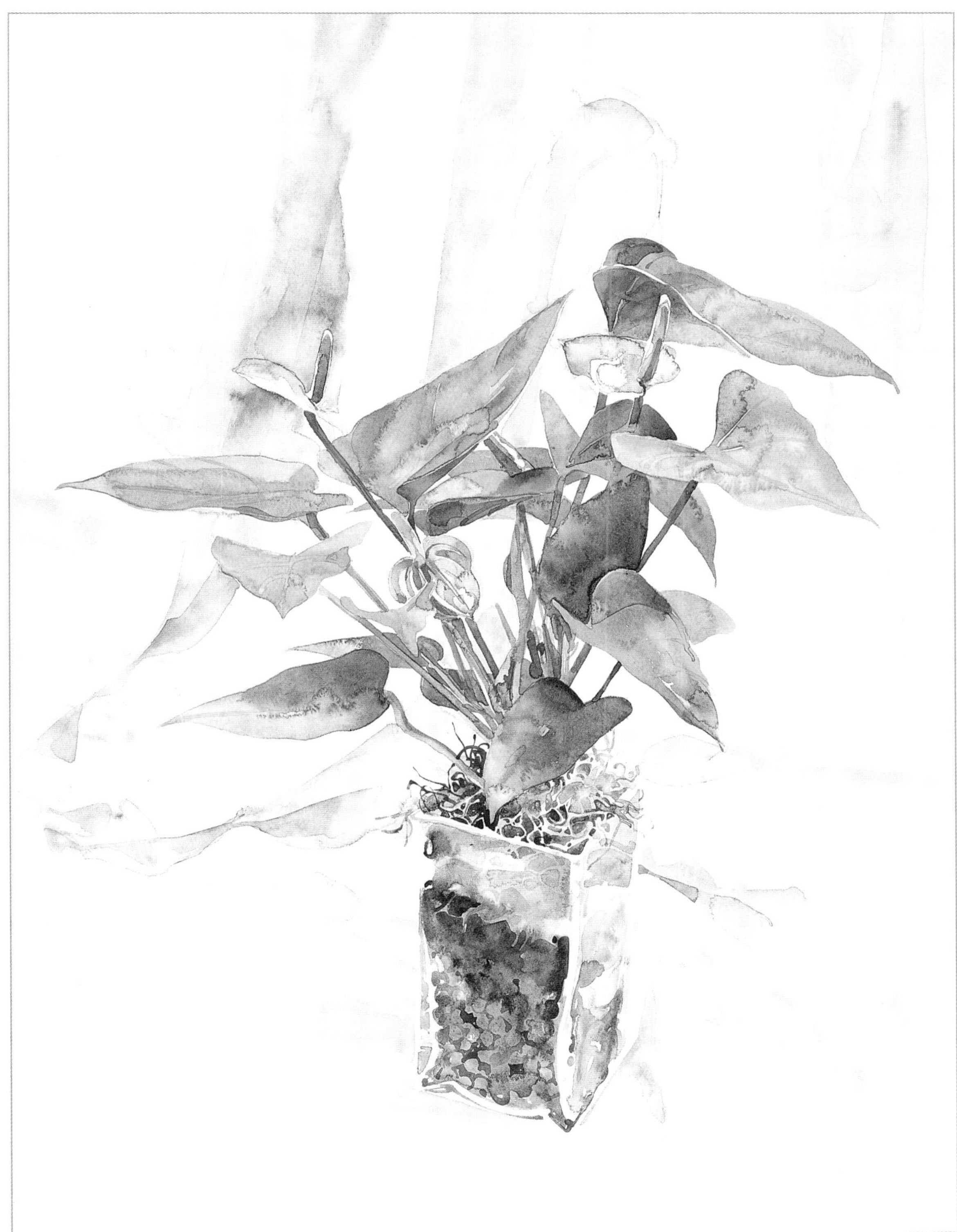

6 Build up the greens of the leaves, adding more shadows and veins, then darken the stems, and deepen the reds where required. Move on to the moss area at the base, adding browns for the details and tonal values, and filling in the negative shapes. Finish by working on the vase, refining the shapes and tones of the pebbles behind the thick glass.

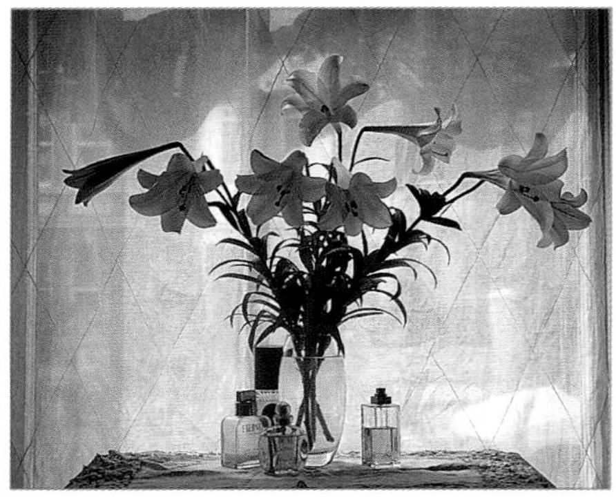

Interior with lilies: colored pencils, pastels, and Conté crayons on gray Ingres paper

The attraction of this scene is that there is a great deal more color in it than is apparent from a quick glance. The area outside the subject matter influences the choice of colors. The rich, gray paper is ideal for drawing negative shapes, to set the composition and find the tonal balance.

Materials

- Gray Ingres paper
- Colored pencils
- Pastels
- Conté crayons
- Fixative

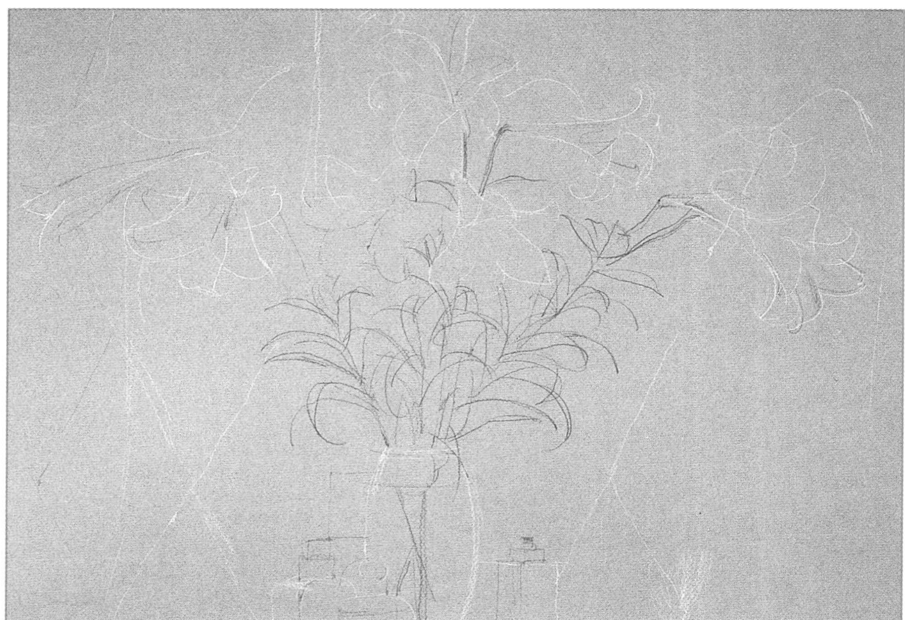

1 Start by using green, white, and blue colored pencils to make a very loose guide composition. This needs to be no more than the basic shapes of the still-life set-up because you will be creating the negative shapes first.

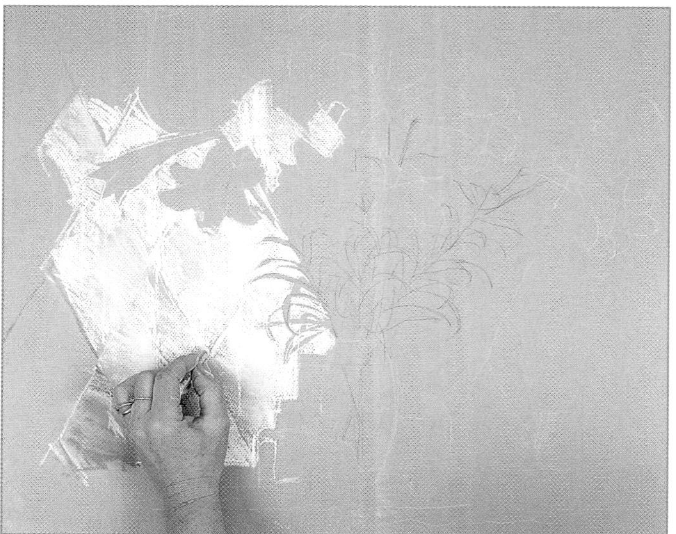

2 Establish the patterns of the shadows and folds on the muslin curtains with a slightly off-white pastel, and then a very pale blue. The darker colors at the base are indigo overlaid with blues. Press the pastels hard into the paper to reduce the effect of the tooth, and add warm and cool colors equally across the white.

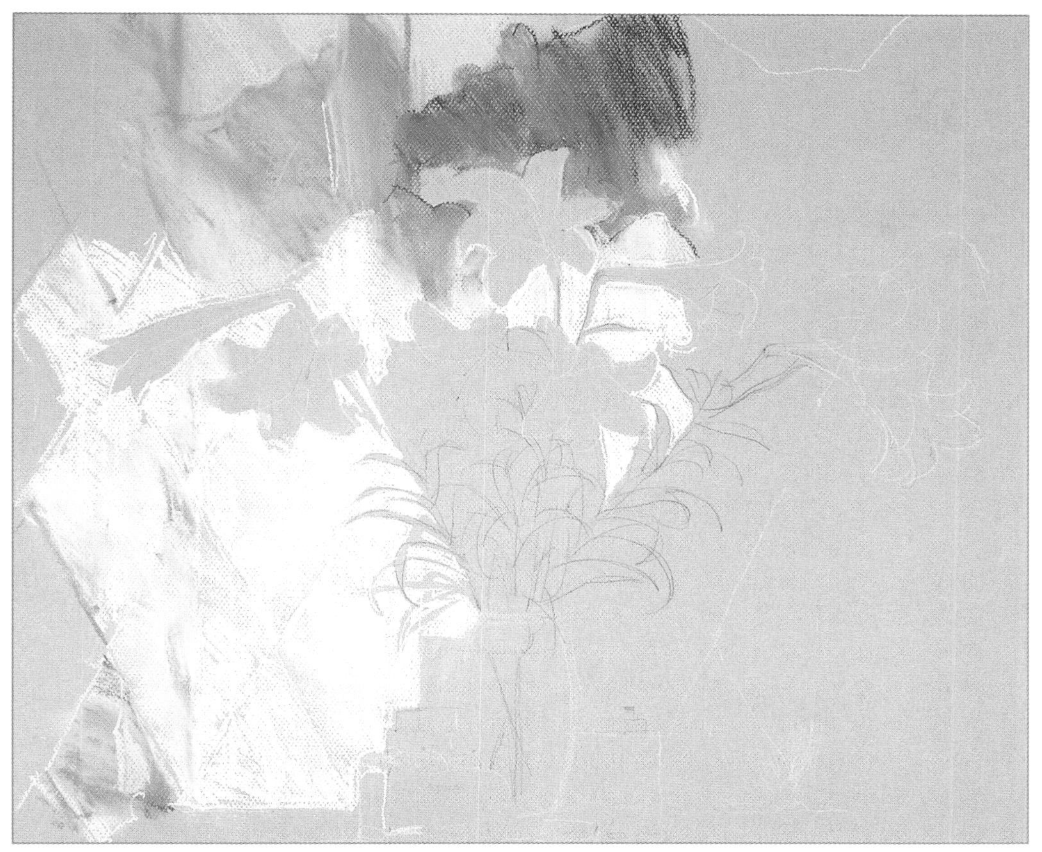

3 Drawing around the negative shapes, use as many pastels as you need to build up the layers of color—there is much more than white here. The curved shadows at the top are pale blue warmed up by olive green and brown, and the lighter, unshadowed area above is another negative space.

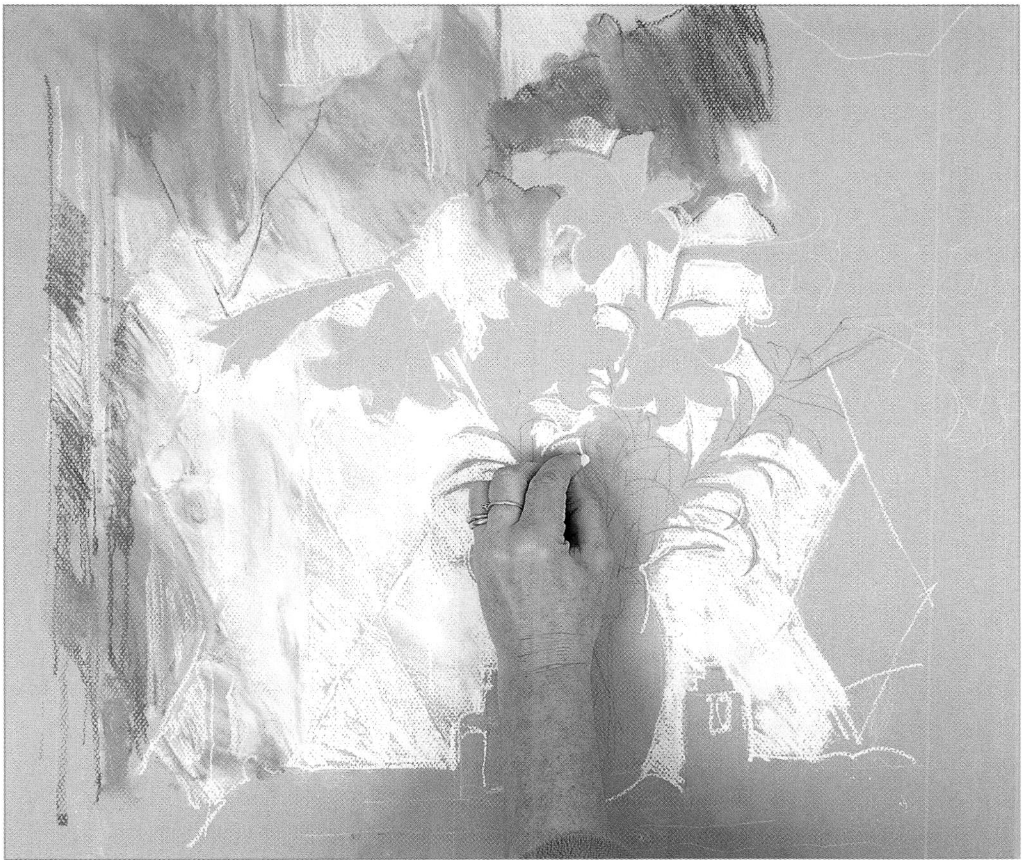

4 Concentrate on the small, negative shapes between the leaves and flowers—in the sunlit areas, these are a bright, but muted off-white. Use long, free strokes to capture the upper shadow areas, and blend pastels around the left-hand window frame vertical. Knock back whites and yellows with cool blues.

5 Draw around the negative shapes to the right of the vase, including the perfume bottle, and out to the edge of the composition. As you do this, move outward into the shadows and light areas, layering light green over the off-white to mute it. Apply just a few lines of purple Conté crayon for the sharp folds at bottom right.

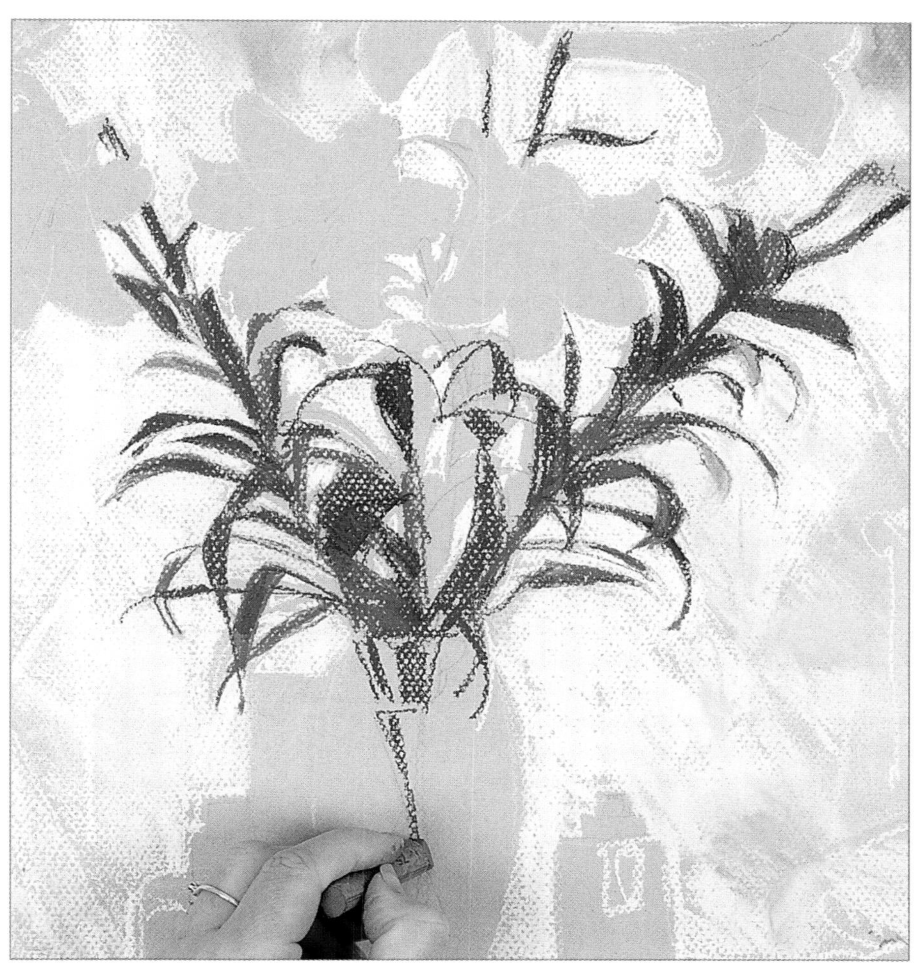

6 With the negative shapes set, use a blue-green Conté crayon, or trim a pastel, for the thin, dark leaves and stalks—if necessary, work over the muslin colors. Even at this early stage of filling in, set the darker and lighter shades and colors in these silhouetted shapes.

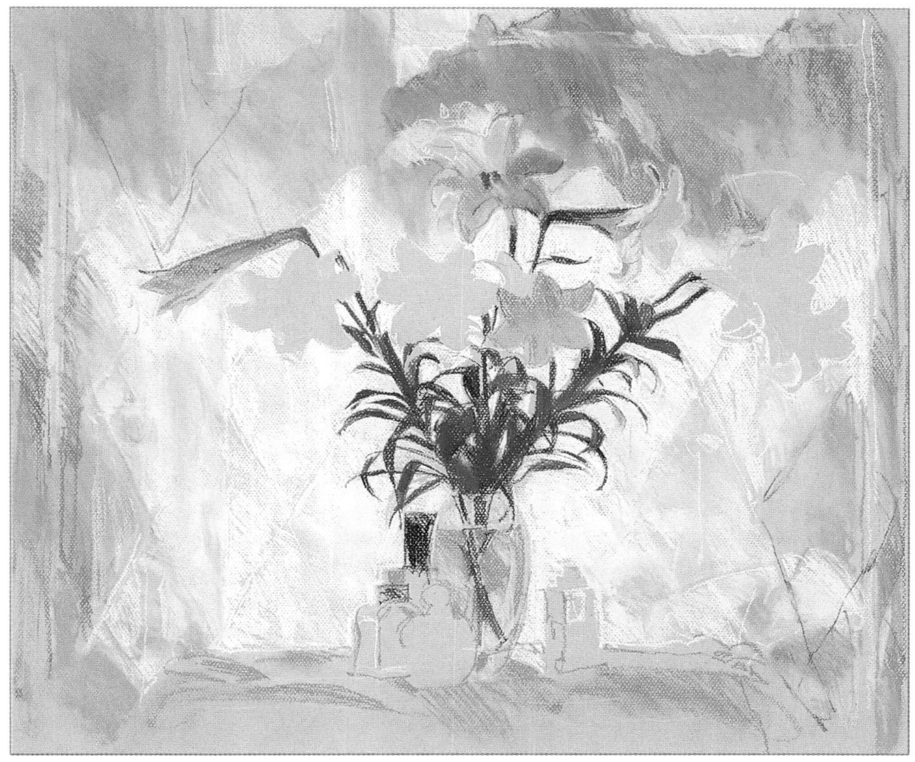

7 The stalk colors are muted where they pass behind the glass of the vase—use grays for the basic vase, whites to capture the glassy sheen, and blue-greens for the water. Apply light side strokes to establish the cloth on the table, draw in the perfume bottle shapes, and darken the tops.

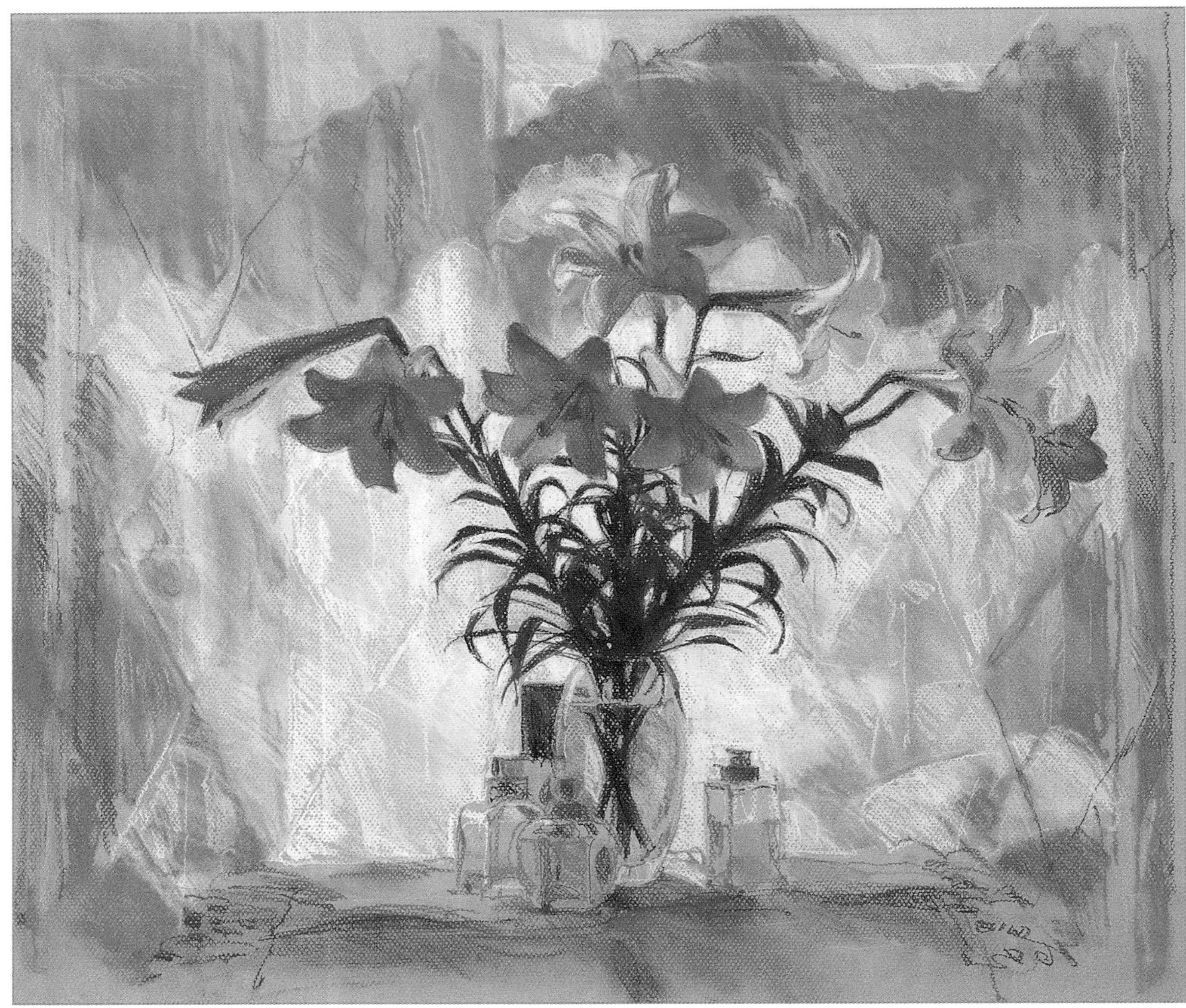

8 Start to fill in the flower heads, working between the grays, blues, and greens. As you progress across the flowers, look for the balance of color and shape, and the differences in the fall of light, adding warm reds and yellows. Fill in the colors of the bottles, and stop before the composition becomes overworked. Spray with fixative to finish.

Dried flowers: Conté crayons, oil pastels, and watercolor inks on heavy, Arches watercolor paper

Using a mixture of mediums means that your method of working may change. Putting in both the lightest and darkest parts of a picture from the start is not standard procedure, but the mediums make this the most effective solution. The rough deckle edges of heavy-duty Arches paper make an attractive frame.

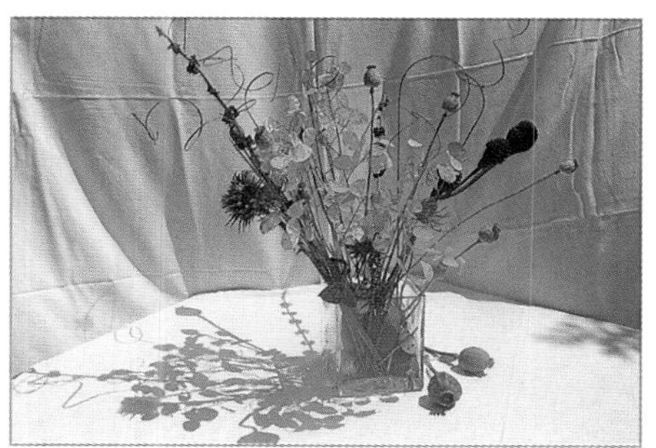

MATERIALS

- Heavy, deckle-edged Arches watercolor paper
- 3B pencil
- Conté crayons
- Oil pastels
- Watercolor inks
- Large oriental brush
- Reed pen
- Clean water

1 Include the shapes of the reflections on the table in the initial drawing. Use the pencil lightly, but don't draw into the darkest areas at this stage—Conté crayons don't go well over pencil.

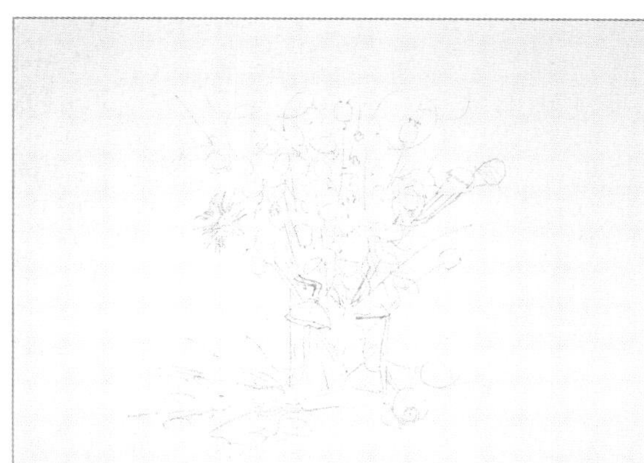

2 Work very lightly with black Conté crayon to find the thinnest lines—this is the only time black is used. Concentrate on making the shapes of the stalks and flowers, and only add shadowed lines where necessary. Use oil pastels to highlight the lightest parts, blending to make color gradations.

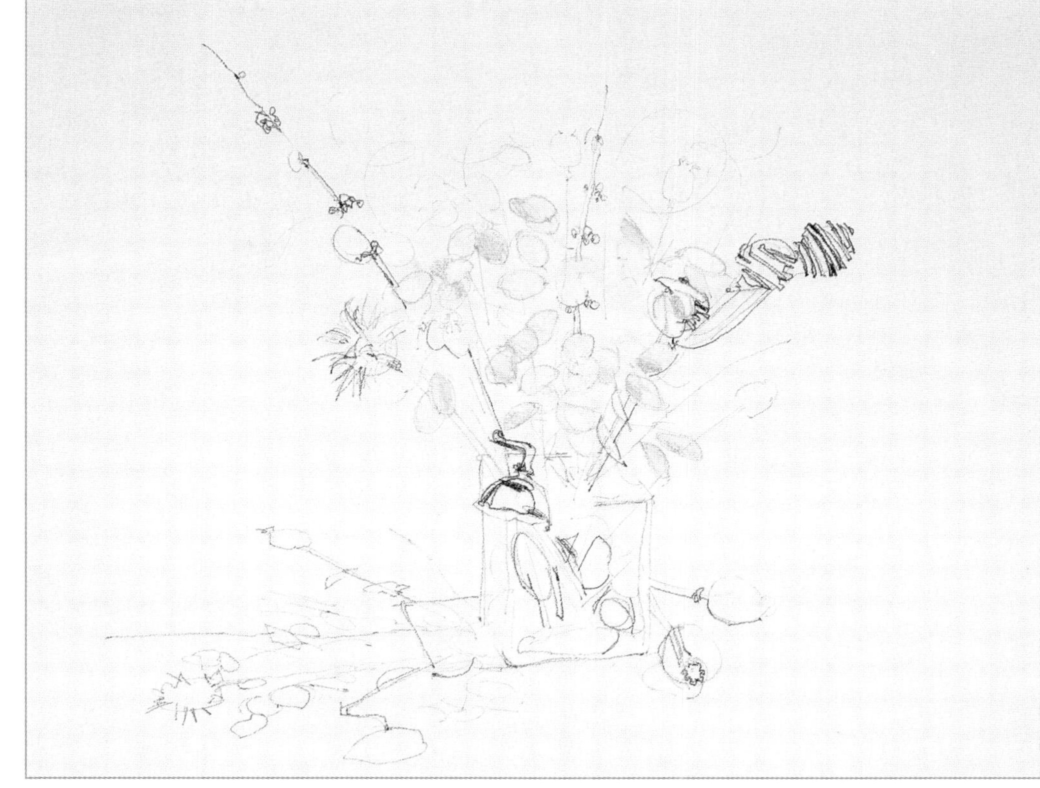

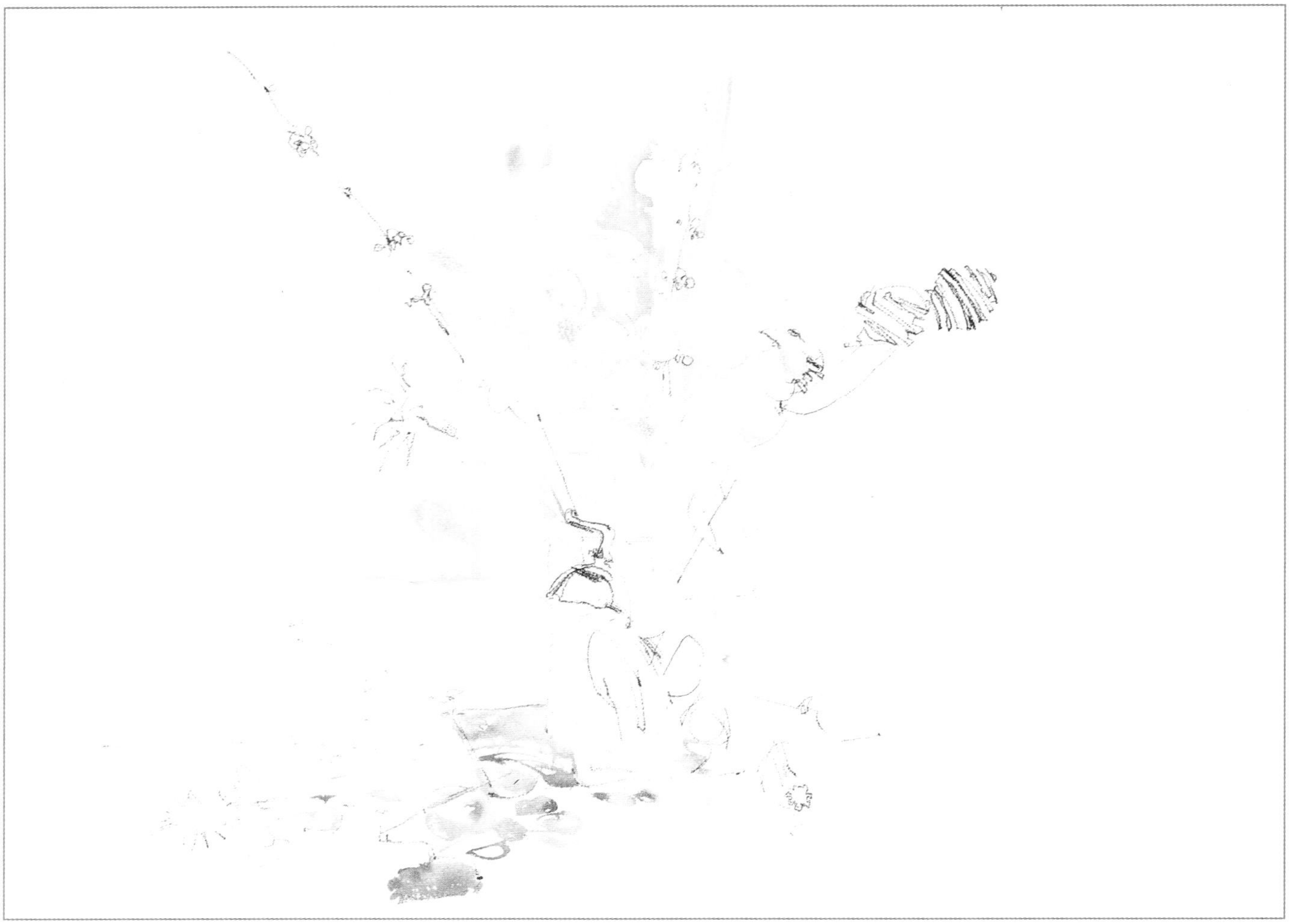

3 Mix a blend of blue and gray watercolor inks, and use a large oriental brush to apply pale, diluted washes. Draw around the shapes already on the paper, varying the depths and tones, and suggesting some of the background. Add a little purple to the mixture, and draw the shadows on the tablecloth.

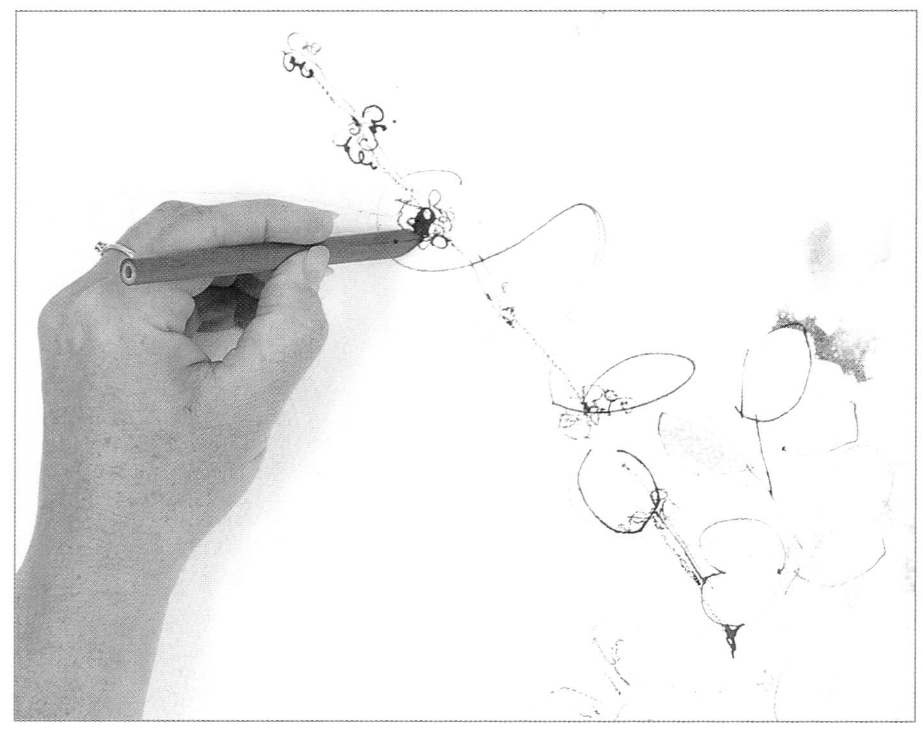

4 Use a reed pen and brown watercolor ink to draw in the darkest petals and swirls at the top of the paper—the ink makes muted tones that are far more effective than using black.

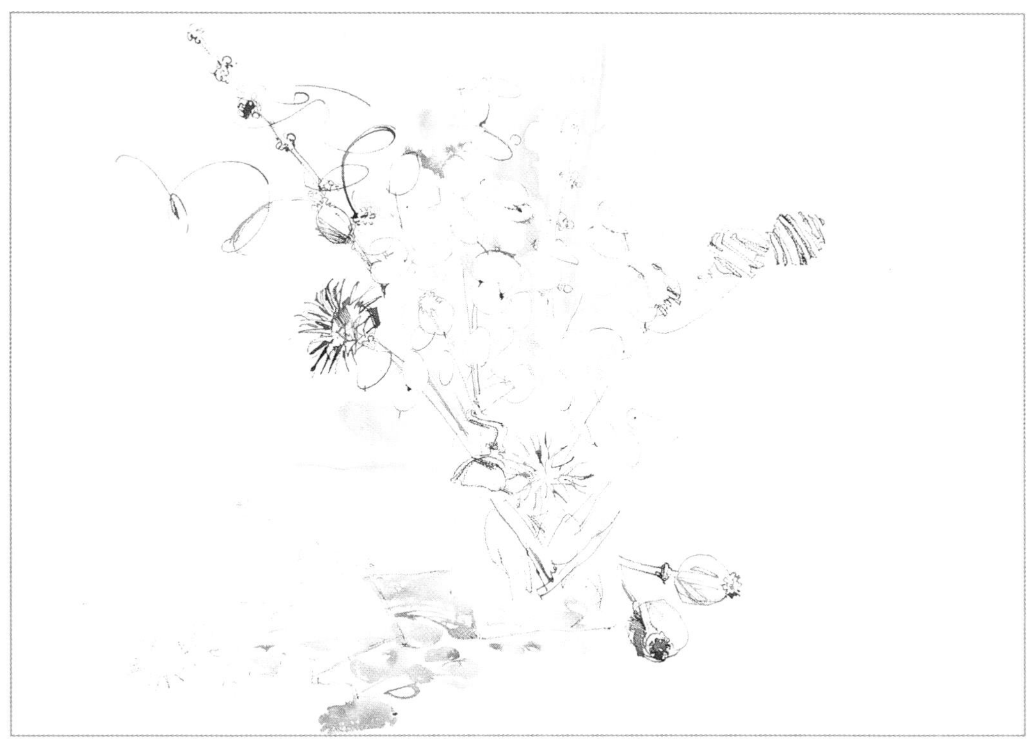

5 You can now work in two ways with the pen—quite loosely for the larger shapes, where you can add some hatching for tone and volume, and tighter to capture the linear stems and spikes. Use blends of light brown and ocher for the lighter shapes, and look for the contours as well as the lines. Add the first basic shapes in the vase.

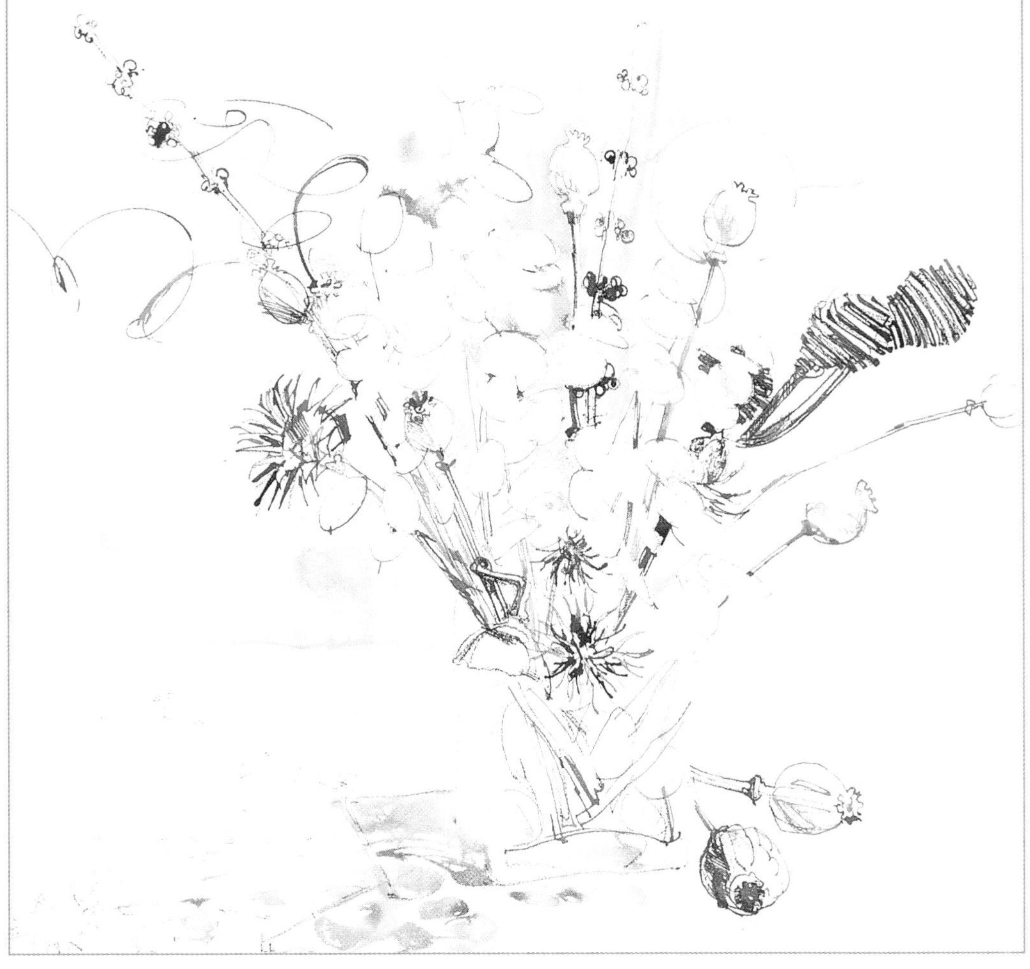

6 Using ink to reinforce the right-hand flowers, draw the lines over and around the underdrawing and brush washes. Blend and dilute the inks as you go, and use the pen to outline the white of the paper for the very brightest highlights.

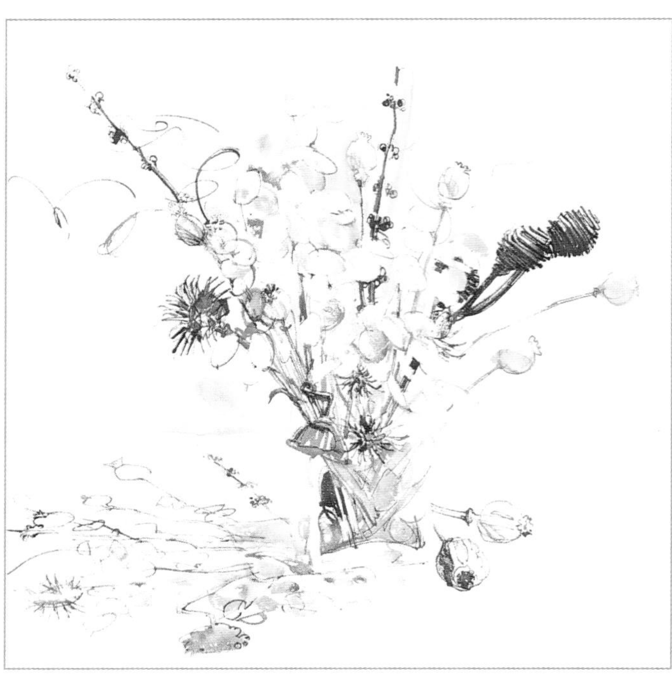

7 Use the oriental brush and ink to fill in some of the white areas, and add the tonal values across the whole drawing. The purple and blue washes give a cool shadow effect in contrast to the warmer browns and yellows. Switch back to the reed pen and use the cool mixtures to create the cast shadows.

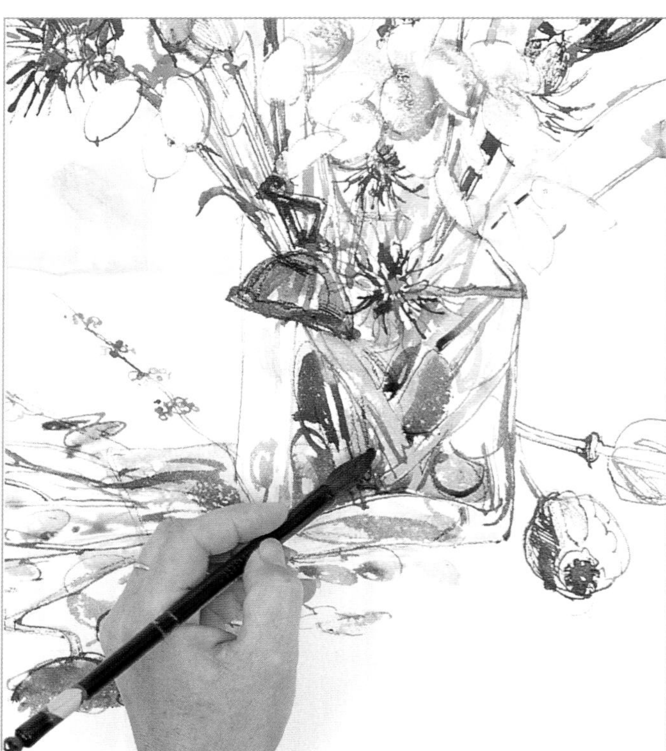

8 Fill in the blues and purples of the cast shadows with the oriental brush, then build up the lines and colors in the vase. This forms a pivotal base to the composition. Draw in the cast shadows on the right-hand side, and refine and darken the ones on the left, then fill them in.

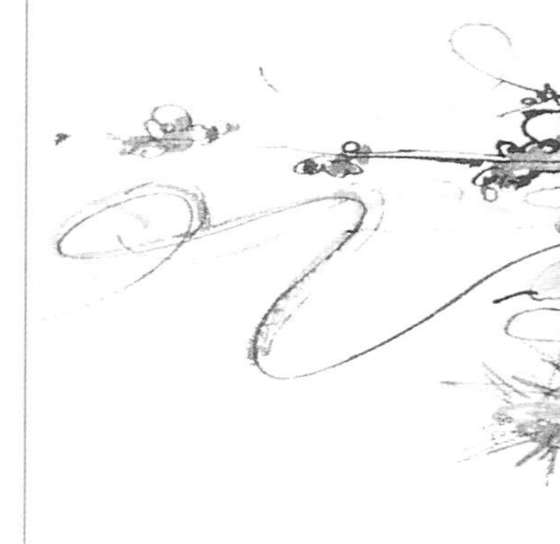

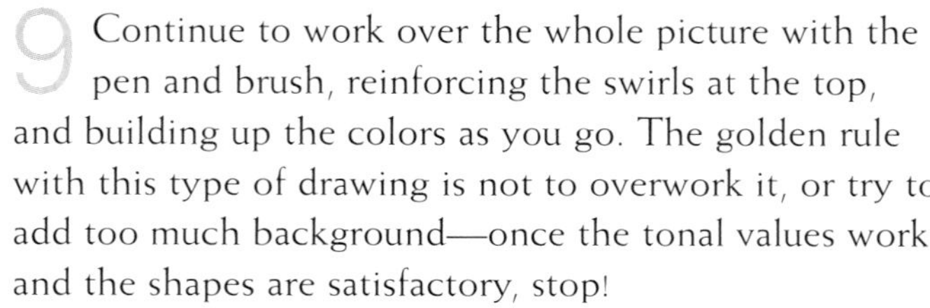

9 Continue to work over the whole picture with the pen and brush, reinforcing the swirls at the top, and building up the colors as you go. The golden rule with this type of drawing is not to overwork it, or try to add too much background—once the tonal values work and the shapes are satisfactory, stop!

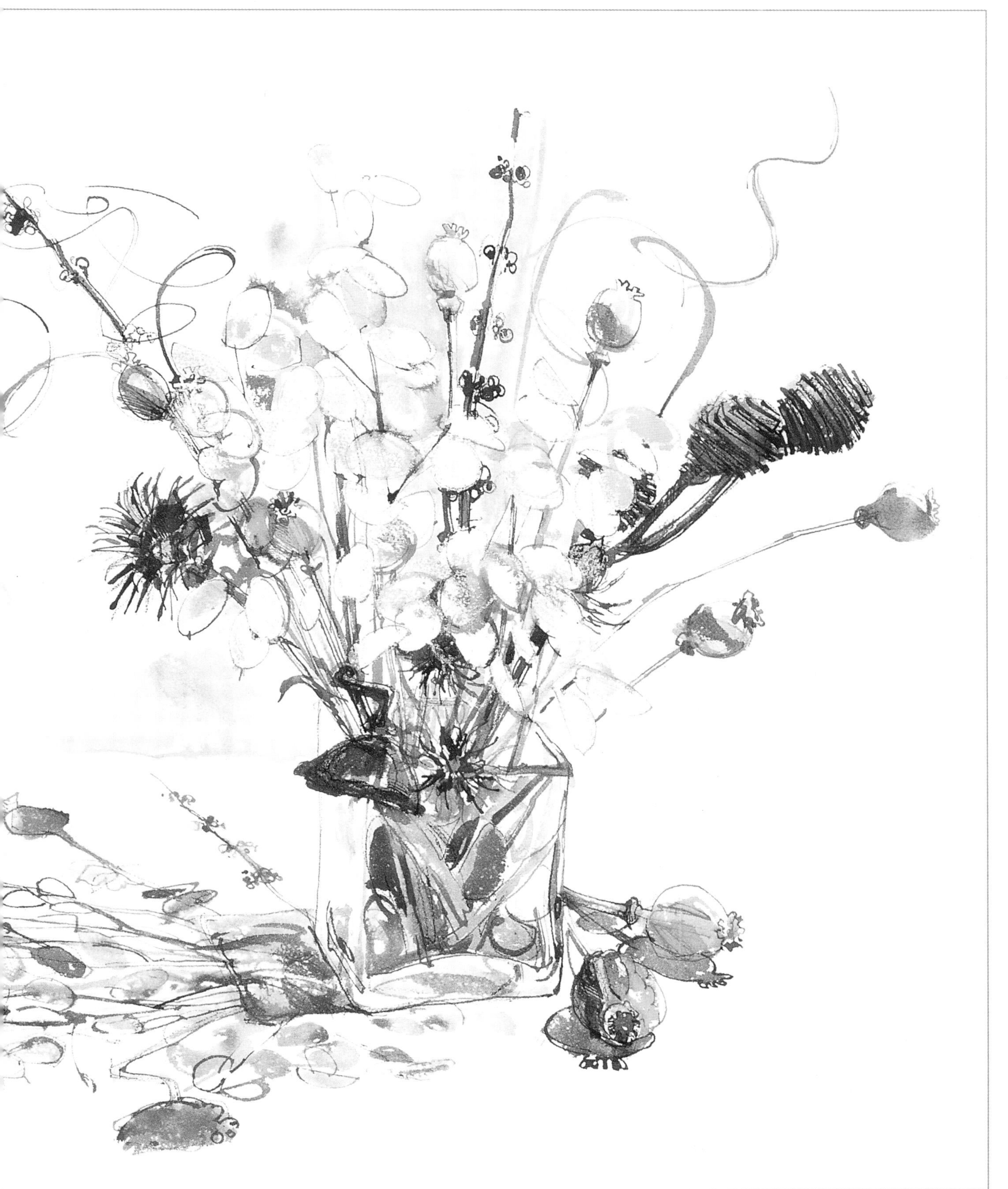

Interior and exterior set-up:
acrylics on gessoed masonite

This project comes at the end of the book because it has the most going on in its composition—an interior still life in semi-contre-jour lighting, a framing pair of French windows, and a garden seen through them. You can work both from light to dark and vice versa with acrylics, which can be very useful in a complex situation that might require second thoughts.

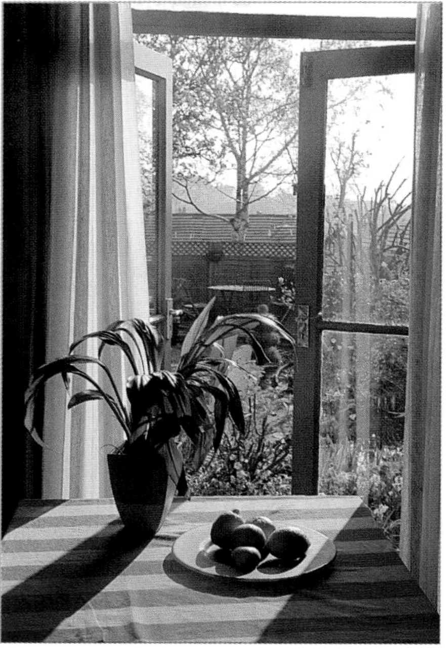

Materials

- Gessoed masonite
- Sable brushes
- Acrylic paints
- Clean water

1 Use a diluted wash of acrylic paint to sketch out the composition in its entirety—you can use any color, but a classic, neutral blue works as a guide that does not take much effort to paint over subsequently. At this stage work lightly, to discover the elements and their proportions and relationships to each other.

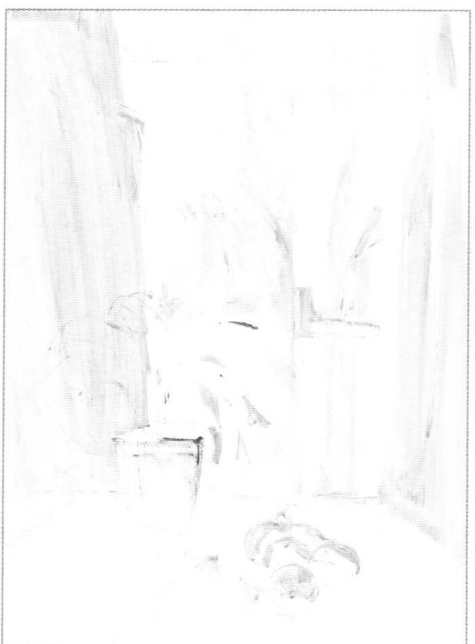

2 Make a diluted mixture of yellow, brown, and a little red. Paint this over the curtain areas, where the warmest parts of the scene are, and very lightly on the sky, seen both through the glass and straight out—don't forget the reflections in the glass. Use a small brush to add the warmest areas on the fruit and between the potted plant's leaves.

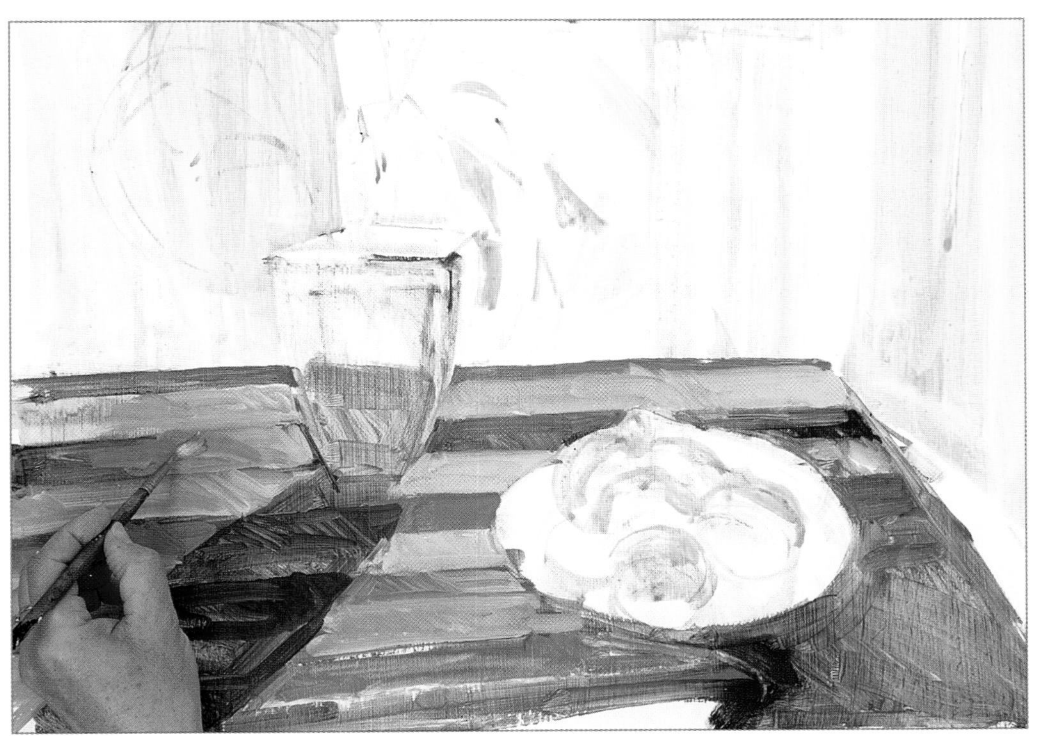

3 Lay in the dark blue stripes on the tablecloth that provide the coolest basis in the picture—concentrate on capturing the effects of perspective. Use the same color to shape the cast shadows, then mix the other stripe color and apply it. Use white to lighten all the stripes, and build them up to their final tones.

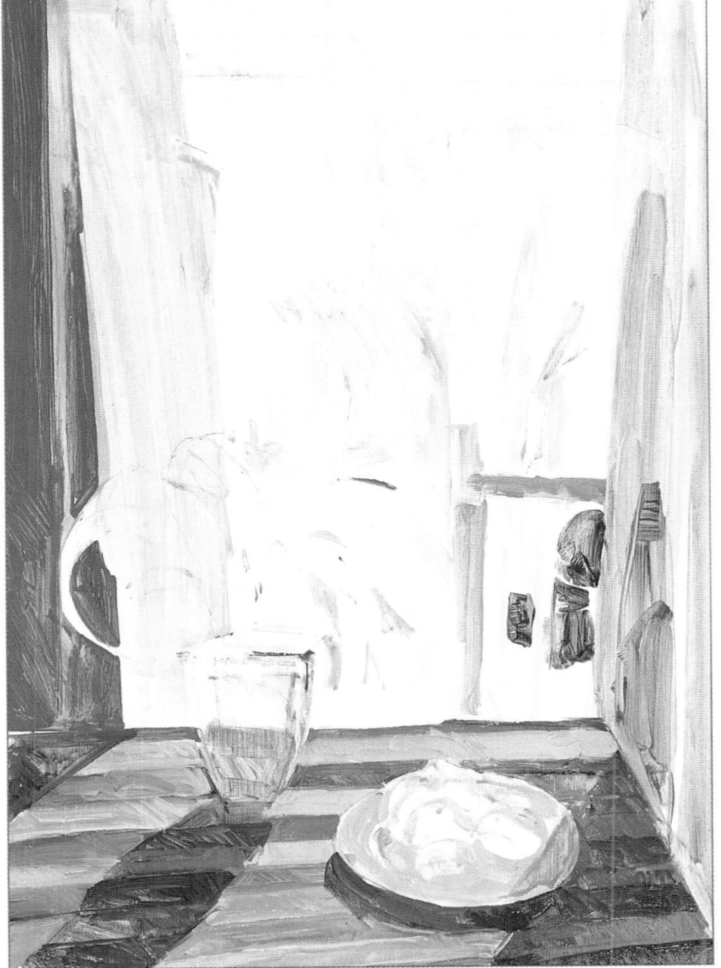

4 Paint the plate a cool green, taking account of the shadow across it. The tablecloth stripes still show under the darkest cast shadows from the right, so keep the color and tonal variations. Use a thin wash on the window frame, and start to put in tones for the garden scene, before adding purple to the curtain shadows on the left.

5 Add the other vertical shadows, and amend the shades of yellow to warm them up against the cool purples. Apply green to the left-hand frames, and then blue for the darkest leaves going to the left. Use brighter colors for the other leaves, finding their shapes across the whole plant.

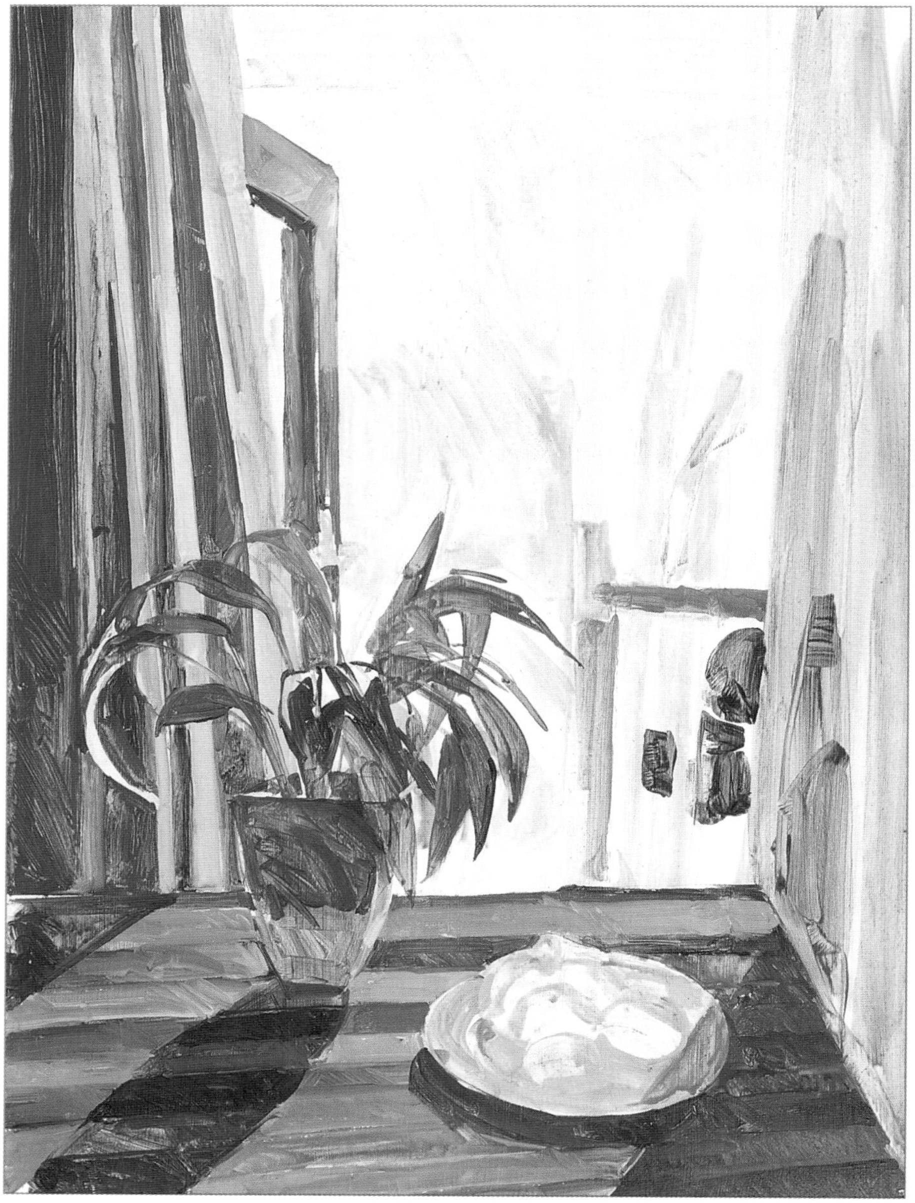

6 Apply a very pale wash of gray-blue over the sky area, to knock back the yellow and introduce the effect of early-morning light. While this wash is still wet, add layers of washes for the background shapes in the garden, and allow these to dry without hard edges—don't forget to do this above the horizontal transom in the frame.

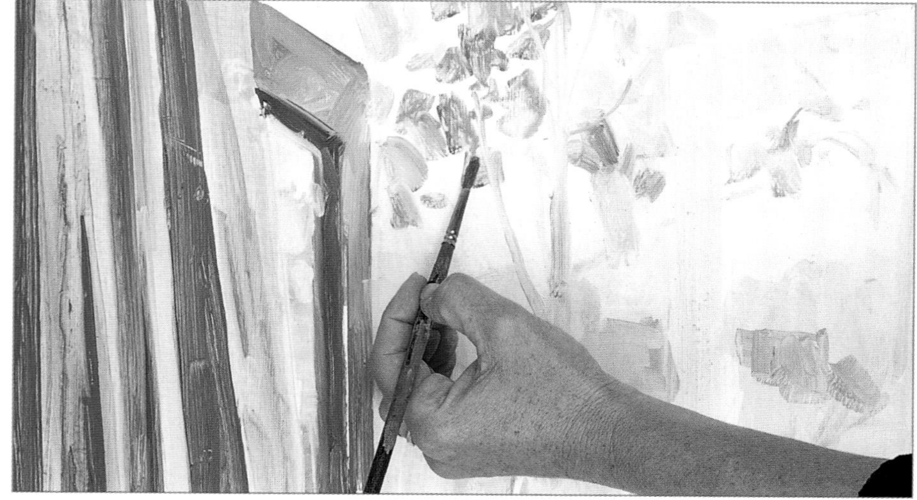

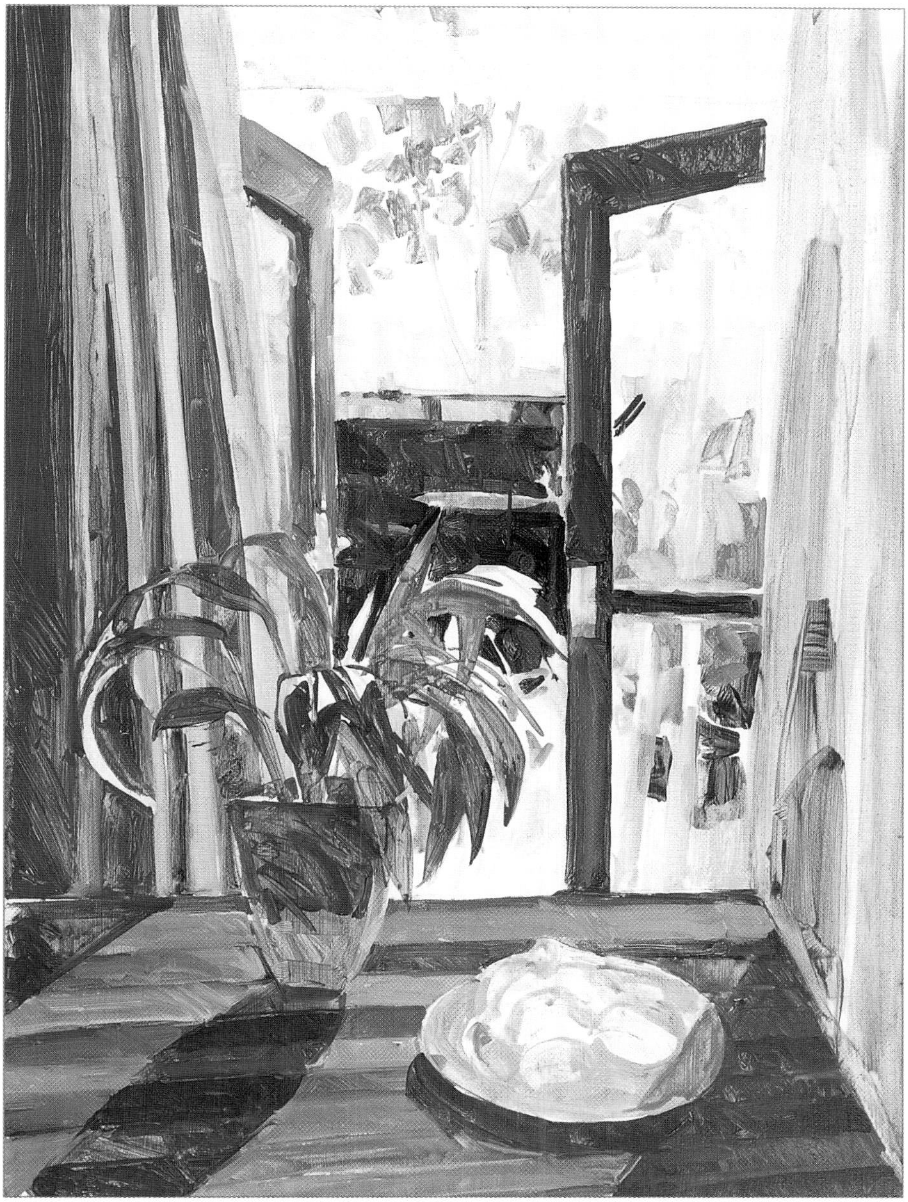

7 Introduce warm tones of brown, purple, and blue to the wall and table in the garden, then add similar shades around the leaves of the interior potted plant. The right-hand door frame is not in the sunlight, so use darker shades than on the left-hand one—also darken the area seen through the right-hand glass.

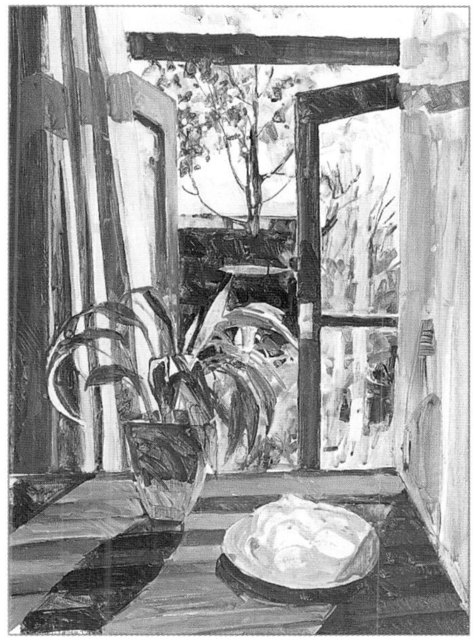

8 Use light greens and yellows to reinforce the lines of the potted plant leaves against the curtains. Paint the transom bar wholly in shadow—its purple-blue color is reflected onto the right-hand door and curtain in warm colors, and the shadow is very light on the left-hand curtain. Add similar colors to the garden scene.

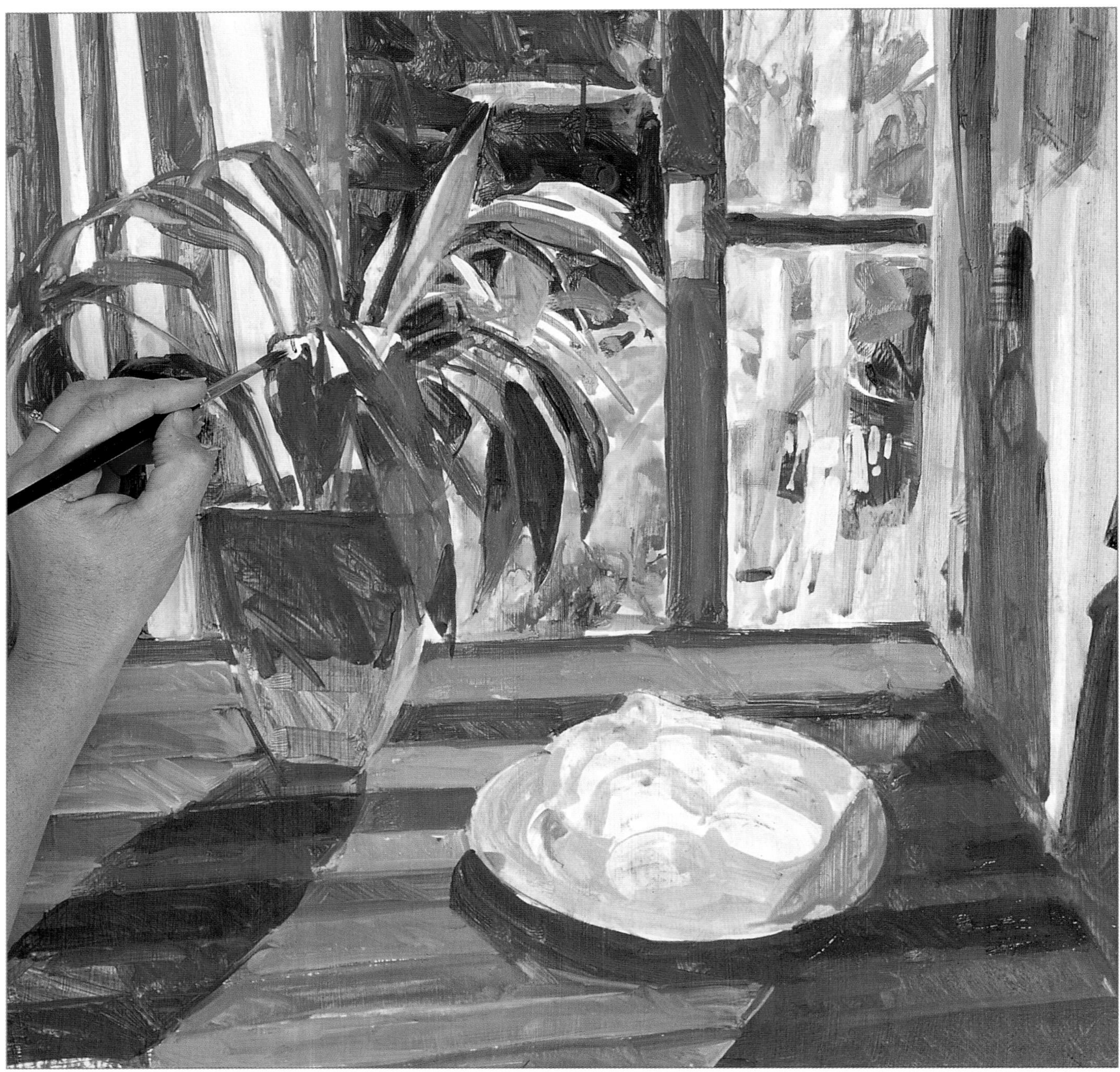

9 Stand back to check out the tonal values, then strengthen the potted plant leaf colors across the whole plant, and add lighter colors for the highlights, which help to bring the plant forward in the picture. Keep the right-hand leaves quite loose, adding dark, vertical shadows that go down into the cast shadow at the bottom.

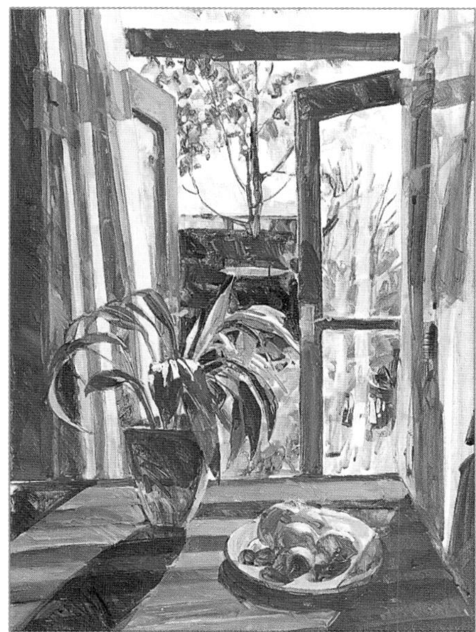

10 Apply orange-red to the sunlit parts of the fruit, and then tone it down with yellows and ochers. Blend browns, ochers, and reds for the fruit's shadow areas, then add a little reflected color from the tablecloth and the cast shadows.

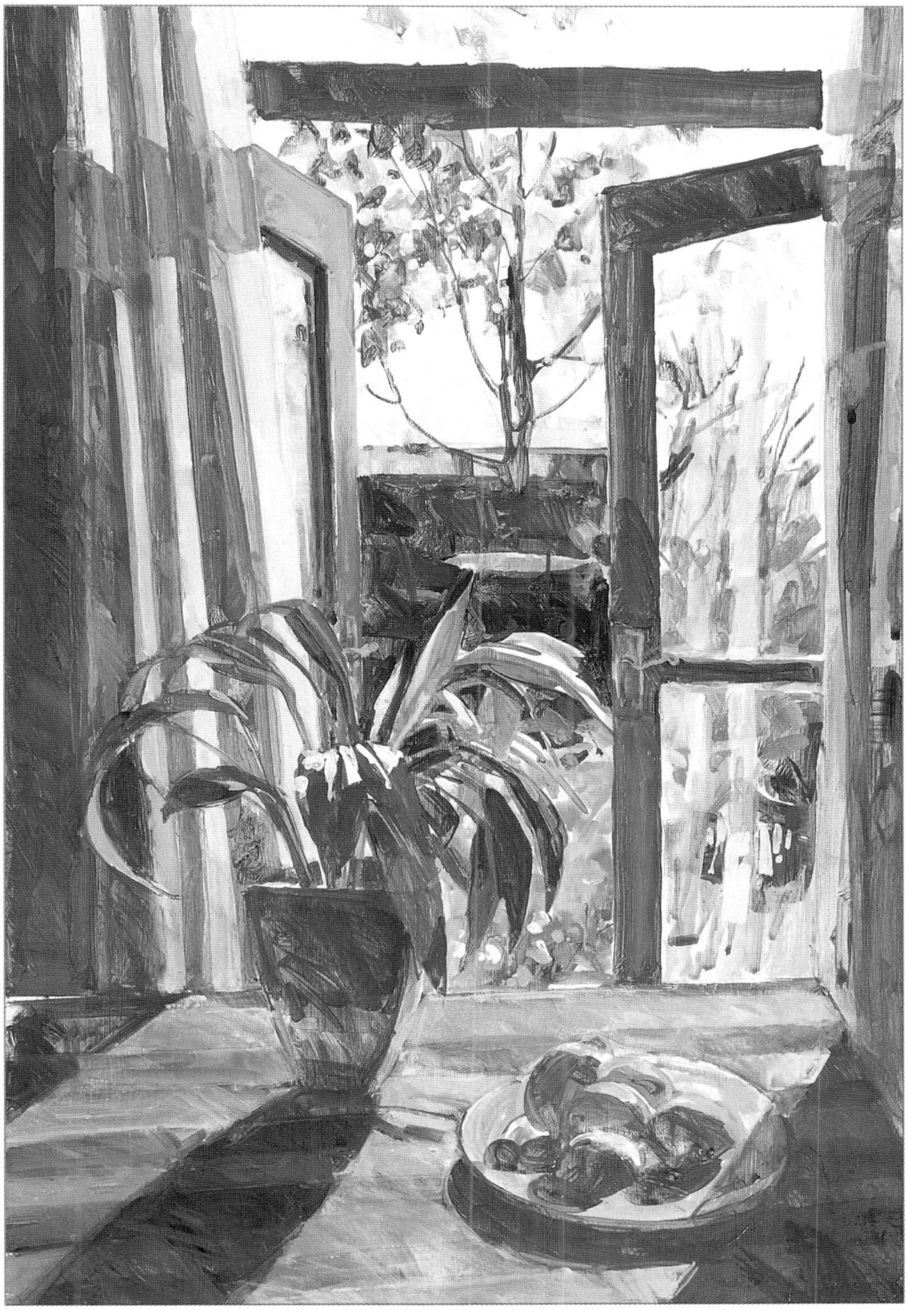

11 Use a small brush to go over the tablecloth with a scratchy, scumbling glaze of white and a little blue, and dab off and move excess paint with a clean piece of paper towel. Add mauve to the white if required. Look at the highlights on the pot, and strengthen both the shadows on it and the one it casts.

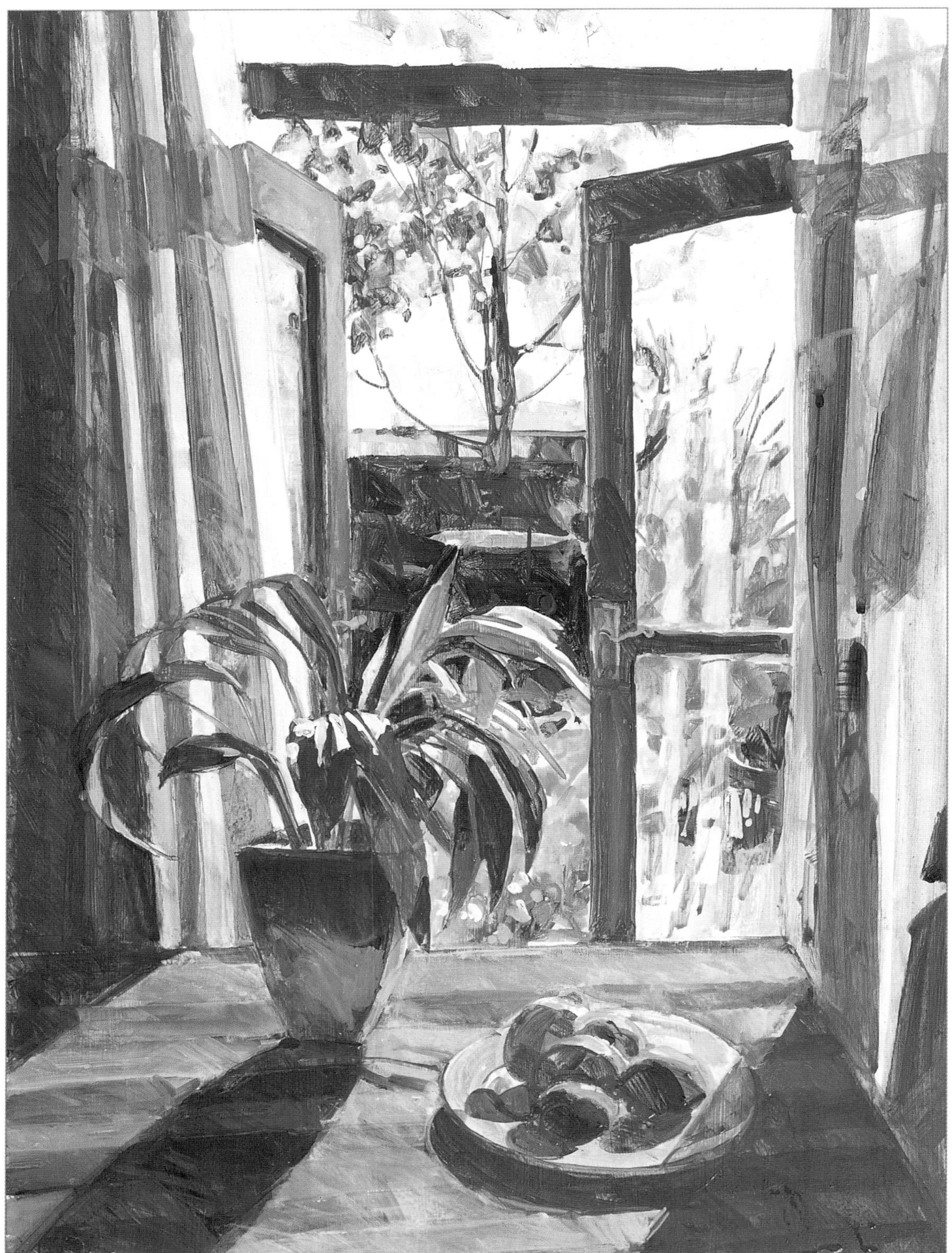

12 Add highlights to the lowest background flowers and then to the fruit, strengthening and refining them until you are satisfied. Now all that remains is to look at the whole picture and add small details, and refine the color and tones.

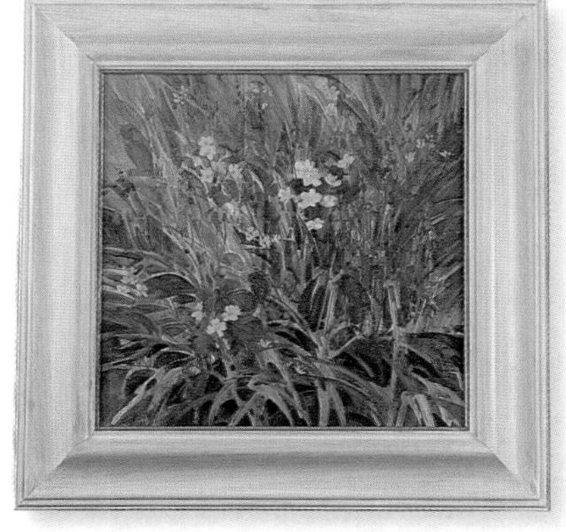

Presentation and framing

Displaying your finished artwork can be as individual as the artwork itself. The interior in which it is to be hung can also affect your choice. Different frames can alter the character, light, and atmosphere of a painting. They can bring out certain colors and tones, help a painting to appear light and airy, or enrich the artwork by emphasizing the strong shading or structure.

MATTING AND MOUNTING

The standard method of preparing artwork on paper for framing is to mat it. A mat is a card window frame that gives the artwork a structure and isolating space around the image.

Matting board comes in a huge range of colors, and the window matt is usually cut with a beveled edge. I find that a neutral, light-tone card works well for most situations, especially when framing for an exhibition. It sits comfortably in most rooms without unbalancing either the color of the artwork or the interior.

Sometimes, however, it is very effective to lay work on top of a sheet of mounting board. If your paper has a deckle edge it is nice to show this, or perhaps the work has a decorative edge or texture through it.

FRAMING

Artwork mounted on paper is protected with glass on the front and hardboard on the back, so a frame has to be able to safely support all this weight. Moulding for framing can be made of metal, wood, or even plastic, perhaps with applied detail made of plaster, resin, or layers of paint. The choice can be confusing, so if possible, take your picture in and place it against different examples of moulding.

At all times the important thing to remember is that the frame is there to complement the picture, not overpower it. So although a frame is undeniably important to give the work its own space within the interior, if it is too bold or heavy it can weaken the picture's impact.

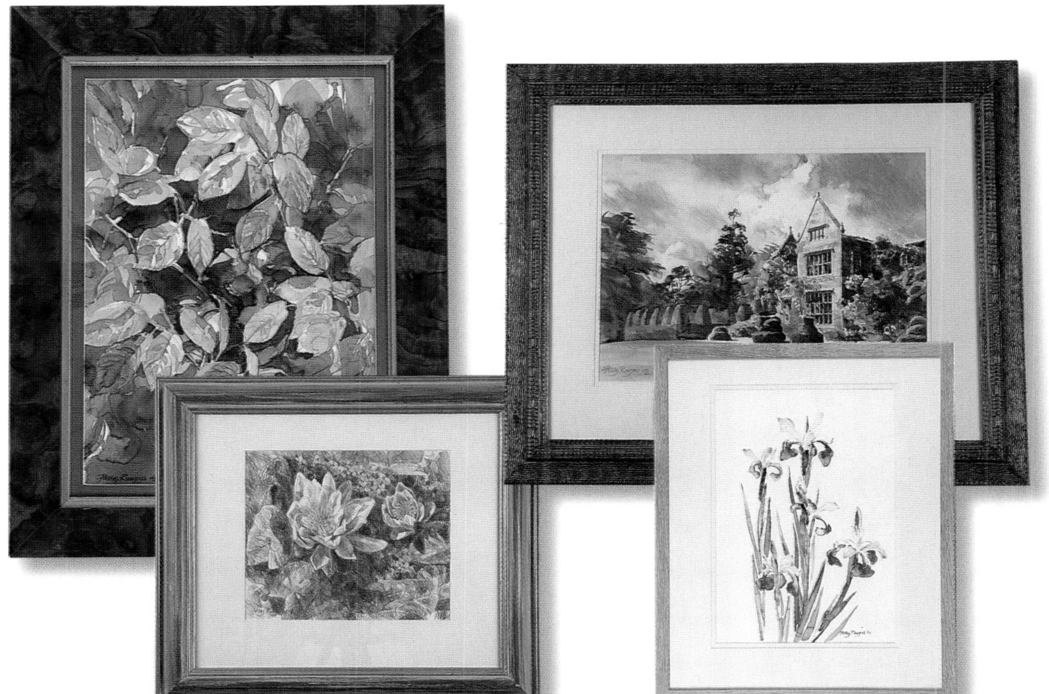

FRAMES

Framing on a big scale, or using a complicated moulding, is often best left to the professionals. There is a huge range of readymade frames on the market, often at very reasonable prices. You can adapt the size with new matts and mounts to fit your artwork, and if the frame is not exactly right, you can repaint or sand it down to your own requirements. Markets, garage sales, and antique shops are also very good hunting grounds for frames. Even broken or chipped frames can be repaired—or even left as they are, to add character to a picture.

Index

3B pencils 52–5, 69–73, 74–8, 88–92, 104–7

A

accessories 28
acrylics 32–3, 34, 56–60, 118–24
additives 28–9
  acrylics 33
anatomy 18–19
architectural settings 69–73
Aristotle 6
arum lilies 104–7

B

backgrounds 20–1, 102
  flattening 59
bamboo pens 12, 28
binder, acrylics 32
bluebells 21
bog orchids 12
bonsai 38, 46
botanical drawing 7
botanical gardens 93–8
box shapes 42
broken washes 31
brushes 27
  flat 69–73
  oriental 27, 52–5, 61–98, 113–17
  sable 27, 52–60, 64–8
buildings 69–73

C

candelabra primulas 20
chalk 34
chalk pastels 24
circular shapes 42
color 13, 40–1, 44–7
  and emotions 46–7
  pen work 12
  religious symbolism 7
  seasons 47
color wheel 44
colored pencils 13, 23, 34, 79–83, 99–103, 108–12
colors
  complementary 45
  fall 49, 88–92
  knocking back 60, 64, 73, 87, 120
  primary 44
  strengthening 60, 68
complementary colors 45
composition 20–1, 36–47
  indoor 38–9
  outdoor 40–1
Conté 34
  crayons 61–3, 69–73, 108–17
  pastels 24
  pencils 10–11
contour drawing 12
cotton balls 28, 31, 77
crayons
  Conté 61–3, 69–73, 108–17
  watercolor 25
  wax 23, 24–5, 34
crocuses 21, 39
cropping 38
curves 39

D

daisies 15, 61–3
decision making 48–9
drawing 22–3
  botanical 7
  contour 12
  paper 16
see also preliminary drawings; sketches
drawing boards 17
dried flowers 113–17
drying, with a hairdryer 57, 71, 81, 84, 89

E

enjoyment 49
erasers 69–73, 74–8, 84–7
experimentation 48
exteriors 22–3, 69–73

F

fall colors 49, 88–92
fashion 7
flat brushes 69–73
flat washes 31
flowerbeds 52–5
flowers
  anatomy 18
  as gifts 7
focal points 36, 38, 40
foliage 52–5, 69–73
fountains 53
framing 125

G

gardens
  botanical 93–8
  public 52–5
gel medium 33
gessoed masonite 56–60, 118–24
gifts, flowers as 7
gloss medium 33
Golden Rule 36, 39
grasses 56–60
gray Ingres paper 108–12
gum arabic 29, 84–7

H

hair dryers 57, 71, 81, 84, 89
Hale, Ann 6
heavy watercolor paper 113–17
hedges 69–73, 74–8
highlights 28, 55, 65, 70, 73, 115, 123, 124
history 6
horizons 39
hue 44

I

ice 74
indoor composition 38–9
informal set-up 99–103
inks 12
interiors 20–1, 104–7, 108–12
  and exteriors 118–24

K

knocking back colors 60, 64, 73, 87, 120

L

landscape sketchbooks 17
lavender beds 23
leaves 19
light 39, 46
lilies 7, 13, 15, 19, 108–12
liquid acrylics 32
liquid frisket 28
liquid watercolors 26
location equipment 17

M

marks 15
masking fluid 52–5, 74, 84–7
materials 9, 48
preparation 22
matte medium 33

matting 125
medicinal properties, plants 6
mediums
  acrylics 33
  choosing 10–11
mixing 15, 34
monochrome 10–11
monochrome mediums 10–11
mounting 125

N
negative shapes 38, 62, 79, 80, 90, 95, 97, 101, 104, 108, 109, 110
neutral tones 45
nibs 12

O
oil-based materials 34
oil pastels 23, 25, 113–17
one-point perspective 42
orchids 21, 41
oriental brushes 27, 52–5, 61–98, 113–17
outdoor composition 40–1
ox gall liquid 29

P
painting studies 22
palettes 27
palm trees 22, 47
pans, paint 26
paper 16, 25, 30
  drawing 16
  gray Ingres 108–12
  smooth 11, 30, 104
  stretching 30
  textured 11, 25, 30
  watercolor see watercolor paper
  weight of 16
paper towels 28
paste 33
pastels 23, 34, 69–73, 108–12
pen and ink 12, 34, 88–92
pencils 10–11
  3B 52–5, 69–73, 74–8, 88–92, 104–7
  colored 13, 23, 34, 79–83, 99–103, 108–12
  Conté 10–11
  plus another medium 11, 35
  watercolor 13, 25, 99–103
pens
  bamboo 12, 28
  reed 113–17
  steel-nib dip 88–92
perspective 42–3
photographs 23
planes 39
planning 17, 48
plants
  medicinal properties 6
  names 7
pomegranates 33
ponds 64–8
poppies 7, 25, 37
preliminary drawings 64, 69, 74, 79, 88, 99, 104
  see also drawing; sketches
preparation 37, 48
presentation 125
"Pride of London" flowers 84–7
primary colors 44
public gardens 52–5

R
rags 28
recession 42
Redouté 7
reed pens 113–17
religious symbolism, color 7
rose hips 14
roses 19, 20
rubber-tipped color shapers 84–7

S
sable brushes 27, 52–60, 64–8
salt 31
saturation 44
seasons 51
  color 47
shadows 41, 54, 64, 68, 71, 75, 79, 83, 91, 92, 96, 106, 116, 119, 122
shapers, rubber-tipped color 84–7
sketchbooks 17
sketches 37, 40, 48, 69
  see also drawing; preliminary drawings
skies 52–5, 69–73
smooth paper 11, 30, 104
smooth watercolor paper 104–7
snow 74
spiral–bound sketchbooks 17
sponges 28
spring scene 79–83
steel-nib dip pens 88–92
strengthening colors 60, 68
studies 22–3
  developing 24–35
  interior 20–1
summer scene 84–7
suppliers 126
surfaces 11, 25

T
techniques 9, 48
textured paper 11, 25, 30
textures, acrylics 33
thumbnail sketches 37
tonal values 44
toothbrushes 28, 31
topiary 52–5, 69–73, 74–8
trees 22, 47, 52–5, 69–73
tubes, paint 26
tulips 15
two-point perspective 43

U
underpainting 56, 72

V
vanishing points 42, 43
variegated wash 31
vertical planes 39
viewfinders 40
violas 13

W
Warhol, Andy 7
washes 31
water 64–8
water lilies 22, 64–8
watercolor crayons 25
watercolor inks 88–92, 113–17
watercolor paints *see* watercolors
watercolor paper 16, 25
  heavy 113–17
  semi-rough 52–5, 61–102
  smooth 104–7
watercolor pastels 14, 93–8
watercolor pencils 13, 25, 99–103
watercolor sketchbooks 17
watercolors 26–31, 34, 52–5, 61–87, 104–7
wax crayons 23, 24–5, 34
wet-in-wet 31, 61
wild plants 56–60
winter scene 74–8

Acknowledgements

The publishers would like to thank Weidenfeld & Nicolson Ltd and Andrew Lawson for permission to use the photograph on page 72.

The author would like to thank Ann Hale, for permission to use the drawing at the top of page 6, and for her tremendous help with botanical work; and Lauren, for letting me borrow her wax crayons.

Suppliers

USA

Asel Art Supply
2701 Cedar Springs
Dallas, TX 75201
Toll-free: 1-888-ASELART
www.aselart.com

Caran d'ache of Switzerland Inc. *(for Neocolor watercolor pastels)*
38–52, 43rd Street
Long Island City, NY 11101
Tel: 718 482 7500
Email: CdAofS@aol.com

Daler-Rowney USA
4 Corporate Drive
Cranbury, NJ 08512-9584
Toll-free: 1-800-278-1783
www.daler-rowney.com

Dick Blick Art Materials
P.O. Box 1267
695 US Highway 150 East
Galesburg, IL 61402-1267
Toll-free: 1-800-828-4548
www.dickblick.com

Jerry's Artarama
P.O. Box 58638
Raleigh, NC 27658
Toll-free: 1-800-827-8478
www.jerryscatalog.com

Paper & Ink Books *(for reed pens)*
P.O. Box 35
3 North Second Street
Woodsboro, MD 21798
Toll-free: 1-800 736 7772
www.paperinkarts.com

Winsor & Newton Inc.
P.O. Box 1396
11 Constitution Avenue
Piscataway, NY 08855
Toll-free: 1-800-445-4278
www.winsornewton.com

UK

Blot Pen & Ink Supplies *(for reed pens)*
14 Lyndhurst Avenue
Prestwich
Manchester, M25 OGF
Tel: 0161 720 6916
www.blotspens.co.uk
Email: sales@blotspens.co.uk

Daler-Rowney
P.O. Box 10
Bracknell
Berks, RG12 8ST
Tel: 01344 424621
www.daler-rowney.com

Jakar International Ltd (Caran d'Ache)
Hillside House
2–6 Friern Park
London, N12 9BX
Tel: 020 8445 6376
Email: info@jakar.co.uk

John Purcell Paper
15 Rumsey Road
London, SW9 0TR
Tel: 020 7737 5199
www.johnpurcell.net

Oasis Arts and Crafts
Goldthorn Road
Kidderminster
Worcs, DY11 7JN
Tel: 01562 744522
sales@oasisarts.co.uk

Simonart
122–150 Hackney Road
London, E2 7QL
Tel: 020 7739 3744

Winsor & Newton
Whitefriars Avenue
Wealdstone
Middx, HA3 5RH
Tel: 020 8427 4343
www.winsornewton.com